THE BIG PICTURE

FINDING THE FATHER IN THE BIBLE

TREVOR GALPIN

Copyright ©2021

The Big Picture: Finding the Father in the Bible
by Trevor Galpin

Published by TLG Mins

Design and Layout by Tom Carroll

ISBN: 978-1-8380570-4-6

All rights reserved. No part of this publication may be reproduced, stored in a retrieval system or transmitted in any form or by any means - for example, electronic, photocopy, recording - without the prior written permission of the author or publisher. The only exception is brief quotation in printed reviews.

All Scripture quotations, unless otherwise indicated, are taken from The Holy Bible, New International Version®, NIV® Copyright ©1973, 1978, 1984, 2011 by Biblica, Inc.®. Used by permission. All rights reserved worldwide.

For more information and resources by Trevor and Linda Galpin please visit: **www.trevorlindafhm.com**

CONTENTS

Foreword V

Introduction VII

1. Revelation 10
2. The Creation 28
3. The Garden Of Eden 42
4. The Fall 55
5. The Father In The Old Testament 77
6. The Coming Of The Son 99
7. Jesus Begins To Reveal The Father 120
8. The Father in John's Gospel 142
9. The Events in the Upper Room 160
10. The Cross 178
11. Resurrection and Ascension 190
12. Pentecost And Beyond 208
13. Paul The Apostle 221
14. The Gospel 239
15. Sonship 259
16. The Last Word 274

    Other Books by Trevor Galpin 283

    Recommended Reading List 287

    Resources 289

FOREWORD

What has begun to emerge in our experience in the last number of decades is a new landscape. We have departed the once familiar shores of an orphan-based Christianity and embarked on a perilous journey across the seas of transition. That voyage has been fraught with many perils, strong winds have whipped the waves into a frenzy, oftentimes we feared that we would drown in confusion and insecurity. There was nothing to stand on. Would we ever find solidity under our feet and a place to rest and build from?

Suddenly, the cry was heard from the prow of the ship, "Land Ahoy!" Could it possibly true? Then out of the mists and fog appeared a solid form—LAND!

Dragging our bedraggled ships onto shore we are relieved, but we wonder what this new land is like. The more we push outwards from that initial beach of prophetic revelation we begin to discover that this new and undiscovered land is very large. It is abundant with lush forests, verdant pastures, rocky crags, rivers and a lot more to be discovered. It is a good land, a land of full Trinitarian relationship. It is new and undiscovered, but it is, at the same time, deeply familiar. It is our ancient homeland.

The Father's love experienced in the heart, the mind, the soul, the body has and continues to transform our individual lives. But it will do more than that. It will transform us individually into those who are truly family and who really cannot exist without one another. Rugged individualism is no longer possible. The full revelation of who God really is needs a corporate Body to contain and express it.

The Big Picture is a theological approach to the Good News of God's love, but it is a *heart-theology*; the heart of revelation channelled through the ability of a mind surrendered to the love of God. Christianity needs theologians. I contend that they are needed more than ever, albeit not theologians who are generated out of orphaness. Tragically we have been led down the garden path and up the wrong Tree by theology that is not rooted in the heart of the Father. Thanks be to God a new theology is emerging that is in contradistinction to the old orphan theology, but it also retains a continuity with what the Holy Spirit has deposited in the historical Church.

I have to say that, for me and many others, Trevor Galpin has emerged (out of a deep process of Divine Spirit in his own life) to be one of our guides in helping us explore this vast continent of the Father's love. Trevor has a deft touch, handling big topics with lightness, depth of insight, scholarship and with his characteristic mischievous humour. I believe this book is an important part of what Paul the apostle called "The whole counsel of God" (Acts 20:27). It is a resource for now and for the future and many treasures are contained therein.

Stephen Hill, Tauranga 2021

INTRODUCTION

Over the last few years, I have had the privilege to teach at a number of week-long Schools as part of Fatherheart Ministries (FHM). These Schools known as A Schools are followed by B Schools sometime later. They are opportunities for people to sit under prophetic teaching and have an experience of being loved by God as their Father.

My wife Linda and I had the opportunity of attending both of these events in 2007 while we were living in New Zealand. These Schools were led by James and Denise Jordan, the founders of Fatherheart Ministries. It is not an exaggeration to say these were life changing weeks for us both. I have written about my personal experience at the A School in my book *Falling from grace and being caught by the Father* (2013). In 2008, we became associated more closely with FHM, joining the team with the Jordans. Over the next few years, we transitioned from being team to speakers to finally being released to lead and teach the A Schools and then to speak alongside James at B Schools and then to lead and teach B Schools on behalf of FHM.

Throughout these years I have had a growing understanding in my heart of the nature of God as Father, his Son Jesus and the work of the Holy Spirit. I studied in the 1970's for a degree in Theology in the UK and have loved studying and exploring the Scriptures. I began to see in many ways I had very much missed the point about what God was doing and revealing through his Word, the Bible. I was a product of my background as a Baptist and charismatic. As time went by, I wrote and dug deeper into the scriptures. I wanted to see how the revelation of God as the Father was revealed through the life and ministry of Jesus. My next book *Jesus and his Father* (2014) emerged out of this exploration. Then came a look at the story of the Church throughout

INTRODUCTION

history and how we had seemingly lost touch with this truth. I had taught a number of times on Church History and so the book appeared *Finding the Father in the story of the Church* (2016).

I found Father was opening the eyes of my heart to new and exciting revelation in the scriptures and had the privilege of teaching these truths. By 2018, God had taken me to look at the Apostle Paul and how he had a revelation of the Fatherhood of God leading us back into our true identity as sons. It was exciting and challenging as my theology was being turned upside down or rather as I was once told by a group of pastors in Africa, it was being turned the right way up. One of them said it was as if he had been struggling all his life to walk on his hands and failing continually then he discovered he had feet. Like so many, I too had found my feet, took tentative steps and began to walk and run and jump for joy. So, the next book, *The Story of Paul – the Early Years* (2018) came out followed by the second part, *The Story of Paul, the middle years* (2020).

Revelation is an uncovering of truth that has always been true. We just had not seen it. Our eyes were closed and only when God the Father gives us the gift of revelation can we see. In this season I drank deeply of the flow of revelation coming through James and Denise Jordan's ministry. Their teaching on the nature of the two trees in the Garden of Eden, and the eyes of our hearts being opened was profound. I was encouraged by them to teach what I had seen, and I had the joy of doing this on a number of B Schools.

As I taught and reflected, I began to see how all the teachings being taught in A and B Schools were linked. They were not just stand-alone teachings. They were all parts of a greater whole. I describe the process like doing a jigsaw puzzle. Like many, I have rediscovered jigsaw puzzles during the COVID pandemic while locked down and at home. When doing a puzzle, we usually look for all the edge pieces

INTRODUCTION

first and join them. Then we move on to the coloured sections. Often, they sit there, not joined, floating. Then little by little pieces are found to link them to each other. Finally, as the last piece is found we stand back and look at the big picture with great satisfaction. Out of this came this book, *The Big Picture finding the Father in the Bible*. I am not claiming that I have found all the pieces, but I do feel there is a coming together of many of these great truths God is graciously showing us in these days. I feel too, our theology is continuing to be transformed and is becoming full of life and light. Theology used to bore me but now as truth leaps out of the Word, it thrills me beyond what I could ever have imagined. I hope I can share this joy and thrill with you as you read.

I remember the words of John Robinson in 1630, who encouraged the Pilgrim Fathers as they crossed the Atlantic to the New World: "The Lord has yet more light and truth to break forth from his word."

Trevor Galpin, 2021

CHAPTER 1

REVELATION

WHAT IS REVELATION?

When the Apostle Paul sits down to dictate the letter which we know as the Letter to the Ephesians, his heart is full to bursting with amazing truth about the nature of God and his great plan for humanity. As Tychicus takes up his stylus to transcribe for Paul, he probably has no idea the depth of revelation about to tumble out of Paul's overflowing heart. It is to be a profound moment because the words written will change our whole understanding of God.

In his usual style of letter writing, Paul introduces himself as the author of the letter and his appointment by God as an ambassador of Christ Jesus. He uses the word apostle to describe his role. In this early period of the Christian era the word is commonly used to describe someone who is commissioned by a person in authority to represent them in some way. So, as in his other letters, Paul explains his appointment is by the expressed will and appointment of God.

He then goes on to greet the recipients of the letter, and he uses one of his favourite expressions to describe them: They are the holy people of God, the faithful in Christ Jesus. In this description he sees them as '*hagioi*', the saints, the specially set apart ones who by faith are united and at home in Christ. Ever since he wrote the letter to the Galatians many years earlier, Paul has described believers as being 'in Christ.'

In his customary way he blesses them with grace and peace from God who he explains is the Father of the Lord Jesus Christ. This description of God being the Father of Jesus is at the core of Paul's teaching and writing. It is the truth Jesus himself has revealed and passed on to his followers, commissioning them as his ambassadors to spread all over the world.

Paul, at this point, dictates a sentence which Tychicus probably struggles to write. His stylus must have shot across the sheet of papyrus as the words tumble out of Paul's mouth. Paul is so excited he barely pauses for breath. His sentence grows longer and longer; phrase follows phrase; punctuation is hardly used. Finally, Paul stops. Tychicus is likely out of breath as the sentence is two hundred and fifty-seven words long.

This sentence has been described as the greatest sentence ever written. The truths revealed by Paul in this extraordinary sentence in Ephesians chapter 1 will be explored in detail in subsequent chapters of this book. This magnificent outpouring forms the foundation of the revelation of God the Father and his eternal plan for us as his sons. Then Paul begins to pray.

WHAT DOES PAUL PRAY?

Paul's longing and desire for his readers is summed up in a prayer he inserts at the end of the great sentence. Whenever Paul writes, he has his audience clearly in mind and does not just write theoretically. He writes personally and from his own experience. He wants his readers to receive this revelation in the same way he has received it.

> *"For this reason, ever since I heard about your faith in the Lord Jesus and your love for all God's people, I have not stopped giving thanks for you, remembering you in my prayers. I keep asking that the God of our Lord Jesus Christ, the glorious Father, may give you the Spirit of wisdom and revelation, so that you may know him better. I pray that the eyes of your heart may be enlightened in order that you may know the hope to which he has called you, the riches of his glorious inheritance in his holy people" (Ephesians 1:15 – 18).*

Paul addresses his prayer to the "God of our Lord Jesus" and then goes on to clarify this God is "the Father of glory" or the glorious Father. Paul is asking God the Father of Jesus to give them the Spirit of wisdom and revelation to know him better. This prayer is full of truth about the nature of God.

When Paul talks about God, he consistently describes God as personal and relational. It is as if he is saying, being God is his job. Who he is, however, is a Father and a Son and a Spirit. This is totally in accord with all the other New Testament writers. From their Jewish heritage, they believe God is one. This is known as monotheism. This is in stark contrast to the beliefs of all the other people at this time who worshipped multitudes of gods.

The defining difference for the New Testament writers is their belief that Jesus is the divine son of God who has come into the world and lived among us as a human being sharing our nature and experience. They believe God's Spirit is a distinct person and the agent of God's activity in the world. This is known as the Trinity.

DOES PAUL USE THE WORD TRINITY?

Nearly two hundred years later the first Christian writer who wrote in Latin was a North African Roman lawyer named Tertullian. He coined the term trinity to describe this complex and profound nature of the God who is fully one and expresses his nature through three equally distinct persons, Father, Son and Holy Spirit. The purpose of this book is not to write a theological treatise on the Trinity rather to look specifically at the nature and work of the Father in this relationship.

What is significant is the ease in which Paul and others write about God without having to go into complicated definitions of the theology of trinity. Instead, they write about what they have seen and experienced for themselves in their dealings with God. The Apostle John writing in his first letter expresses it like this,

> *"That which was from the beginning, which we have heard, which we have seen with our eyes, which we have looked at and our hands have touched, this we proclaim concerning the Word of life. The life appeared; we have seen it and testify to it, and we proclaim to you the eternal life, which was with the Father and has appeared to us. We proclaim to you what we have seen and heard, so that you also may have fellowship with us. And our fellowship is with the Father and with his Son, Jesus Christ" (1 John 1:1-3).*

Getting back to Paul's prayer, he addresses it to the Father of Jesus and the heart of the prayer is for us to receive from the Holy Spirit, wisdom and revelation in order to know the Father better. In this prayer he is saying there is so much more to know of the nature of God as our Father than has been known. Before we go deeper into this, I want to say something about the Spirit and how he is involved in revealing truth.

WHAT IS THE HOLY SPIRIT'S ROLE IN GIVING REVELATION?

On the last occasion with his disciples before going to the cross, Jesus spoke to them in the upper room about the Holy Spirit.

> *"When the Comforter comes, whom I will send to you from the Father, the Spirit of truth who goes out from the Father, he will testify about me" (John 15:26).*

He continues a little later in the evening by adding,

> *"But when he, the Spirit of truth, comes, he will guide you into all the truth. He will not speak on his own; he will speak only what he hears, and he will tell you what is yet to come. He will glorify me because it is from me that he will receive what he will make known to you. All that belongs to the Father is mine. That is why I said the Spirit will receive from me what he will make known to you" (John 16:13 – 15).*

Jesus shows the disciples how the Holy Spirit will speak in exactly the same way as he had, only saying what he hears the Father say. The Holy Spirit will also speak the things Jesus gives him to say. Jesus has revealed many things from the Father to his followers and the Spirit will continue doing this after Jesus has returned to the Father.

Paul sees how revelation comes as a gift from God's Holy Spirit. It is one of the activities of the Spirit. In his first letter to the Corinthians, he said,

> *"These are the things God has revealed to us by his Spirit. The Spirit searches all things, even the deep things of God. For who knows a person's thoughts except their own spirit within them? In the same way no one knows the thoughts of God except the Spirit of God" (1 Cor 2:10 – 11).*

The apostle Peter also wrote of revelation coming from God's Spirit in a similar way,

> *"Above all, you must understand that no prophecy of Scripture came about by the prophet's own interpretation of things. For prophecy never had its origin in the human will, but prophets, though human, spoke from God as they were carried along by the Holy Spirit" (2 Peter 1:20-21).*

With all this in mind, Paul is asking God, the Father of Jesus, to give us the Spirit of wisdom and revelation to know him better. The gifts of the Spirit in this prayer are wisdom and revelation. Before looking in detail at what he means by revelation, I want to take a look at wisdom.

WHAT WISDOM IS PAUL TALKING ABOUT?

Paul uses the Greek word *"sophia,"* which is a feminine noun and is translated in English as wisdom. In the Bible, the source of wisdom is God, which is why it is his gift to us. This should not be confused with the world's wisdom. Paul says in 1 Corinthians 3:19, the wisdom of this world is foolishness in God's sight. The world's wisdom is more to do with intelligence, knowledge or understanding which come from study, examination, and the efforts of our minds. Wisdom like this is the ability to rationally think and act in a way for common sense to prevail and for us to make good choices that are helpful and productive. This is not the wisdom Paul means.

Paul's focus, as we shall see, is on the heart rather than the mind, and the gift of wisdom he is asking for is an experience rather than a concept or learned ability that comes with age. There is a place for this sort of wisdom. I wish I knew when I was seventeen what I know now. But in this context, wisdom is a wisdom of the heart, which is a gift of the Father to us. The difference is like going for swimming lessons where we read all about swimming, watch videos, study the various strokes, and understand the laws of the buoyancy of water from observation. All this acquired wisdom and knowledge counts for nothing when you jump in the water. You start to experience swimming… hopefully!

God's gift of wisdom is more than just experience. Paul says the gift of wisdom and revelation is to bring us to a deeper knowledge or knowing of the Father.

I want to come back to the word knowledge or knowing, but first I want us to look at the big Bible word Revelation.

WHAT DOES THE BIBLE MEAN BY REVELATION?

Paul is asking the Father to give us the Spirit of revelation. We have already seen one of the activities of the Holy Spirit is to bring revelation from God the Father. Paul's description of the Holy Spirit is specific. He is the Spirit of revelation. He is not talking about a spirit of revelation which is like an attitude or ability to operate in revelation. This is a misconception often heard and observed in Christian circles where an individual claims a special status based on this sort of thinking.

Sometimes the language speaks of "my revelation" or might be accompanied by dramatic and flamboyant behaviour. All this is designed to enhance the reputation of the speaker. However, Paul is talking about the Holy Spirit as the embodiment of revelation.

When Christians talk about revelation, we often think of the last book of the Bible known as Revelation, or the Revelation of John. In this case it is referring to the author, the apostle John, the beloved disciple who also wrote the fourth Gospel and three letters. John's book begins by saying it is the revelation of Jesus given to him. However, there is so much more to revelation than just the last book of the Bible.

What exactly does the word mean? In Greek, the word is *"apokalupsis."* English speakers will recognise this word as it is often translated in English as apocalypse. The Book of Revelation speaks about cataclysmic future events surrounding the end times and the second coming of Christ using vivid language and images. These mysterious and strange pictures were never intended to be anything other than an encouragement for the faithful as they faced hardship in their present circumstances. However, many have sought to find all sorts of hidden clues and secret messages in these pages about the date of the second coming of Jesus. This has given birth to a whole genre of Christian literature which at best is very fanciful and at worst has led to fear and discouragement. Some interpretations of these end time revelations are close to the early heresy of Gnosticism in which only the favoured super spiritual few could ever understand or interpret. As we shall see, this is the opposite of what the word revelation means.

The way the Book of Revelation is interpreted by many has added to this misunderstanding as the images and language have been taken up into everyday language and in popular culture. Armageddon, doomsday, apocalypse, the mark of the beast, end times, judgment day, the eschaton, are just some of them. In contemporary news reports,

CHAPTER 1

English speakers commonly refer to any large-scale catastrophic event or disaster as apocalyptic. Serious floods or events are described as "of biblical proportions." All these words feed the misconceptions around the word revelation.

The original meaning of the word *"apokalupsis"* means a disclosure, an unveiling or uncovering. It is used in other contexts to describe the unveiling of a statue that has been covered or hidden by a cloth. It carries the idea of uncovering something that has not been seen before. In the context in which it is used in the Bible, something of the nature and eternal character of God is uncovered or revealed so it can be seen. Something that has always and eternally been true but not seen or known by mankind. It is essentially the work of God who reveals truth about himself to us by means of his Spirit.

This is what Paul is asking for when he prays. He is praying for us to receive the Spirit of wisdom and revelation. What is revealed to us, we have not previously seen before. It is all to do with the eternal nature of God as Father. His longing is for us to know him better as a result of this revelation.

HOW CAN WE KNOW THE FATHER BETTER?

As in all of Paul's writing every word is carefully chosen. At the end of verse 17, the phrase "you may know him better" or as is sometimes translated, "the knowledge of him" is one such case in point. Paul carefully uses the word *"epignosi"* which we translate in English as "know." He could have used another word *"oida"* which we also translate as "know." Each word has a different meaning. We shall see why Paul used one and not the other.

"*Epignosi*" comes from the verb "*ginosko*" which is most often translated as "know" or "known." This word implies a certain type of knowing best explained in several English words a knowing of something or someone personally, intimately and through experience. It doesn't just mean to know about something, to know facts about someone but to know it through personal experience. Paul is using it here to indicate knowing the Father better comes from experiencing him in an intimate and personal way. He is using it to indicate knowing which is heart based.

The other word "*oida*" is also translated as to "know" in English Bibles. However, this word means something altogether different than "*ginosko*," which is personal or experiential knowledge. "*Oida*" means head knowledge or perhaps to understand something through observation and is probably better understood as knowledge coming through the rational mind rather than the heart. An example of "*oida*" is this paragraph I have just written. We need "*oida*," but "*ginosko*" or "*epiginosko*" enables us to know in our hearts.

In Romans 12 verse 2, Paul says we are to be transformed by the renewing of our minds. This is often quoted as prooftext to justify all manner of study and learning. We hear it said we need to get truth into our heads so it will go down into our hearts. Preachers like to say the journey from the head to the heart is the longest journey of all. I've said it myself in the past. It is utter nonsense! Chapter 12 of Romans follows eleven chapters about the truth of God being received in our hearts. When our hearts hear and see truth, it changes the way we think, and our minds are renewed.

Paul is constantly praying for us to grow in knowledge and "knowing" throughout his letters and he uses various forms of "*ginosko*." When the New Testament encourages us to know God the Father, it is not "*oida*" that is used. In fact, we aren't called to understand God; we are called to "*ginosko*" him. To experience him in a personal and intimate way. Amazingly, this means we are not called to observe him and know things about him but instead to experience him personally and intimately. Sadly, so much Christian teaching and the goal of much of contemporary Christianity has focused on knowing about God rather than knowing him personally. Many know about God as a Father but do not relate to him as a loving Father. Knowing about God has its place of course, but it is not the starting point. Knowing him through relationship at the heart level comes first. When our hearts know him, it changes us, and we become like him. In turn, this changes the way we think and how we understand him.

My own personal experience of God as a Father was similar. I knew a great deal about him but in reality, I kept him at a distance. I viewed him through the lens of my broken experience with my own dad. I have written about this in my first book *Falling from grace and being caught by the Father* (2013). As the years have gone by and my heart is at peace and at home in my relationship with God as my real Father, it has changed me and the way I now think. When I pen a book like this, I am writing from my heart with a new understanding of his nature and ways. The big picture has emerged through experiencing this revelation not the other way around, by studying it.

HOW DO WE GET THIS REVELATION?

This question is one I often hear people asking. It comes from a place of trying to get answers and to get understanding through the rational mind. So much of our western mindset has elevated the mind over the heart. However, the Spirit of wisdom and revelation in order to know the Father better is not received through intellectual study or rational debate. It is received by our hearts. Paul continues in his prayer,

"I pray that the eyes of your heart may be enlightened"
(Ephesians 1:18).

Here, he gives the clue on how we receive this gift. It is by having the eyes of our hearts enlightened or opened. In the next chapters, we will look at how the eyes of our hearts became closed and are now being opened. It is central to receiving revelation.

Before we move on, I want to be clear. Revelation is the opposite of scientific research or human reasoning. The knowledge God reveals about himself to mankind can never be attained through any type of scientific research, logical reasoning or theological debate. It is entirely a supernatural disclosure from God given to our hearts. Only God uncovers the truth of his eternal nature through revelation. He alone is the source of knowledge about himself and his plan. Revelation is, therefore, an act of God.

Jesus confirms this during his ministry:

"All things have been given to me by my Father; and no one knows the Son except the Father, and no one knows the Father except the Son and those to whom the Son chooses to reveal him" (Matthew 11:27).

In the same way, the true identity of Jesus can only be known through the gift of revelation. When Jesus asks his disciples who they thought he was, Simon Peter answers,

"You are the Messiah, the Son of the living God."

> *Jesus said to him, "Blessed are you, Simon son of Jonah! For flesh and blood has not revealed this to you, but my Father in heaven" (Matthew 16:16 -17).*

He also explains how the Holy Spirit will be the bringer of revelation.

> *"When the Comforter comes, whom I will send to you from the Father, the Spirit of truth who goes out from the Father, he will testify about me" (John 15:26).*

Later the same evening, Jesus says something significant about the way revelation will continue to be given to his followers after he has returned to the Father.

> *"I have much more to say to you, more than you can now bear. But when he, the Spirit of truth, comes, he will guide you into all the truth. He will not speak on his own; he will speak only what he hears, and he will tell you what is yet to come. He will glorify me because it is from me that he will receive what he will make known to you. All that belongs to the Father is mine. That is why I said the Spirit will receive from me what he will make known to you" (John 16:12 – 16).*

When writing to the Church in Corinth, Paul explains how the wisdom and revelation of God is the Spirit's work:

> *"We do, however, speak a message of wisdom among the mature, but not the wisdom of this age or of the rulers of this age, who are coming to nothing. No, we declare God's wisdom, a mystery that has been hidden and that God destined for our glory before time began. None of the rulers of this age understood it, for if they had, they would not have crucified the Lord of glory. However, as it is written: "What no eye has seen, what no ear has heard, and what no human mind*

has conceived," the things God has prepared for those who love him, these are the things God has revealed to us by his Spirit.

The Spirit searches all things, even the deep things of God. For who knows a person's thoughts except their own spirit within them? In the same way no one knows the thoughts of God except the Spirit of God. What we have received is not the spirit of the world, but the Spirit who is from God, so that we may understand what God has freely given us. This is what we speak, not in words taught us by human wisdom but in words taught by the Spirit, explaining spiritual realities with Spirit-taught words" (1 Corinthians 2:6 – 13).

WHERE DID PAUL GET THIS REVELATION FROM?

This is a question addressed to Paul particularly by those who question his authority and his teaching. When he writes the first of his letters, the letter to the Galatians, it is one of the things he responds to. He is writing to draw the Galatians back to the true gospel, away from a law-based corruption of the gospel. In the opening statement of the letter, he says,

"I am astonished that you are so quickly deserting the one who called you to live in the grace of Christ and are turning to a different gospel, which is really no gospel at all. Evidently some people are throwing you into confusion and are trying to pervert the gospel of Christ" (Galatians 1:6 – 7).

He then explains the source of his teaching.

CHAPTER 1

> *"I want you to know, brothers and sisters, that the gospel I preached is not of human origin. I did not receive it from any man, nor was I taught it; rather, I received it by revelation from Jesus Christ." (Galatians 1:11 -12).*

Paul's confidence rests on this astonishing claim. He is absolutely convinced the things he sees and then teaches find their origin and source in a revelation he receives personally from the Lord Jesus.

For a man who starts off as one totally refusing to believe Jesus is the Son of God and has risen from the dead, to make a statement like this shows the depth of change wrought in his heart by the Spirit.

We read in several places what happens to Paul and how this change came about in him. One of his travelling companions, Luke writes about the events surrounding Paul's dramatic conversion in chapter 9 of the Acts of the Apostles. It is a brief and concise account. Later, Paul adds his own personal perspective of the events when he writes to the Galatians. In this account in Galatians, he says,

> *"For you have heard of my previous way of life in Judaism, how intensely I persecuted the church of God and tried to destroy it. I was advancing in Judaism beyond many of my own age among my people and was extremely zealous for the traditions of my fathers. But when God, who set me apart from my mother's womb and called me by his grace, was pleased to reveal his Son through me so that I might preach him among the Gentiles, my immediate response was not to consult any human being. I did not go up to Jerusalem to see those who were apostles before I was, but I went into Arabia. Later I returned to Damascus" (Galatians 1:13 – 17).*

The salient point he is making in this passage is his calling to preach to the nations came because God set him apart from birth and is delighted to reveal his son Jesus to him. The unveiling takes place for Paul when he meets the risen Jesus on the road to Damascus. This personal encounter is a great revelation to Paul. It changes him. He experiences Jesus personally and tangibly, so much so, when he preaches, he reveals Jesus in and through his own life and ministry.

On two other occasions, probably twenty or more years later when he is on trial before the Jewish authorities in Jerusalem, and two years later before the Roman authorities and Jewish king Agrippa in Caesarea, he adds more detail. In particular when on trial before Agrippa and the Roman governor Festus, Paul relates what Jesus said to him when he appears to him on the road.

> *"On one of these journeys I was going to Damascus with the authority and commission of the chief priests. About noon, King Agrippa, as I was on the road, I saw a light from heaven, brighter than the sun, blazing around me and my companions. We all fell to the ground, and I heard a voice saying to me in Aramaic, 'Saul, Saul, why do you persecute me? It is hard for you to kick against the goads.'*
>
> *Then I asked, 'Who are you, Lord?'*
>
> *"'I am Jesus, whom you are persecuting,' the Lord replied. 'Now get up and stand on your feet. I have appeared to you to appoint you as a servant and as a witness of what you have seen and the things I have yet to reveal to you. I will rescue you from your own people and from the Gentiles. I am sending you to them to open their eyes and turn them from darkness to light, and from the power of Satan to God, so that they may receive forgiveness of sins and a place among those who are sanctified by faith in me" (Acts 26:15 – 18).*

CHAPTER 1

The words Jesus speaks to Paul are extremely significant. "I have appeared to you to appoint you as a servant and as a witness of what you have seen and the things I have yet to reveal to you." I have written about this passage in detail in my book, *The Story of Paul – the Early Years* (2018).

In this exploration of the nature of revelation Paul receives, it is the final phrase which is the most important. Jesus promises to give Paul revelation. "Things I have yet to reveal to you," has been translated in various ways because the word Jesus used is unusual. It means 'to allow one's self to be seen.' It means Jesus is going to deliberately allow Paul to see things about his nature by revealing them to him. In light of everything else Jesus says about the Holy Spirit revealing truth, it is clear he is going to reveal more truth in and through Paul's teaching and preaching.

Paul sees this being worked out in his ministry and teaching. He describes it as a mystery that has been hidden but has now been revealed or made known. In his letter to the Ephesians, he writes of God giving truth to him by divine revelation.

> *"Surely you have heard about the administration of God's grace that was given to me for you, that is, the mystery made known to me by revelation, as I have already written briefly. In reading this, then, you will be able to understand my insight into the mystery of Christ, which was not made known to people in other generations as it has now been revealed by the Spirit to God's holy apostles and prophets" (Ephesians 3:2 -5).*

In his letter to the Romans, chapter 16 verse 25, Paul talks about "the revelation of the mystery that was hidden for long ages past but is now revealed." In the letter to the Colossians, he writes,

> *"I have become its servant by the commission God gave me to present to you the word of God in its fullness, the mystery that has been kept hidden for ages and generations but is now disclosed to the Lord's people. To them God has chosen to make known among the Gentiles the glorious riches of this mystery, which is Christ in you, the hope of glory" (Colossians 1:25 – 27).*

IS THIS ONLY FOR THE EPHESIANS?

I want to return briefly to the prayer Paul prays for the Ephesians in his magnificent letter. The letter is the Word of God to the Ephesians and to all believers in every age. This prayer, I believe, will be the backdrop for the rest of this book. Paul asks the Father of the Lord Jesus to give you the Spirit of wisdom and revelation so that you will know him better. He asks too for the eyes of your heart to be enlightened. I want to encourage you as you read these pages and begin to "see" the big picture, to allow the Father full access to your heart and the light will go on for you in order to receive more from him. I am sure you already know the Father and his ways and plans for you, but Paul is praying for more. There is always more.

As the dots are joined, as the pieces of the puzzle come together, and maybe your mind is challenged and stretched, my prayer is exactly the same as Paul's. I am praying for the light to go on in your heart to know the Father better.

CHAPTER 2

THE CREATION

Not many people are in the habit of picking up a book on Systematic Theology. These books are not bedtime reading nor are they for the faint hearted. I think they should come with a government health warning. But just in case you do read them, I hope you are not offended by my comments. If you look at these books, you may have noticed, as I have, most of these great works begin with the doctrine of God. This is a good place to start. The majority begin their description of God with him being the creator God. The reason for this is because Genesis Chapter 1 verse 1 begins with these well-known and majestic lines,

> *"In the beginning God created the heavens and the earth. Now the earth was formless and empty, darkness was over the surface of the deep, and the Spirit of God was hovering over the waters" (Genesis 1: 1 - 2).*

The writer of these words in Genesis recognises God's creative activity also includes the Spirit of God.

The Apostle John begins his gospel with equally memorable and majestic words,

> *"In the beginning was the Word, and the Word was with God, and the Word was God. He was with God in the beginning.*

Through him all things were made; without him nothing was made that has been made" (John 1: 1 - 3).

John is flowing in the great river of revelation as he pens these verses at the beginning of his gospel. He firmly places the Word, Jesus the Son of God, there in the beginning with God.

The writer to the letter to the Hebrews begins his great chapter on the heroes of faith with a reference to God creating the universe.

"By faith we understand that the universe was formed at God's command, so that what is seen was not made out of what was visible" (Hebrews 11:3).

None of these writers use the word Father at this point, but the Son and the Spirit together with the Father are all actively involved in creation. The creation is seen as an activity and work of God. It is about what he does. But what was he doing before this?

WHAT WAS GOD DOING BEFORE HE CREATED EVERYTHING?

The question is one I have wondered about for some time. We believe God is eternal which by definition means he existed before anything in his creation. I was going to say in the world, but of course his creation is universal and not just limited to our terrestrial ball, the earth. I have wondered what God was doing before he began his work of creating the universe.

Our earthbound understanding of time and distance wants us to put boundaries around ourselves so we can locate events in a humanity focused framework. We call it history. All of science records everything based on the time it takes for the earth to circle our star, the sun. Distance is based on an earth-bound measurement defined arbitrarily by scientists. Consequently, we struggle with the idea of something eternal or the concept of eternity. The mind and rational thought are brought to bear on these activities with interesting results. Theology was considered the only true Science in the Middle Ages, and therefore theology began with creation as its starting point. One gentleman, James Ussher, the Archbishop of Armagh and the Primate of All Ireland between 1625 and 1656 was a prolific scholar who is famous for his chronology sought to establish the exact time and date of creation. He said, "The entrance of the night preceding the 23rd day of October... the year before Christ 4004." According to Ussher, creation began around 6 pm on 22 October 4004 BC. To twenty-first century minds, this sounds utterly ridiculous. In reality, science has not changed much in its quest for the beginning. Whilst many do not believe in creation, they speak nonetheless about a big bang kickstarting everything as we know it. It is located many millions of years ago. Even if there was a big bang, when it was is somewhat irrelevant. The question is still valid, what was the eternal God doing before creation?

As the Apostle Paul grows in his knowledge of the ways of God, he receives incredible revelation about the nature of God himself. When he starts to write the letter to the Ephesians, he is in an amazing flow of revelation. In chapter one, the great opening sentence preceding his prayer in verse 17 is full of revelation. It is truth about God that has always been true throughout eternity but has not been seen by the human heart until the Father reveals it by means of his Spirit to Paul.

WHAT REVELATION DID PAUL 'SEE'?

I have already shared the original sentence Paul dictates to Tychicus is two hundred and fifty-seven words long. Thankfully modern Bible translators breaks it up with punctuation marks and divides it into sentences for ease of reading. However, there is a downside to this. Translators, however skilled at their craft, are not just translating, they are interpreting according to their understanding. All translation carries this risk. The vast majority do an outstanding job in seeking to be faithful to the original words and intentions of the biblical authors. But from time-to-time, translators deliberately impose their preconceived theological position on the biblical text making it say what they want it to say rather than what the original author actually said.

One example of this is the Latin Vulgate translated by Jerome around 385 AD. It became the standard text used by the Roman Catholic Church until the 1950's when the Second Vatican Council encouraged Catholics to read versions of the Bible in their own languages. Jerome's translation is strongly influenced by his belief in the perpetual virginity of Mary. Consequently, he translates references to Jesus's brothers as his cousins, thus mistranslating to suit his personal theology.

Another example is the NIV. A revised English edition titled Today's New International Version (TNIV) was published in February 2005. This version introduced gender-neutral language such as "human beings" and "people" instead of "mankind" and "man." A number of Paul's words were changed, i.e., "son" became "child." This clearly illustrates how interpretation by translators reflects their bias. This shows the importance of being careful with translations. We will see other examples of this later.

CHAPTER 2

As is his custom in all his letters, Paul greets his readers with this delightful greeting, "Grace and peace to you from God our Father and the Lord Jesus Christ." Then he launches into this great opening statement which begins with a paean of praise addressed to God the Father.

> *"Praise be to the God and Father of our Lord Jesus Christ, who has blessed us in the heavenly realms with every spiritual blessing in Christ" (Ephesians 1:3).*

What follows is an astonishing revelation.

> *"For he chose us in him before the creation of the world to be holy and blameless in his sight" (Ephesians 1:4).*

Paul is saying God the Father chose us before he created the world. Paul has seen what God was doing before he created anything. This revelation shows something in the intention and desire of God that is pre-creation. His intention focuses on us, the human race. His plan is for us to be holy and blameless. Holy does not mean religious but unique or set apart for special purpose. As blameless, it means there is no guilt or accusation to stain or spoil us.

Then Paul adds,

> *"In love he predetermined us to be placed as sons through Jesus Christ, in accordance with his pleasure and will" (Ephesians 1:5).*

Paul is shown something extraordinary by the Holy Spirit about the nature of human beings. Simply put, before God the Father creates anything, he plans to have sons to be the focus of his love. He plans for us as objects of his love, to be guilt-free and special. And this would be accomplished in and through his Son Jesus. The way Paul describes God's motivation as being "in love" clearly shows the nature of God.

The Apostle John also saw this and writes,

> *"See what great love the Father has lavished on us, that we should be called children of God" (1 John 3:1)!*

Also seeing something of God's eternal nature, John sums it up in the beautiful and succinct statement, "God is Love" (1 John 4:8).

When Paul writes to the Corinthian Church some years before, he has glimpsed part of this truth and expresses it as being a mystery which God had intended for our good before time began.

> *"A mystery that has been hidden and that God destined for our glory before time began" (1 Corinthians 2:7).*

The way the New Testament writers use the word mystery is a little different from the modern usage. Today, we tend to think a mystery is something that cannot be discovered. It alludes us. It is the opposite in the Bible. A mystery is something that has been hidden, or its meaning lost or forgotten but will be revealed in time. Therefore, it is closely associated with revelation, which by definition is an uncovering. In this way revelation uncovers a mystery so it can be seen with the eyes of our hearts.

Paul receives this amazing and astonishing revelation of the eternal God, Father, Son and Spirit in the glorious and loving unity of their oneness having a plan to have children. God creates humanity in his heart and imagination before he creates anything physically. We were conceived in his heart, known by him and intended to live in a special relationship with him as our Father, faultless and blame free. The motivation for all of this comes from the nature of God who is eternally love.

It not only shows us God's motivation and nature of love; it shows too, God has eternally been Father. He does not become Father; he has eternally been Father. He is Father by nature. I used to think he became my Father when I became a Christian. Yet this revelation shows he has always been Father, my Father, even before I knew him. His Fatherhood does not depend on me knowing it. He conceived me in his heart before my parents conceived me. Before the creation of the world, Father conceived me. This is true for everyone one of us, for all humanity. Even those who deny his existence. He does not need them to acknowledge him as Father. He is their Father anyway. His longing is for all of mankind to know him as Father and the rest of the story is how this is being worked.

It is no surprise, given the scale of these revelations, it causes Paul's tongue to run away with him and the words just kept tumbling out. The rest of the great long sentence will be picked up in other chapters in this book.

I can imagine the glorious dance of Father, Son and Spirit rejoicing in loving embrace and unity, revelling in the thought of beautiful sons and daughters. Then the thought becomes a glorious action as the writer to the Hebrews says the universe is formed at God's command. As it says in Genesis 1:3, the Spirit hovered, then God speaks, "Let there be…"

Father, Son and Spirit joyfully create not just one universe but if astronomers are to be believed, many universes. God created countless galaxies. Again, if they are to be believed, there are 200 billion galaxies in our universe. God created our sun and its planets among 2,500 solar systems in our galaxy. Then he created the blue planet we call Earth. A tiny spec in myriads of stars and planets. He created the perfect environment to place his sons and daughters. The best place to raise his family and for us to call home. As John says in the beginning of his gospel through Jesus the Word all things were made; without him nothing was made that has been made (John 1:3).

One of the most ancient books in the Old Testament which some suggest comes from a similar age as Moses composing Genesis is the book of Job. In the last few chapters, God speaks to Job and questions him. In this he reveals how he created the earth.

> *"Where were you when I laid the earth's foundation? Tell me, if you understand. Who marked off its dimensions? Surely you know! Who stretched a measuring line across it? On what were its footings set, or who laid its cornerstone while the morning stars sang together and all the angels shouted for joy?*
>
> *"Who shut up the sea behind doors when it burst forth from the womb, when I made the clouds its garment and wrapped it in thick darkness, when I fixed limits for it and set its doors and bars in place, when I said, 'This far you may come and no farther; here is where your proud waves halt'" (Job 38: 4 – 11).*

WHEN DID GOD CREATE MAN?

The book of Genesis in the Bible is the first of the five books referred to in Jewish and Christian tradition as the books of Moses. Moses appears in the book of Exodus which recounts the stories of the people of God, the Israelites leaving captivity in Egypt. Moses is the one who leads them out. He figures in all but the first book.

Nonetheless, he is credited with writing these books. Obviously, because Genesis predates Moses, he would have been drawing on stories passed down the generations by the Jewish people. This is referred to as the oral tradition.

Genesis literally means beginnings. It is a book of beginnings.

CHAPTER 2

The largest part of the book deals with the family of Abraham and his descendants. It describes his relationship with God and how his grandchildren end up in Egypt. The early chapters of Genesis take the reader back to the creation of the world. In Genesis chapters 1 to 3, we have the stories of creation, the first human beings, the Garden of Eden and what is called the Fall of man. These passages are significant because they answer some of the great questions mankind has always asked. They contain the mysteries, the hidden things, Paul would later write about. Jesus refers to these stories and quotes from these early chapters. As far as Jesus is concerned, they are true stories containing great truth.

Many have doubted the historicity of these early chapters of Genesis, but they are coming from a place of unbelief and a rational mind set. They claim they are fables and myths arising out of primitive thinking and cannot be relied upon. Undoubtedly, they are ancient in origin and quite probably reflect more than one source or voice. But to discount them is to miss the point of revelation. God reveals these things by his Holy Spirit to show us his nature and the origins of humanity and to explain the reason for the problems at the heart of man.

Genesis chapter 1 to chapter 2 verse 3 describes in beautiful poetic Hebrew the creation of the world in six days and God's day of rest on the seventh day. Chapter 2 from verse 4 reflects another account of creation that compliments and sits alongside chapter 1. In particular it gives a more detailed account of the first man Adam and his wife. There is a third brief account in Genesis chapter 5 verses 1 to 2 which summarizes the earlier accounts. These are not contradictory but complimentary and may reflect the various oral traditions Moses is drawing on as he composed Genesis, the book of beginnings.

All three accounts agree God creates man. Genesis chapter 1 places this on the sixth day of creation.

> *"Then God said, "Let us make man in our image, in our likeness, so that they may rule over the fish in the sea and the birds in the sky, over the livestock and all the wild animals, and over all the creatures that move along the ground. So God created man in his own image, in the image of God he created them; male and female he created them" (Genesis 1:26 – 27).*

The second account gives much more specific detail on the actual mode of creation God uses to create man.

> *"Then the LORD God formed a man from the dust of the ground and breathed into his nostrils the breath of life, and the man became a living being" (Genesis 2:7).*

Finally, in chapter 5, we read the summary.

> *"When God created mankind, he made them in the likeness of God. He created them male and female and blessed them. And he named them "Mankind" when they were created" (Genesis 5:1 – 2).*

The Hebrew word for "man" used in all three passages is the noun 'Adam'. It is a fully inclusive word not meant to be gender specific unless the context makes it male. It is best translated therefore as the generic term 'man' or 'mankind' or at a push, 'humanity,' though both these words are collective nouns. It can be translated 'human beings,' but maybe this is stretching it too much.

The point is God creates mankind collectively, and in his creation of us he made males and females. The important thing is together as males and females we are described as being made in his image and in his likeness. This is not just about being a man or a woman. In a very real way, it is saying masculinity and femininity are part of God's nature and we are made in his image.

Paul sees God the Father's plan is to have sons and daughters as the object of his love. The plan is conceived in the Father's heart before creation and in the moment of creation recorded in Genesis, we see mankind being created like him, made in his image as males and females. Collectively and individually, we are made in his image.

This does not mean we are gods. Instead, it is like looking in a mirror. When we do this, we see our image. The real us is standing looking in the mirror. What we see is not the real us but our reflection. So, it is in our creation by God. We are not gods but are a reflection of him, his nature and character. When Adam has a son, it is described in the same way: "He had a son in his own likeness, in his own image; and he named him Seth" (Gen 5:3). We are made in God's image. We are made for his love and this is in our nature because we are like God our Father.

HOW DID GOD CREATE THE FIRST MAN?

On the sixth day of creation God announces,

"Let us make man in our image" (Gen. 1:26).

All the other descriptions of God's creative activity begin with a command, "Let there be..." But here is an announced intention of the Trinity, "Let us." The next chapter of Genesis gives us a beautiful description and amplification of the actual moment of creation. It is unique. Unlike the creation of animals, birds or fish, God creates man differently.

THE CREATION

> *"Then the LORD God formed a man from the dust of the ground and breathed into his nostrils the breath of life, and the man became a living being"* (Genesis 2:7).

All other created things are created by the command of God out of nothing, but man is made out of a substance, the dust of the earth, the mud and soil covering the surface of the earth. The picture Genesis paints is of God getting down in the dust. The eternal God is described in very human terms. It does not have the feel of a vast presence or some spooky mystical force. It is close up and personal. He gathers a pile of mud or earth and fashions it together. Bringing it all together it takes shape and form. Unlike any other creature God has made, this pile of mud looks like him. When the Son of God came into our world, Paul says he was made in human likeness, was found in appearance as a man (Philippians 2:7). The eternal God is Spirit, but he takes on human flesh in Christ which is the template he uses to make the first man.

When God the Father finishes forming the shape of an adult male human being, he bends even lower. He breathes into the man's nostrils. The language of the writer of Genesis gives God humanlike characteristics to help us understand better. This is called "anthropomorphism." The writer sees God breathing through his mouth into the nostrils of the mud man. As God's breath enters the man, the life-giving breath of the eternal God fills his lungs. His heart begins to beat. Oxygen infused blood rushes through his body. Muscles flex and move as the life-giving blood flows through him. His brain explodes with life as synapses leap at one another, creating sensations and feelings, pulsating with quickened energy. Maybe his eye lids flicker as the man becomes more fully alive. His mind is a blank sheet, no memories, no thoughts, no experiences. Then slowly as God the Father continues to fill his creation with his life-giving breath, the man opens his eyes. As his eyes focus and become accustom to the astonishing light filling him, he finds himself gazing into the loving eyes of his Father.

CHAPTER 2

The thought conceived in the heart of God the Father, Son and Spirit has taken form and shape and is now a living being made in the image of God. Absolute pure love fills the heart of the man as they gaze at one another.

When Paul is speaking to a group of pagan Athenian thinkers in the Areopagus of Athens, he talks to them about how God created us, not referencing the Jewish Scriptures, but their own poets and philosophers.

> *"The God who made the world and everything in it is the Lord of heaven and earth and does not live in temples built by human hands. And he is not served by human hands, as if he needed anything. Rather, he himself gives everyone life and breath and everything else. From one man he made all the nations, that they should inhabit the whole earth; and he marked out their appointed times in history and the boundaries of their lands. God did this so that they would seek him and perhaps reach out for him and find him, though he is not far from any one of us. 'For in him we live and move and have our being.' As some of your own poets have said, 'We are his offspring'" (Acts 17:24 – 28).*

Those Greek poets Paul quotes, in some way deep within them, touch the very essence of our creation. In him, we indeed live and move and have our being. They unwittingly grasp a profound truth; all humanity are the offspring of God. This astonishing revelation is at the heart of the gospel. God loves the world because he is the Father of all. And all are made in his image and his likeness, the objects of his love. This has never changed. It will be forgotten, denied and ignored but nonetheless, it is an eternal truth that remains true for all time and will be revealed in the fullness of time when God sends his Son.

This glorious truth uncovered and revealed to Paul by God make up the edge pieces of the jigsaw of the Big Picture. It gives a framework for every other truth and revelation in the Bible. Without this essential foundational truth, all other truths, however wonderful, tend to float in a rather disconnected way.

CHAPTER 3

THE GARDEN OF EDEN

The major focus of Chapters 2 and 3 of Genesis revolves around events taking place in a garden in the east called Eden. We are told this is where God put the man he created.

WHAT WAS THE FIRST THING GOD DID AFTER CREATING ADAM?

There are some significant things in the text in Genesis 1 which are important to note since they form the backdrop of life in the Garden of Eden and are a fundamental part of the revelation of God, especially as he is revealed as Father.

Genesis 1:27 beautifully and poetically records the creation of Man,

"So God created mankind in his own image,

in the image of God he created them;

male and female he created them."

The next verse says, "God blessed them." The summary in Genesis 5:2 also says,

> *"When God created mankind, he made them in the likeness of God. He created them male and female and blessed them. And he named them "Mankind" when they were created."*

After God creates them, he blesses them. It is easy to read this and go straight to the next part of the story. To do so means we have passed over something fundamental about the nature and character of God. It is quite simply he is a Father who delights to bless his children. Our first reaction might be to think, *Well, yes, that's obvious, everyone knows that! Yes, of course it is true he blesses us.* However, in practice we tend to think the blessing of God comes as a reward for something good or something of merit we do. It is rather like prizes given out at school at the end of the year. Only the good and favoured few get the prizes. In many ways God has been viewed as the headmaster who gives out the prizes.

We hear this in the way things are said and taught in contemporary Christianity. Blessing is linked to our behaviour and obedience rather than the nature of the one who blesses. It is as if we have to qualify to receive God's blessing. I saw a post on Facebook recently which simple said, "OBEY TO BE BLESSED." In later chapters of this book we will see how this attitude and belief system has developed, and the damaging effect it has on us and the way we perceive God.

God blesses mankind whom he has just created before they do anything. His blessing on them is unconditional and not based on behaviour or merit. God does not change; this is still his nature. He is a Father by nature who delights and wants the very best for his offspring. The next few verses are all examples of his nature as the Father who blesses.

Genesis 1:28 says,

> *"God blessed them and said to them, "Be fruitful and increase in number; fill the earth and subdue it. Rule over the fish in the sea and the birds in the sky and over every living creature that moves on the ground."*

Two clear instructions are given by God to man. The first is to be fruitful and increase in numbers, the second to rule over the created world.

The first of these is to go and make babies! The Father wants his children to be like him and have the delight of children made in our image. He will later explain how a man and a woman come together as a couple to form a family. As part of our humanity, we are created as males and females and sexuality is part of this nature. The instruction to multiply obviously has a sexual context. God is blessing this sexual component of our nature. After the Fall, sexuality along with everything else was damaged and corrupted. Some have been taught sex in of itself is evil and only permitted as a necessary evil for the procreation of children and is never intended to be enjoyable and give pleasure. Yet, God's original plan remains in place to bless our sexuality. We shall see more detail on this issue in Genesis 2.

The other instruction God gives in Genesis 1 is for mankind to rule over the created order, over creation itself. This includes all the animals, birds and fish, every living thing from blue whale to the tiniest microbe. Implicit in this instruction is the whole idea of being custodians and carers of the planet. We are intrinsically linked to the earth, especially as we are formed from the dust. Creation also suffers the consequences of the Fall and looking at the devastation human beings have wrought on the planet and its ecosystems is tragic. However, in the revelation God gave to Paul, which he talks about in his letter to the Romans, there is hope for creation in Christ. Paul says,

"For the creation waits in eager expectation for the sons of God to be revealed. For the creation was subjected to frustration, not by its own choice, but by the will of the one who subjected it, in hope that the creation itself will be liberated from its bondage to decay and brought into the freedom and glory of the children of God. We know that the whole creation has been groaning as in the pains of childbirth right up to the present time" (Romans 8:19 – 22).

All of this happened on the sixth day. Then comes day seven. The day of rest. Genesis 2 begins with the familiar lines,

"Thus the heavens and the earth were completed in all their vast array. By the seventh day God had finished the work he had been doing; so on the seventh day he rested from all his work. Then God blessed the seventh day and made it holy, because on it he rested from all the work of creating that he had done" (Genesis 2:1 – 3).

WHAT DID ADAM DO WHILE GOD RESTED?

The simple answer is we are not told. I think the answer is simple. Nothing. He rested too. It has been said God rested from his labours because he wanted to spend time with his beloved creation. He did not want to be seen as a working father. This is a delightful idea, but it comes from a twenty-first century perspective of absent working fathers who are never at home. This is understandable. Having said this, God nonetheless is the perfect Father. He meets every need of his newly created offspring.

The idea of enjoying rest is quite foreign to many who have been brought up to work hard and not waste a minute of precious time. All sorts of statements are made to lay guilt on those who are not diligently pursuing every opportunity. Verses to back up the idea of work are plucked out of context and added to the mix. Here's a great one to dump guilt on someone.

"Go to the ant, you sluggard, consider its ways and be wise" *(Proverbs 6:6)!*

There is no suggestion of work being wrong in what God is doing and giving by way of example. He is not resting because he needs it as if he lacks something because he lacks nothing. We, however, are completely different. The way we are made requires us to sleep for about eight hours in every twenty-four. In addition, God the Father puts in place a principle of regular time to be set aside from activity to just be, to rest. He models it for us.

What's more, he commends it, blesses it and makes the weekly rest day special, or holy. It is not just a good principle, a nice idea if we can fit in. It is what we need, and God thoroughly approves of and endorses rest.

The Jewish people call this day the Sabbath. They take this day seriously. Countless rules were built around the day, which took all the joy out of the rest day and poured guilt on those who broke these rules. Christianity fares hardly any better as the rest day, which is the day following the Sabbath, becomes a day of intense religious activity and busyness. Employed work is replaced by religious work, and there is great expectation put on to "the committed" to make every second count.

I was brought up in an earnest religious family. Sitting down to put your feet up on a Sunday afternoon was permitted, but I was instructed to read a wholesome book rather than a frivolous comic. I was pointed in the direction of missionary biographies. I recall one Saturday cutting up a comic and inserting the pieces between the pages of a book about Albert Schweitzer. Unfortunately, I was caught on Sunday afternoon as some of the pages fell out and revealed my sin. Spanking my bottom was not considered work by my father.

God blesses rest. It is his idea in the first place. The writer to the Hebrews talks about God's rest as the place where we are at home in him, resting in his comfort and in his presence. He says,

> *"There remains, then, a Sabbath-rest for the people of God; for anyone who enters God's rest also rests from their works, just as God did from his. Let us, therefore, make every effort to enter that rest" (Hebrews 4:9 – 11).*

The writer is also addressing the thinking creeping into the early Church that good works are necessary for salvation, whereas the believer's life is at rest in God.

The compiler of Genesis begins the parallel account of creation in Genesis 2 verse 4. We read about God's general creative work, then it moves to the beautiful image of God forming man out of the dust and breathing life into him. The rest of the chapter describes events happening in the idyllic environment in the Garden of Eden where God places the man. In this parallel account, a number of significant things happen. The story focuses on two things, the first is the garden where the man is placed and the second is the man himself.

WHERE WAS THE GARDEN OF EDEN?

Genesis 2 tells us God plants the garden and locates it east in a place called Eden. In verses 10 – 14, it says a river flowed from Eden and watered the garden. It then says as the river flowed on it divided into four tributaries. The first readers of Genesis would have recognised the names of these rivers and had an idea of their whereabouts. Bible scholars who translate the passage have sought to identify them and give them names. It is not very clear where these rivers are except somewhere in the area known as the Fertile Crescent in the north of modern-day Syria and Iraq.

There is little point in trying to find an exact location. If the account of Noah's flood is to be believed, the location would have been swept away in the deluge.

More important than trying to find the geographical location of the garden is to see the truth God is revealing through these stories of our beginnings and his dealing with mankind.

Genesis 2:9 records,

> *"The LORD God made all kinds of trees grow out of the ground, trees that were pleasing to the eye and good for food. In the middle of the garden were the tree of life and the tree of the knowledge of good and evil."*

In his desire to provide the best possible place for the man to live, as someone has said, the best place to raise a family, God plants a garden.

Genesis describes the garden as containing all manner of beautiful trees producing good edible fruit. In Genesis 1:30, God says, "I give every green plant for food." Some have tried to suggest this is biblical prooftext to say we should all be vegans. Some have even gone so far as to suggest that before the Fall all the animals were herbivores and became meat eating carnivores as a result of the Fall. However, if you look at God's account of creation given to Job, he asks if Job was there when he created the earth. Did Job see the lioness hunt her prey and satisfy the hunger of the lions. This clearly knocks this one on the head. I know many people who are relieved we don't have to eat only green things.

The Genesis account continues, "In the middle of the garden were the tree of life and the tree of the knowledge of good and evil.

WHAT IS SO SPECIAL ABOUT THESE TWO TREES?

These two trees become a major focus of the events about to unfold in Chapter 2 and 3 of Genesis. The tree of life is mentioned first. In Chapter 3 verse 22, God says the fruit of the tree is life-giving, and to eat of its fruit enables us to live forever. It is mentioned three times in Genesis 2, four times in Revelation, three of those in the final chapter. We are told the tree of life is in the "paradise of God" in Revelation 2:7. This means it is in "heaven." In Revelation 21:2, the New Jerusalem, which is also in the present heaven, will be brought down, including the tree of life and will be placed on the new earth. In Revelation 22:1, John is shown by an angel a river of life-giving water flowing from the throne of God and of Jesus the Lamb of God down the middle of the street of the New Jerusalem. And there is the tree of life.

CHAPTER 3

> *"On each side of the river stood the tree of life, bearing twelve crops of fruit, yielding its fruit every month. And the leaves of the tree are for the healing of the nations" (Revelation 22:2).*

In the Garden of Eden the tree appears to have been a source of ongoing physical life. Its presence suggests a supernatural provision of life as Adam and his wife are free to eat its fruit. Adam and his wife were designed to live forever, but to do so they likely needed to eat from the tree of life.

The other tree in the garden is the tree of the knowledge of good and evil. This tree is entirely different. The story in Genesis 2 says,

> *"The LORD God took the man and put him in the Garden of Eden to work it and take care of it. And the LORD God commanded the man, "You are free to eat from any tree in the garden; but you must not eat from the tree of the knowledge of good and evil, for when you eat from it you will certainly die" (Genesis 2:15 – 17).*

The tree is dangerous. To eat of its fruit will result in the physical death of the man. The man is free to cultivate the garden and eat of all the other fruits and plants with the exception of this tree. Adam has been intended to physically live forever and not die. He would have seen death in the natural order of creation. He quite likely has seen the lioness catch its prey as Job describes. But he has no idea what death is like for a human being.

WHY WOULD GOD ALLOW SOMETHING SO DANGEROUS IN THE GARDEN?

If God is a Father who wants the best for his children, people wonder why he allowed such a dangerous tree right in the middle of the garden? The tree presents a challenge to the man. It is a gift to him of freedom, free will and choice. God's creation includes boundaries, natural laws and consequences, all of which need to be learned. The man needs to learn certain things in the natural world are dangerous. This tree carries the warning and the instruction not to eat its fruit. God's love for his children is such he wants us to be free to love him and follow his instruction. He does not intend for us to be robots who have no choices. Instead, he offers us freedom to choose life rather than death. To love him from open hearts. He does not force us to love or demand it. He gives freedom. It is part of his nature. God is free and we are made in his image to be free. In this sense, the tree of the knowledge of good and evil is a good thing but also a dangerous thing.

In our homes we have things like this. A log fire burning in the grate is comforting, creating a cosy atmosphere, giving warmth and pleasure. At the same time, we need to teach our children the fire is dangerous and not to touch it, otherwise they will get burnt.

With the tree of the knowledge of good and evil, God the Father carefully explains the consequence of eating its fruit to the man.

This tree is only mentioned in Genesis 2 and 3, but its impact is on virtually every page of the Bible. Its presence is felt throughout the Bible and human history. The devastating consequences of eating the fruit by the first man and woman changed everything. The effects of this tree have been revealed powerfully in recent years to a number of people, most notably to my friends James and Denise Jordan, the founders of Fatherheart Ministries in New Zealand. God revealed this to them over a number of years as they have taught about the Revelation of God as Father and written about it in their books. James's book *The Ancient Road Rediscovered* (2012) and Denise's book *The Forgotten Feminine* (2013) have greatly influenced my understanding and opened my heart to see this truth. We shall look at this in the next chapter.

In terms of the Big Picture being like a jigsaw puzzle, these two trees are very much like the 'blue bits,' the pieces critical to bringing all the coloured bits together and making sense of the whole picture, but often left until the end.

Before we move into chapter 3 of Genesis, I want to look at a couple of other things. I have said Genesis 2 is a parallel account of creation, amplifying and complimenting the creation account in Genesis 1. In it we get more detail about the creation of the man and the woman. In Genesis 2:7, we read the man is made from the dust of the earth by God and has the life of God breathed into him. In the latter part of the chapter, the story describes the creation of the woman. Here is the whole passage.

> *"The LORD God said, "It is not good for the man to be alone. I will make a helper suitable for him."*
>
> *Now the LORD God had formed out of the ground all the wild animals and all the birds in the sky. He brought them to the man to see what he would name them; and whatever the man called each living creature, that was its name. So the man gave names to all the livestock, the birds in the sky and all the wild animals. But for Adam no suitable helper was found. So the LORD God caused the man to fall into a deep sleep; and while he was sleeping, he took one of the man's ribs*

and then closed up the place with flesh. Then the LORD God made a woman from the rib he had taken out of the man, and he brought her to the man.

The man said, "This is now bone of my bones and flesh of my flesh; she shall be called 'woman,' for she was taken out of man."

That is why a man leaves his father and mother and is united to his wife, and they become one flesh. Adam and his wife were both naked, and they felt no shame" (Genesis 2:18 – 25).

My friend John Macdonald has written a book *Made in his Image* (2020), which is a very helpful work looking in detail at the nature of men and women being made in the image of God. It is a masterful book bringing great light on this subject. I don't intend to start quoting from it as I wouldn't know what to include and what to leave out. Instead, I recommend you get John's book.

The other question which comes up is to do with angels. In the beginning of Genesis 3, we encounter an angelic being. Where does this creature come from? When were angels created?

WHEN DID GOD CREATE ANGELS?

The answer is quite straightforward. The Bible doesn't say. We look at the creation of the material world or the universe as we know it. In the passage already quoted from the book of Job Chapter 38, God asks Job the question about being there when he created the earth.

"Where were you when I laid the earth's foundation? Tell me, if you understand. Who marked off its dimensions? Surely you know! Who stretched a measuring line across it? On what

were its footings set, or who laid its cornerstone while the morning stars sang together and all the angels shouted for joy" (Job 38: 4 -7)?

From this passage we see the angelic hosts shouting for joy as God creates the earth. Therefore, they were created sometime in eternity before the creation of the world.

The writer to the Hebrews in his first chapter looks at the eternal sonship of Jesus and his superiority to the angels. He quotes,

"In speaking of the angels, he says, "He makes his angels spirits, and his servants flames of fire" (Hebrews 1:7).

Then he elaborates further about the nature of angels,

"Are not all angels ministering spirits sent to serve those who will inherit salvation" (Hebrews 1:14)?

What is evident from these passages is angels are spirit beings created by God to be his servants and to serve us, his sons and daughters. Put another way, angels were created to be servants. We were created to be sons.

When we move into Chapter 3 of Genesis, we are introduced without explanation to one of these strange angelic creatures.

CHAPTER 4

THE FALL

Chapter 3 of Genesis begins with a conversation between the woman and a creature described as a talking snake.

> *"Now the serpent was more crafty than any of the wild creatures the LORD God had made. He said to the woman, "Did God really say, 'You must not eat from any tree in the garden'"* (Genesis 3:1)?

WHERE DID THIS SNAKE COME FROM?

Everyone knows the story of Eve and the serpent in the Garden. It has been the subject of countless works of art and pictures. It is deeply embedded in the psyche of Western literature and culture. Yet, our view of it mostly comes from many of these medieval pictures. A more careful look at this story raises many questions more than the one I highlighted. How does the serpent speak? Snakes don't have vocal cords. Wasn't Eve surprised when the snake speaks to her? Before it is cursed to crawl on its belly, how many legs did it have? Did it stand on two legs or walk on four?

CHAPTER 4

A number of these questions hinge around the word snake or serpent. At best the Hebrew language can be challenging to translate. This one line, "Now the serpent was more crafty than any of the wild creatures the LORD God had made," is one of those challenges.

Working backwards towards the word snake is the phrase *'wild animal'* (NIV) or *'any beast of the field'* (KJV). This translates a word *"chay"* in Hebrew which means simply *"living things."* Then there is the word translated as *"crafty"* or *"cunning."* It can also be translated as subtle, or prudent. Putting all these things together we see the creature speaking to the woman is one of the most cunning and subtle creatures created by God.

What about the word usually translated as snake? The Hebrew word is *"nawshash,"* which is literally *'shining one.'* So why is it translated snake? Later in the chapter God curses the creature and says it will crawl on its belly. This is where the image of a snake comes from. Consequently, from the earliest times the word *"nawshash"* has been translated almost in hindsight as snake.

In reality, the cunning creature later identified as Satan by other biblical writers was a shining one. In what sense is this meant and is there other biblical evidence to help shed light on it?

WHO IS THE SHINING ONE?

There are two key passages, both are in the prophetic section of the Old Testament. The first is in Ezekiel 28:12 – 17. The second is Isaiah 14:12 – 15. Prophecy in the Old Testament is rooted in a context and time in which it is spoken. Both of these passages are spoken when God's people were surrounded by enemies. In Isaiah's case it is the

Babylonians and in Ezekiel's case, he is thinking about the King of Tyre. However, the nature of prophecy is more than just a word for the present. There are many times when the prophets saw something beyond and bigger than the immediate. This is the case in both these passages. As they prophesy against the evils of Babylon and Tyre in their present age, the Spirit of God gave them insight into the source of greater evil from a much earlier era. They both see something about the source of evil embodied in the *'morning-star, son of the dawn'* as Isaiah calls him, and the magnificent creature described by Ezekiel.

Ezekiel gives a lot of detail about this creature. This is not the King of Tyre he is describing. He is "seeing" something else.

> *"You were the seal of perfection, full of wisdom and perfect in beauty. You were in Eden, the garden of God; every precious stone adorned you: carnelian, chrysolite and emerald, topaz, onyx and jasper, lapis lazuli, turquoise and beryl. Your settings and mountings were made of gold; on the day you were created they were prepared.*
>
> *You were anointed as a guardian cherub, for so I ordained you. You were on the holy mount of God; you walked among the fiery stones. You were blameless in your ways from the day you were created till wickedness was found in you" (Ezekiel 28: 12 – 15).*

From this prophetic utterance we see this creature is perfection personified, full of wisdom and beauty. It is covered in jewels set in gold, a shining one indeed. Made by God, dazzling and beautiful from its creation, it is in Eden, God's garden. It is described as a *"guardian cherub."* The Hebrew word *"cherub"* is transliterated as cherub and considered one of the angelic beings created by God. Its task is to *"cover"* in the sense of protect. Hence, the translation a guardian cherub. The prophet Ezekiel does not see what it is guarding or if its guardianship relates to anything specific in Eden.

Then in verse 15, Ezekiel sees his fall. He says, "wickedness was found in you."

> *"Your heart became proud on account of your beauty, and you corrupted your wisdom because of your splendour" (Ezekiel 28:17).*

The significant words here are pride on account of his beauty and his corrupted wisdom. Corrupted wisdom becomes a feature of everything this fallen angelic being touches hereafter, as we shall see.

Isaiah's prophecy gives more insight and revelation on the nature of the creature's rebellion and fall.

> *"How you have fallen from heaven, morning star, son of the dawn! You have been cast down to the earth, you who once laid low the nations! You said in your heart, I will ascend to the heavens; I will raise my throne above the stars of God; I will sit enthroned on the mount of assembly, on the utmost heights of Mount Zaphon. I will ascend above the tops of the clouds;*
>
> *I will make myself like the Most High" (Isaiah 14: 12 – 14).*

The seven statements beginning with "I will" all illustrate the pride in which he held himself and show his desire to usurp the place of God, Most High. He wants to be above God; he wants to be worshipped as God.

Isaiah calls this creature, *"morning star, son of the dawn."* This translation refers to the bright shining star seen at dawn. This links this passage to the shining one of Genesis 3.

When Jerome translated this passage in the Latin Vulgate in 385

AD, he adds another name which is not in the original Hebrew text. It is the name Lucifer. There is no justification for this addition whatsoever. The name Lucifer was a common name in the Roman world. It means Light Bringer. Interestingly, it is the name of Jerome's bishop with whom he had just had a serious disagreement. Jerome is not known for suffering fools gladly and was not above using his position to make points. One can only wonder! As a result of this addition and mistranslation by Jerome, Lucifer has come to be believed to be the name of Satan.

After the Fall, the fruit of the Tree of Life becomes dangerous to Adam and his wife. If they eat the fruit post fall, they will live forever in their broken sinful state and God loves them too much to let that happen. Therefore, God sets a number of cherubs or cherubim to guard the way to this tree. I believe the shining guardian cherub in Eden was supposed to guard the tree of the knowledge of good and evil. The shining one appears in Genesis 3 speaking to the woman very near the dangerous tree of the knowledge of good and evil.

When Paul writes to the Corinthians about Satan's deceptive tactics, he references the Fall, writing how Eve is deceived by the serpent's cunning (2 Corinthians 11:3). A little further he describes Satan himself masquerading as an angel of light (2 Corinthians 11:14). This is further evidence of this fallen satanic creature's cunning appearance as the shining one.

HOW WAS THE WOMAN DECEIVED?

The way the creature speaks to the woman and how she responds suggests very strongly this is not their first conversation. His opening remarks are a foretaste of what is to come.

Before looking at this I want to look at what Jesus says about Satan in John chapter 8. In this story Jesus is talking with the Pharisees and he is being questioned about his father. In the ensuing exchange they claim Abraham as their father.

> *"If you were Abraham's children," said Jesus, "then you would do what Abraham did. As it is, you are looking for a way to kill me, a man who has told you the truth that I heard from God. Abraham did not do such things. You are doing the works of your own father" (John 8:39 – 41).*

They angrily attack Jesus by questioning his legitimacy. The rumours about his unusual parentage still circulate.

> *"We are not illegitimate children," they protested. "The only Father we have is God himself."*

> *Jesus said to them, "If God were your Father, you would love me, for I have come here from God. I have not come on my own; God sent me. Why is my language not clear to you? Because you are unable to hear what I say. You belong to your father, the devil, and you want to carry out your father's desires. He was a murderer from the beginning, not holding to the truth, for there is no truth in him. When he lies, he speaks his native language, for he is a liar and the father of lies" (John 8:41 – 44).*

Jesus shows very clearly the nature of the devil, Satan. He is a murderer and a liar, the father of lies. He wants to destroy God's children.

When the satanic creature speaks to the woman, he insinuates lies and half-truths to sow doubts in her mind about the trustworthiness of God.

THE FALL

"Did God really say, 'You must not eat from any tree in the garden'" (Genesis 3:1)?

What looks like a harmless question creates doubt. He is questioning God's word. Did God really say you must not eat of the fruit trees in the garden? No, God did not say this, the woman answers. She repeats God's instruction given to her husband Adam word for word with one exception. She says they must not eat the fruit of the tree in the middle of the garden, the tree of the knowledge of good and evil, and adds they must not touch it either or they will die. The question asked by the creature creates doubt and sows confusion which he builds on.

"You will not certainly die," the serpent said to the woman. "For God knows that when you eat from it your eyes will be opened, and you will be like God, knowing good and evil" (Genesis 3:4 – 5).

In this statement he declares his real intention. He says God has lied to them. He says they will not die. Instead, they will become like God by eating the fruit. Their eyes will be opened to know good and evil.

The subtlety of his words and the appeal he is making is clever. He is questioning the goodness of God. He is implying God is holding something back from them. He is trying to undermine the Fatherly nature of the God who is providing the best for his children. The creature dangles a carrot so to speak before the woman, eating the fruit will make her like God. This touches a deep longing in all of our hearts. Many Christians say they just want to be like Jesus. But they, like the woman in Eden, overlook the fact we are already like God. We are made in his image, in his likeness. As Christians, we are in Christ and his Spirit is within us. But this is jumping ahead. This is a truth the Father reveals to the Apostle Paul, which we will look at later.

CHAPTER 4

For the woman, the appeal to be like God is a huge attraction. It is a temptation set up by this satanic creature, but it is also a hidden temptation covered in deception and lies. As Jesus says about the devil, lies are his native language.

The deception goes to another level as the woman looks at the attractive fruit. She is thinking about their next meal. It will be good to eat. Add to this, in her mind is the idea of eating the fruit to make them wise. This beautiful shining creature lost his place in the realms of heaven because his wisdom became corrupted. The woman is on the receiving end of this corrupted wisdom.

> *"When the woman saw that the fruit of the tree was good for food and pleasing to the eye, and also desirable for gaining wisdom, she took some and ate it. She also gave some to her husband, who was with her, and he ate it" (Gen 3:6).*

WHERE WAS ADAM DURING THIS EXCHANGE?

In centuries to come many would lay the blame for the Fall squarely on the shoulders of the woman. They take Paul's words about Eve being deceived out of context. She has been blamed by much of Christianity's teaching for the Fall and led to dreadful suppression of woman and indeed hatred of women. I would again point you to Denise Jordan's book *The Forgotten Feminine* and John MacDonald's book *Made in his Image* for a much more detailed exploration of the effect of the Fall on women in particular.

Where is Adam? It has been suggested he is not there. Perhaps he is across the other side of the garden cultivating or naming more animals.

He has been given a job by God. He is a gardener, cultivating and tending the earth. It seems reasonable to think he is not there when his wife has this encounter with the shining one. When human reason comes into play, all manner of speculation and supposition results. Men in particular have sought to justify their misogynistic attitude and behaviour using this corrupted wisdom of Satan.

The truth is Adam is there at his wife's side. When she takes a mouthful of the fruit, she immediately gives some to her husband who is with her. The Hebrew is quite specific. Regardless of whether he is with her the whole time or not, he eats too. This whole event does not take long, from the shining one's deception to when Eve desires the fruit and speaks to her husband and then his eating as well. I am going to refrain from being dogmatic about whether Adam is there the whole time or not, because so little is given in Scripture. Without question though, Adam is with his wife when she eats, so he has no excuse for not knowing what he ate. He knows it is fruit from the tree of the knowledge of good and evil and therefore knowingly goes against God's clear instruction when he ate.

However, it is only when they both eat the fruit things change for them. They are so united in their pre-fallen state as husband and wife, so connected as one that the consequences of their actions kick in only after they both ate. Their eyes are open to a completely different way of seeing when they both eat the fruit.

> *"Then the eyes of both of them were opened, and they realized they were naked; so they sewed fig leaves together and made coverings for themselves" (Genesis 3:7).*

CHAPTER 4

WHAT EYES WERE OPENED?

The first person I heard ask this question was my friend Denise Jordan. She has the amazing ability to ask very penetrating questions. As far as the Big Picture is concerned the issue of these eyes is like doing a very colourful part of the jigsaw.

What eyes are opened when they eat the fruit of the tree of knowledge of good and evil? Adam and his wife can obviously see with their natural eyes already, so it does not mean their physical eyes. Before the Fall, mankind is created in God's image. We are created to "see" not just with our physical eyes but with inner eyes. Paul uses an expression to explain this inner way of seeing in his prayer in Ephesians 1:18. He prays for the eyes of our hearts to be enlightened. When he is called by Jesus to be his witness on the road to Damascus Jesus commissions him to go and preach to his own people, the Jews and also the Gentiles,

> *"I am sending you to them to open their eyes and turn them from darkness to light, and from the power of Satan to God"* (Acts 26:17 – 18).

Jesus's words to Paul show through this how the eyes of our hearts are closed and consequently we live in darkness under Satan's power. Part of the freedom that comes when we are received back as God's children through the work of Jesus is we see as we were intended to see in the first place with the eyes of our hearts. This enables us to "see" revelation and truth from our hearts rather than from rational thought and understanding.

When Adam and his wife eat the fruit, Scripture says the eyes of both of them were opened. From what Jesus says to Paul, it shows the eyes of our hearts are closed but other eyes opened. A new way of "seeing" happens in the Fall. The impact of eating the fruit changes the way they see everything. It is as if from this moment on all humanity begins to see things from a darkened satanic perspective rather than from a God given perspective we were created for.

WHAT DID THEY SEE WITH THESE NEW EYES?

The first thing they see with these new eyes is each other, stark naked. They have been naked since their creation and felt no awkwardness or shame about being naked together. Like a virus ripping through their hearts, this new way of seeing changes everything. Innocence turns to shame; the beauty of human nakedness turns to embarrassment and shyness. They see each other differently. Within a short time, they will start to blame shift and accuse each other. The first consequence of having eaten from the "Wrong Tree," the tree of knowledge of good and evil is they begin to judge each other. This would accelerate in each succeeding generation. People are judged based on lists of good things they should do and evil things they have done. This flows from Satan's corrupted wisdom.

The next thing they see is themselves. They see their own nakedness and feel ashamed of themselves. They are no longer able to see themselves as God their Father sees them, objects of his love. Instead, their inclination is to cover themselves and hide. To hide their nakedness and feeling of exposure, the Bible says they take fig leaves and sew them together to make rudimentary clothes. This is an absurd action. Apart from the somewhat phallic shape of the fig leaf, they are a bizarre choice as a covering. I can't even begin to imagine how they sew them together. The utter futility of this exercise exposes the devastating consequence of their actions.

Fig leaves are an attempt to hide their new broken identities. They illustrate the struggle ever since of people afraid to face the reality of who they are. We create false identities to hide behind. We are afraid to confront our own brokenness and think we can fool people into thinking we are something other than we really are by dressing up in fig leaves.

The whole world plays this game of dressing up. It is not just little children who have boxes of dressing up clothes. We have sophisticated sets of designer clothes hanging in our wardrobes. The fig leaves of titles and descriptions of ourselves. Our occupations can become major sets of fig leaves. Our status in society or communities, our reputation is a huge fig leaf. When people of rank or importance are exposed as being fake underneath their fig leaves, the collective anger heaped on them can be viscous. They are vilified by public self-righteous condemnation. We all play the game of dressing up, but society has disgust for those who are exposed. We look at one another through fallen eyes and have little mercy. It's all part of the Fall.

Religion takes this game of dressing up to a whole new level. Religious fig leaves are designed to hide ourselves not only from other people but also God. Satan's corrupted wisdom in the Wrong Tree makes us think religious activity, which is perceived as "good" will fix the problem of our alienation from God. All manner of religious games are invented under the cloak of trying to be good. We believe if we do enough and behave in the right way God will be pleased with us. He may even bless us. We have come to believe God's blessing is a reward for good behaviour. Troubles, hardships and sickness are interpreted as punishment by the angry God.

Dressing up in religious clothes becomes so much more than fig leaves in nearly all religions. The robes and special outfits become all part of the drama of man-made religion. It's interesting how clerical sin and failure comes in for special condemnation. When caught, they are often described as being defrocked!

When the eyes of our hearts are opened by the love of God, we see how like little children we have been, thinking we can hide behind our fake identities.

Adam and his wife see each other and themselves in the wrong way, they are ashamed and are trying to cover up the failure when they hear a familiar sound. Suddenly Adam and his wife hear God approaching.

> *"Then the man and his wife heard the sound of the LORD God as he was walking in the garden in the cool of the day, and they hid from the LORD God among the trees of the garden"* (Genesis 3:8).

Adam and Eve lost many things in the Fall but one thing they did not lose was the recognition of God's presence. They hear him in the garden. Mankind has never lost this deep inner knowledge. It is what gave rise to religion. It is also in those who do not believe in God. The sense of spirituality or otherness. They may not have words for it, but it is deep in all people and every culture. Actually, they do have a word for it, it is 'numinous.' Not that many people use it! It is the deep knowledge of something bigger outside of ourselves. It is in us all because we are made in the image of God. It is like his spiritual DNA within each one of us.

The reaction of the man and his wife to God's presence is to hide from him. They see themselves through fallen eyes, they see each other through fallen eyes. Now they see God through fallen eyes. It is perhaps

CHAPTER 4

the most devastating consequence of the Fall. It changes how we see God. The God who creates them, who blesses them, who walks and talks with them, who loves them and plans them to be his children, they now hide from him.

WHAT DID GOD SAY TO THEM?

"Where are you?" asks God. It is not as if he doesn't know. He is not playing Hide and Seek with them. Instead, knowing what happened, he wants them to come out of hiding and face him. Adam's answer is the saddest verse in the whole Bible. It puts into a single sentence the sum total of mankind's problems. It is the root issue in every human being's heart.

> *"He answered, "I heard you in the garden, and I was afraid because I was naked; so I hid""* (Genesis 3:10).

Adam hears God. We have never lost the ability to recognise God's presence. The reality is we long for it, but we seek it through Satan's corrupted wisdom from the Wrong Tree in religious activity and behaviour. On hearing God in the garden, Adam's reaction is to be afraid. They see God through fear rather than love. The context shows Adam's response is born out of terror at being caught. He can no longer see God as a loving Father and is quaking in terror assuming punishment and retribution. The Bible repeatedly tells us, "Don't be afraid." This aspect of fear comes from Wrong Tree thinking and it is where Adam is speaking from when he answers God.

The Bible also uses the term "The fear of the Lord" numerous times as an appropriate response to the presence of God. This means wonder, reverence and awe coming out of our heart relationship with him as

Father. This comes the from the Tree of Life where the fear of the Lord is life-giving.

Standing there, the two of them clutch the fig leaves to their naked bodies. Adam says the reason for his terror is his nakedness. It is not because he has eaten of the dangerous forbidden fruit. He is a picture of guilt and shame, feelings and emotions totally new to him. He is only just beginning to experience the consequences of eating the fruit.

Adam tells God his nakedness caused him to hide. One of the major consequences of the Fall on both of them is its effect on their sexuality. Nakedness now becomes a cause of fear and shame between them. The God given healthy, life-giving relationship between the man and his wife which is evidenced in their comfort and ease in their nakedness together as a man and woman, male and female is disrupted in the Fall. Ever since the Fall, satanic attack has been particularly aimed at sexuality. As male and female, they are made in the image of God. Increasingly, tension between the sexes has grown. Gender has become a dividing issue rather than a uniting issue. Satan attacks everything made in the likeness of God. Family and marriage has become devalued. Male domination of women has become endemic all through the ages. In recent years, gender itself has been attacked repeatedly by the satanic thinking of the world. God made us male and female in his image. In our corrupted wisdom, we are led to believe our gender is our choice.

The man decides he has the solution to his new problem. He makes fig leaf coverings and when they don't work, to run and hide. Man has tried to solve his own problems ever since. The nature of the fruit of the tree of the knowledge of good and evil is to create a belief system based on human wisdom. In reality this is the corrupted wisdom of Satan. At the heart of this is the belief we can fix our broken relationship with God by self-righteousness and human effort. If we do enough good things and not do evil things, we will work our way back into God's favour. Satan has actively promoted this thinking because he knows it can never work. It leaves us as slaves to our own efforts. Its focus is on a distant angry God who can never be satisfied. Instead, through discouragement, despair and desperation, we become more and more entrenched in the kingdom of darkness under Satan's power and control.

Then begins the blame game. "Who told you that you were naked? Have you eaten from the tree that I commanded you not to eat from?" asks God. Adam immediately turns on the woman and blames her.

> *"The man said, "The woman you put here with me —she gave me some fruit from the tree, and I ate it" (Genesis 3:12).*

More than just blaming the woman, he blames God because he gave the woman to him. He accepts no responsibility for his actions. He crosses over totally into the kingdom of darkness.

> *"Then the LORD God said to the woman, "What is this you have done?" The woman said, "The shining one deceived me, and I ate" (Genesis 3:13).*

The woman says it is the shining one's fault. Both responses come from this corrupted wisdom of the Wrong Tree. A common defence made to an accusation of misbehaviour or failure is, "The devil made me do it." Ultimately, he is at the root of sin, but this response hides an abrogation of responsibility. Satan set the trap and tempts them. He set the fruit before them, but it is their desire which births the action.

In the fourth century, a desert Monk called Ephraim the Syrian wrote:

"The tempting would not have led into sin those who were tempted if the tempter had not been guided by their own desire. Even if the tempter had not come, the tree itself by its beauty would have led their desire into battle. Although the first ancestors sought an excuse for themselves in the counsel of the serpent, they were harmed more by their own desire than by the counsel of the serpent."

DID GOD CURSE THEM BECAUSE OF THEIR FALL INTO SIN?

The commonly held belief is God curses the man and his wife because of their sinful actions. Many get their theology second hand and take for granted what some teachers and preachers say without reading what the Bible actually says. A closer examination of the text reveals two things were indeed cursed by God but not the man or the women. They, however, will suffer the consequences of their actions.

The first to be cursed is the serpent, the shining one.

"So the LORD God said to the serpent, Because you have done this, cursed are you above all livestock and all wild animals! You will crawl on your belly and you will eat dust all the days of your life. And I will put enmity between you and the woman, and between your offspring and hers; he will crush your head, and you will strike his heel" (Genesis 3:14 -15).

After Satan fell from heaven following his rebellion and sin, he lashes out at anything God has made to drag it into his realm and sphere of influence. This turns us into broken and alienated orphans who lose our position as sons of God. We remain God's offspring but are no longer able to relate to him with the intimacy of sons and daughters. Satan therefore is cursed for doing this. This includes an eternal antagonism between Satan and his offspring and the offspring of the woman. This describes a war between them which appears to specifically attack the woman.

Many have seen in these damning words a sign of hope. God mentions the offspring of the woman. The Hebrew word used is the word *"seed."* Technically, women do not have seed but eggs. However, Hebraic understanding of conception is the man implants the whole embryo into the woman through his seed and she contributes the womb. So, to describe the seed of the woman is unusual.

This passage has come to be seen as a messianic promise of the coming of God's son, born to a virgin. The seed of "woman" will ultimately crush Satan even though Satan will lash out at him. This is highly symbolic imagery in this part of the story.

The second thing God curses is the land, and this is linked to the consequences of the Fall for the man. There is a deep link for the man to the earth. This is fractured in the Fall. The man who has been formed from the ground will struggle to cultivate it. All of creation is impacted by the Fall. Before, man has been given responsibility to care for the created order. The Fall impacts the man's ability to do this. It becomes harder, wilder and out of control. To produce food, it will take a huge amount of sweaty hard labour.

Paul receives revelation of how this happened and how it will be restored. In Romans 8, he writes,

> *"For the creation waits in eager expectation for the children of God to be revealed. For the creation was subjected to frustration, not by its own choice, but by the will of the one who*

> *subjected it, in hope that the creation itself will be liberated from its bondage to decay and brought into the freedom and glory of the children of God" (Romans 8:19 – 21).*

We need to see how God deals with both the man and the woman. He does not curse them, but shows them more consequences of the Fall. They have already begun to experience it, but there is more.

> *"To the woman he said, "There will be an increase in severe pain in childbirth, as you give birth to children. Your desire will be for your husband, and he will rule over you." And to Adam he said, "Because you listened to your wife and ate fruit from the tree about which I commanded you, 'You must not eat from it,' "Cursed is the ground because of you; through painful toil you will eat food from it all the days of your life. It will produce thorns and thistles for you, and you will eat the plants of the field. By the sweat of your brow you will eat your food until you return to the ground, since from it you were taken; for dust you are and to dust you will return" (Genesis 3:16 - 19).*

The same Hebrew word is used for each of them. It is the word "*etsev.*" There is a lot of debate about this word. It means hard work, toil, painful physical labour, and sorrow. They are both to experience this in their individual spheres. For the woman, it is in childbirth and in her relationship with her man. For Adam, it is his role as provider of food for his family, which he has to get out of the ground through his own effort.

This changes our understanding of the passage. For example, the use of painful hard work instead might not imply God is making childbirth deliberately more painful. It says it is painful before the Fall. After the Fall, bringing children into this life and raising them up will all be hard, painful and difficult work compared to what it was like in

Eden. This is another example of all parts of life being harder because of the original sin.

When the shining one tells the woman the forbidden fruit will make her like God, he fails to mention what she will face when her eyes are opened and she comes to know good and evil. God spells it out. In order for her to "be like God" and know the good of creation, she will also be forced to know hard painful work and danger in the process.

Immediately after this, Adam names his wife for the first time.

> *"Adam named his wife Eve, because she would become the mother of all the living" (Genesis 3:20).*

In childbirth, the woman will come to understand procreation involves sacrifice. The intense love and protectiveness she feels for her new offspring will mirror the way God relates to the creatures made in his image. When she does give birth to her first born, she says,

> *"With the help of the LORD I have brought forth a man" (Genesis 4:1).*

In this first birth, she acknowledges she has not been abandoned by God, but he is with her helping her through it.

WHY DID GOD DRIVE THEM OUT OF THE GARDEN?

There is another consequence to the Fall conveniently ignored by the shining One. Adam and Eve will have to leave the safety and comfort of the Garden of Eden.

> *"The LORD God made garments of skin for Adam and his wife and clothed them. And the LORD God said, "The man has now become like one of us, knowing good and evil. He must not be allowed to reach out his hand and take also from the tree of life and eat, and live forever." So the LORD God drove him from the Garden of Eden to work the ground from which he had been taken. After he drove the man out, he placed on the east side of the Garden of Eden cherubim and a flaming sword flashing back and forth to guard the way to the tree of life" (Genesis 3:21 – 24).*

At first sight this can look harsh, especially if viewed through the eyes opened in the Fall. Those eyes see God not as a loving Father but an angry vengeful God, seeking every opportunity to judge and condemn. The God Adam and all his descendants will be terrified of. However, God has not changed, man has changed. God is still a loving Father who wants to relate to the offspring he has created, to whom he has given life.

This is shown in the way the story unfolds. He makes more appropriate clothes for them rather than the fragile itchy fig leaf outfits. To do this, animals are killed and skinned to make rudimentary clothes. Blood is shed on the ground as a consequence of the Fall. Oceans of blood will be shed in the coming years as generation after generation of descendants of Adam march wilfully away from God. Adam's second son Abel will be the first of myriads upon myriads of human beings who will be slaughtered by each other in an orgy of vengeance, violence, bloodletting, war and genocide. This continues unabated by fallen man right to the present day.

Having clothed them, he drives them out of the garden as an act of great kindness as a loving Father. If they stay in the garden there will be serious risk of them eating the fruit of the Tree of Life. They have been free to eat it before the Fall, but now it becomes dangerous. If they eat it, they will still benefit from its life-giving fruit but in a fallen broken way. They will never be free from its ghastly effect. They will live forever consumed by sin and separated from intimacy with God. Like the creature Gollum in Tolkien's *Lord of the Rings*, they would increasingly become a caricature of their former selves. God loves them too much to leave them like this. So, God drives them out of the garden. Other angelic beings are set to guard the tree from fallen man.

God has not changed. Paul sees the original intention of God is to have sons on whom he can lavish his love. He still loves mankind, but they cannot relate to him as a loving Father because they see him with the wrong eyes. They have eaten from the Wrong Tree and all of their life is defined by this mindset.

In Ephesians 4, Paul continues to write what is revealed to him in his heart by the Spirit of God:

> *"You must no longer live as the Gentiles do, in the futility of their thinking. They are darkened in their understanding and separated from the life of God because of the ignorance that is in them due to the hardening of their hearts. Having lost all sensitivity, they have given themselves over to sensuality so as to indulge in every kind of impurity, and they are full of greed" (Ephesians 4:17 – 19).*

CHAPTER 5

THE FATHER IN THE OLD TESTAMENT

When Adam and Eve leave the Garden of Eden, they leave the security and comfort of the familiar place where life has been good. They have lived there in intimacy with God their Father. Of their own volition, they deliberately choose to question God's goodness and provision for them. Through their own choice they have become alienated from God. They can no longer see him with the eyes of their hearts, but instead they see everything through a skewed way of seeing. Everything is seen and interpreted through these fallen eyes. Nothing will look the same.

The tree of the knowledge of good and evil stays where it is, but its impact is flowing through their spiritual DNA and every thought and action is dictated by its corrupted wisdom. It symbolically represents all man-made attempts to reconnect with God by our own efforts. It is never mentioned again in the Bible. But its influence and impact are seen on every page. I refer to it simply as "the Wrong Tree."

As for the Tree of Life, it remains and continues to be a symbolic source of the life-giving love of God the Father which he pours down on mankind even though the vast majority of the time it is misunderstood and not welcomed or deliberately ignored and denied. The subtlety of the Wrong Tree makes man deny the very existence of the Tree of Life and the nature of the God who gives continuously.

The Tree of Life is symbolic of the true nature of God our real Father who gives us his Son. As Paul says,

> *"The first man Adam became a living being"; the last Adam, that is Jesus, a life-giving spirit" (1 Corinthians 15:45).*

My friend Stephen Hill illustrates the two trees by representing them as arrows. The Wrong Tree's arrow points upwards from Fallen man who is a slave to Satan's power. The upward arrow is man's efforts to solve their own problems and their deep sense of alienation from God. This upward arrow is man-made religion. It cannot satisfy, it is not the way to know God. It is like a ghastly eternal game of Snakes and Ladders.

The Tree of Life's arrow is a downward arrow originating in the character, nature and heart of God the Father who is also Son and Holy Spirit. It flows downwards as a continual gift lavished by the Father on his sons and daughters.

As Adam and Eve begin a different way of life outside the garden, it is tragic to see how quickly the Wrong Tree's influence is felt. Various stories are recorded from these oral traditions collected by Moses. All these stories are influenced by fallen man's perception of God. They see God at work, feel his presence but interpret it from the perspective of the Wrong Tree.

The story of Cain and Abel, the first two sons of Adam and Eve in Genesis 4 describes them making offerings to God. It does not say why they decided to make offerings. Instead, we read how Cain thought God reacts to his offering. He felt it isn't received with favour and he becomes angry and miserable. God does not say the offering is unacceptable to him, instead he asks Cain questions and issues a stark warning.

> *"Then the LORD said to Cain, "Why are you angry? Why is your face downcast? If you do what is right, will you not be accepted? But if you do not do what is right, sin is crouching at your door; it desires to have you, but you must rule over it" (Genesis 4: 6 – 7).*

The gracious life-giving God and Father of Cain asks him questions and warns him about Satan's way of thinking. He says sin is crouching at his door, setting a trap similar to the trap set for his mother. God makes it clear Cain has a choice. In every action man takes, there is a choice. The tragic consequences unfold in the rest of the chapter. Cain murders his brother.

WHAT DID PEOPLE CALL GOD IN THE OLD TESTAMENT?

At the very end of the chapter there is a simple statement, it says at that time people began to call on the name of the LORD (Genesis 4:26).

The word they use for God is the four-letter Hebrew word "Yahweh" "יהוה." This is always translated with the capital letters LORD to indicate this is the word. It is a transliteration of the four letters as *YHWH* or *JHVH* and spoken as "*Yahweh* or *Jehovah*." It sometimes is known as the tetragrammaton, which surprisingly is a Greek word.

The books of Moses and the rest of the Hebrew Bible except Esther,

Ecclesiastes and the Song of Songs contain this name. Observant Jews and those who follow the Talmudic Jewish traditions do not pronounce "יהוה" nor do they read aloud the transcription forms of *Yahweh* or *Jehovah*, instead they replace it with a different term when addressing or referring to the God of Israel. The most common substitution in Hebrew is *"Adonai"* which means the Lord.

Throughout the Bible, God instructs his people to "proclaim his name" as in Isaiah 12:4 and Psalm 105:1. To "chant praises to his Name" in Psalm 68:4. Psalm 91:14 speaks highly of one who "knows my name," and there are countless other references to his name. However, the practice developed particularly during the Jewish exile in Babylon to refrain from saying the name of God. There are a number of reasons given for this, not least because they were afraid of offending him.

When the Jews return from exile led by the priest Ezra, he recovers a copy of the Torah, which is the five books of Moses and read it aloud to the whole nation. From then on, the Jewish scribes start creating copies of the Torah and eventually other books in the Old Testament. The process is carefully organised using clean animal skins to write on. The ink has to be black, and of a special recipe. Each word is verbalised aloud while they are writing.

Significantly, they have to wipe the pen or better still, use a new pen and wash their entire bodies before writing the word "Yahweh." This is done every time they write God's name. Given the number of times the name of the Lord appears in the Old Testament this would involve an awful lot of bathing and mountains of new pens. Whilst we can be amazed at the nature of this reverence, sadly it is indicative of Wrong Tree thinking.

One thing is clear, they do not call God Father and they are in terror of offending him.

DID ANYONE KNOW GOD AS FATHER IN THE OLD TESTAMENT?

The impact of eating the fruit of the tree of the knowledge of good and evil is passed down through the family line and has generational impact. Genesis 5 describes the descendants of Adam who are broken people. Lamech brags about his murderous behaviour. It goes on, chapter after chapter of mankind becoming more and more alienated from God. There is a tragic summary verse in Genesis 6,

> *"The LORD saw how great the wickedness of the human race had become on the earth, and that every inclination of the thoughts of the human heart was only evil all the time"* (Genesis 6:5).

The stories in Genesis from these earliest of days are passed on from generation to generation by word of mouth and eventually lead to the story of one man, Abram. There may have been other stories, some even similar to these in Genesis in other cultures but these stories are collected together by Moses who is beginning to "see" things differently.

We see in the Old Testament a God who is longing to re-establish a connection with fallen humanity. This is totally consistent with his unchanging nature and love for those whom he has made. Often the stories and events the Old Testament describes are seen through the fallen eyes of people who cannot really "see." Instead, they write from a perspective of fear and misunderstanding because the eyes of their hearts are closed.

The first person in the Bible who begins to relate to God in a personal way is Abraham. Isaiah the prophet records the LORD as describing

CHAPTER 5

Abraham as "my friend" in Isaiah 41:8.

Abraham is a key figure throughout the Old and New Testament. His life is characterised by his faith in what he has seen of God. Later in the New Testament, the writer to the Hebrews says of Abraham,

> *"By faith Abraham, when called to go to a place he would later receive as his inheritance, obeyed and went, even though he did not know where he was going. By faith he made his home in the promised land like a stranger in a foreign country; he lived in tents, as did Isaac and Jacob, who were heirs with him of the same promise. For he was looking forward to the city with foundations, whose architect and builder is God"* (Hebrews 11:8 – 10).

Israel as a nation considers Abraham the father of their nation. Through his life the idea of fathering a people begins to be seen. The Jews proudly claim Abraham as their father in their heated discussion with Jesus about fathering.

> *"Abraham is our father,"* they answered.
>
> *"If you were Abraham's children,"* said Jesus, *"then you would do what Abraham did. As it is, you are looking for a way to kill me, a man who has told you the truth that I heard from God. Abraham did not do such things"* (John 8:39 – 40).

However, Israel, who see themselves as God's chosen people, do not see him as Father. Centuries after Abraham, Moses glimpses something about the nature of God.

In his dealings with God over a long life, which culminate in leading the people of Israel out of Egypt through the desert to the doorstep of the promised land, he is shown something by God no one has seen up to this time.

In Deuteronomy 29, when he speaks to the gathered people, he addresses them with these words,

> *"Your eyes have seen all that the LORD did in Egypt to Pharaoh, to all his officials and to all his land. With your own eyes you saw those great trials, those signs and great wonders. But to this day the LORD has not given you a mind that understands or eyes that see or ears that hear" (Deuteronomy 29:2 – 4).*

Moses is explaining what has happened. They see physical things, they know it is God at work, but they do not really "see." The eyes of their hearts are closed. What they see is always through the satanic filter inherited from Adam. This is a very significant statement by Moses because it explains so much of the Old Testament understanding of God by the Jewish people. They see him at work, they know what his presence feels like, but they are in terror of him. Every event becomes judged according to the thinking of the Wrong Tree. Things such as good harvest or victory in battle over an enemy are perceived to be the reward or blessing of God. Undoubtedly, he blesses them, because it is his nature to do so. But the perception is it is because of people doing something right.

In contrast, every calamity, flood, famine, plague, or defeat in battle is perceived to be the judgment or punishment of God on people for their sin and failure. Without doubt, God uses events like this to get people's attention and draw them to himself. But it does not mean he is the instigator of such dreadful events.

This sort of thinking is still alive and well and kicking in modern Christianity. A hurricane devastating New Orleans is perceived by some as God judging the sinful city. An earthquake in Haiti killing a quarter of a million people is God's judgment of them for practicing voodoo and the like. Christians triumphantly claiming God moves a hurricane offshore in Florida because of their prayers may self-righteously congratulate themselves. Perhaps it would be better for them to spare a prayer for the inhabitants of the Bahamas who take the full brunt of the storm and suffer appallingly. Maybe just asking for the hurricane to dissipate rather than go somewhere else might be more in keeping with the heart of God.

In the same address to the people of Israel, Moses speaks a truth no one else has seen up to this point,

> *"Is he not your Father, your Creator, who made you and formed you" (Deuteronomy 32:6)?*

Moses is the first person in the Old Testament to see God in this way. He receives this by revelation. God is Father before he is Creator. It is Moses who also meets with God personally on Mount Sinai and brings to the people of Israel a message from the LORD God. They are referred to as the Ten Commandments.

WHERE DO THE TEN COMMANDMENTS FIT IN?

Moses never actually refers to them as the "ten commandments." They are listed in Exodus Chapter 20. The Hebrew expression, which occurs three times in the Old Testament, literally means "ten words." This is why Exodus 20 is often referred to as the Decalogue, *"deka"* being the Greek word for "ten" and *"logos"* meaning "word."

These Ten Words God gives the Israelites at Mount Sinai represent God's personal interest in bringing out the best in his children so that we may live life to the fullest. These words set God's people apart, identify right from wrong, and uphold the ultimate importance of love for God and our neighbour in promoting peace in this life.

These Ten Words are an expression of God's heart and character. They not only show us what God wants they show us what God is like. They say something about his honour, his worth, and his majesty. They tell us what matters to God. The Israelites were an oppressed people, and it is as if God is saying he hears their cry. He will save them because he loves them.

Love is the binding theme of the Ten Words. This is no surprise when we consider God's perfect love for his creation. As a loving parent lays down ground rules for his child to follow to lead a safe and successful life, God the Father gave the Ten Words to help them lead their lives. They are about relationships mattering the most, mankind's relationship with him and our relationship with each other. They were a gift from God the Father not just to the people of Israel but to all of his offspring.

Over time, the Ten Words become known as the Ten Commandments. Their role is a summary of fundamental principles. They are not as explicit or detailed as rules because they provide guiding principles that apply universally, across changing circumstances. They do not specify punishments for their violation. Their precise import must be worked out in each separate situation and this is what happens.

Hundreds of years after Moses receives what becomes known as the Law, the Jewish people are taken into exile in Babylon. During those centuries of exile, they take these basic Ten Words and start to interpret and codify them. What emerges is an impossible list of hundreds of rules and regulations that rip the heart out of the original Law of Moses. A group, who will be encountered in Jesus's ministry known as Pharisees, emerges in those years. Their interpretation of the Law becomes impossible for people to keep. They are driven by a perception originating in the satanic thinking coming from the Wrong Tree.

Many years later, the Apostle Peter challenges the Pharisees who claim to be followers of Jesus and who are insisting on adherence to the Old Testament law as the core of the gospel,

> *"Why do you try to test God by putting on the necks of Gentiles a yoke that neither we nor our ancestors have been able to bear"* (Acts 15:10)?

This interpretation of the Law of Moses coupled with the law of sin and death at work in us is not life-giving to Paul. He shares his experience of this when he writes in Romans 7.

> *"What a wretched man I am! Who will rescue me from this body that is subject to death?.......I myself in my mind am a slave to God's law, but in my sinful nature a slave to the law of sin"* (Romans 7:24 – 25).

There is a solution, and we will look at it in a later chapter.

DID KING DAVID SEE GOD AS FATHER?

The second King of Israel is David. He is the author of many of the Psalms which are an amazing window into his inner world and thoughts. In the New Testament, Paul describes David when preaching,

> *"God testified concerning him: 'I have found David son of Jesse, a man after my own heart" (Acts 13:22).*

When David is anointed by Samuel to be the next King of Israel, it is not based on his outward appearance but on the state of his heart. God says to Samuel to not look at the externals but at the heart.

> *"Do not consider his appearance or his height, for I have rejected him. The LORD does not look at the things people look at. People look at the outward appearance, but the LORD looks at the heart" (1 Samuel 16:7)*

The human default setting was seeing things through fallen eyes and making judgments on outward appearances. Just as Adam does at the beginning, in this story we see God the Father explaining again how seeing with the eyes of the heart is the life-giving way.

In Psalm 89, which is written by someone called Ethan, the writer describes David as someone found by God.

> *"I have found David my servant; with my sacred oil I have anointed him" (Psalm 89:20).*

Then in verse 26, he speaks prophetically of David,

> *"He will call out to me, 'You are my Father, my God, the Rock My Saviour.'"*

The Psalms written by David are a window into his heart. He opens it up and pours out his thoughts, feelings and emotions. At the same time, he is beginning to see things God is revealing to him. David says,

> *"A father to the fatherless, a defender of widows, is God is his holy dwelling" (Psalm 68:5).*

When he feels abandoned by his own parents, he realises God has not forsaken him.

> *"Though my father and mother forsake me, the LORD will receive me"* (Psalm 27:10).

There are things about his character and behaviour which do not reflect God's heart because he is a fallen man. Yet, he is reaching out to God in a different way from his heart. In his Psalm of repentance, written after his disastrous behaviour with Bathsheba he prays,

> *"Create in me a pure heart, O God, and renew a steadfast spirit within me"* (Psalm 51:10).

> *"You do not delight in sacrifice, or I would bring it; you do not take pleasure in burnt offerings. My sacrifice, O God, is a broken spirit; a broken and contrite heart"* (Psalm 51:16 – 17).

His sees frantic religious activity is not needed to try to gain forgiveness but a changed or a recreated heart. He sees by revelation this is God's work.

WHAT DO THE PROPHETS HAVE TO SAY?

The first of the major prophets is Isaiah. He is prophesying before the conquest of the Kingdom of Judah by the Babylonians. His book is of major importance as he speaks out of a personal experience of God.

In chapter 6, the prophet has an encounter with God which transforms his whole life and ministry. It is a very well-known passage, but I want to quote it in its entirety as it is such a significant part of the

THE FATHER IN THE OLD TESTAMENT

Big Picture.

> *"In the year that King Uzziah died, I saw the Lord, high and exalted, seated on a throne; and the train of his robe filled the temple. Above him were seraphim, each with six wings: With two wings they covered their faces, with two they covered their feet, and with two they were flying. And they were calling to one another:*
>
> *"Holy, holy, holy is the LORD Almighty; the whole earth is full of his glory."*
>
> *At the sound of their voices the doorposts and thresholds shook, and the temple was filled with smoke.*
>
> *"Woe to me!" I cried. "I am ruined! For I am a man of unclean lips, and I live among a people of unclean lips, and my eyes have seen the King, the LORD Almighty."*
>
> *Then one of the seraphim flew to me with a live coal in his hand, which he had taken with tongs from the altar. With it he touched my mouth and said, "See, this has touched your lips; your guilt is taken away and your sin atoned for."*
>
> *Then I heard the voice of the Lord saying, "Whom shall I send? And who will go for us?"*
>
> *And I said, "Here am I. Send me!"*
>
> *He said, "Go and tell this people: "'Be ever hearing, but never understanding; be ever seeing, but never perceiving.' Make the heart of this people calloused; make their ears dull and close their eyes. Otherwise they might see with their eyes, hear*

CHAPTER 5

with their ears, understand with their hearts, and turn and be healed" (Isaiah 6:1 – 10).

His astonishing vision of the majesty and magnificence of Yahweh is unique in the Old Testament. Isaiah is immensely privileged to have this revealed to him. Unsurprisingly, he is overwhelmed by the encounter and feels totally unworthy and unclean before Almighty God. He says, 'my eyes have seen.' God has opened the eyes of his heart to see the reality of who God is. The Lord sends an angel, in this case a seraph with a live coal from the altar which touches his lips, and the angel announces his guilt is taken away and his sin atoned for. This restores him to being a man like the ones God has planned before the Fall, holy and blameless in his sight (Ephesians 1:4).

In this restored state he is able to "see" with the eyes of his heart with a clarity not experienced by anyone up to this point in the history of the world since the Fall. Like Adam, he hears the voice of God, but it does not fill him with fear. Instead, Isaiah effectively runs to God and offers himself in his service.

The commission given to him by the Lord is extraordinary. It is all about the eyes of the heart. Isaiah will preach however the people will hear but not understand, they will see but not perceive. Isaiah will announce truth he is shown by revelation, but no one will really see it. They are locked into their Wrong Tree mindset.

This passage will be very meaningful to Jesus and Paul who both quote it when commenting on the response to their teaching. It characterises the response by the vast majority of people to their ministries.

Jesus says to his disciples,

> *"I speak to them in parables: "Though seeing, they do not see; though hearing, they do not hear or understand. In them is fulfilled the prophecy of Isaiah" (Matthew 13:13).*

Then he continues and says to his disciples,

> *"But blessed are your eyes because they see, and your ears because they hear" (Matthew 13:16).*

For the rest of his life Isaiah speaks to the people of Israel even though they neither understand nor respond to his preaching. Yet his eyes are open, his heart is alive, and he sees things revealed to him by the Spirit. In Chapter 9 of his prophecy, he speaks about things in the immediate and he also sees things of a bigger perspective. God reveals to Isaiah truth about himself and his Son who he is planning to send to the world. Isaiah says,

> *"For to us a child is born, to us a son is given, and the government will be on his shoulders. And he will be called Wonderful, Counsellor, Mighty God, Everlasting Father, Prince of Peace. Of the increase of his government and peace there will be no end" (Isaiah 9:6).*

He catches a glimpse of the hitherto hidden nature of the Eternal God who is Father, Son and Spirit in this passage. He sees the Mighty God as the wonderful Counsellor, words Jesus will echo when speaking of the Holy Spirit. He sees God as the everlasting Father. He sees him as the Prince of Peace. The Son who will be born in the fullness of time. Paul expresses this in his letter to the Galatians,

> *"But when the set time had fully come, God sent his Son, born of a woman, born under the law, to redeem those under the law, that we might be repositioned as sons" (Galatians 4:4 - 6).*

CHAPTER 5

Towards the end of his life and ministry, Isaiah reflects on the kindness of God and his dealings with Israel and uses the word Father specifically.

"You, LORD, are our Father, our Redeemer from of old is your name" (Isaiah 63:16).

"No one calls on your name or strives to lay hold of you; for you have hidden your face from us and have given us over to our sins. Yet you, LORD, are our Father. We are the clay; you are the potter; we are all the work of your hand" (Isaiah 64:7 – 8).

In calling God Father, Isaiah acknowledges a particular relationship with him. God is addressed as Father, not because he is Israel's Creator, but because he is also Israel's Redeemer. Isaiah sees this by revelation. It reveals the nature of the special relationship God has with his chosen ones.

WHAT DID THEY SAY ABOUT GOD'S MOTHERLY QUALITIES?

In Genesis, Moses describes the creation of mankind.

"So God created mankind in his own image, in the image of God he created them; male and female he created them" (Genesis 1: 27).

It specifically says the image of God includes masculinity and femininity. Mankind together as male and female reflect something at the heart of the Godhead. Whilst the Bible is clear, God is not a man but is Spirit, it strongly reveals qualities in his nature we recognise as both masculine and also feminine. David, when writing his Psalms, sees this as did Isaiah and Zephaniah.

David's experience comes from his own unusual relationship with his mother and father. In his growing understanding of God, he recognises God's provision more than made up for what is lost with his natural parents. He writes in Psalm 27,

> "Though my father and mother forsake me, the LORD will receive me"

Then in Psalm 131, David compares himself to being like a satiated child who has been suckling at his mother's breast in his relationship with God.

> "But I have calmed and quieted myself, I am like a weaned child with its mother; like a weaned child I am content."

In Psalm 42, when writing about God's love for him he compares it to being sung over by the LORD. Whilst this is not exclusively the province of a mother, many will identify with the lullaby sung over us as we drift off to sleep in our mother's arms.

> "By day the LORD directs his love, at night his song is with me" (Psalm 42:8).

The prophet Zephaniah expresses similar sentiments.

> "He will take great delight in you; in his love he will no longer rebuke you but will rejoice over you with singing" (Zephaniah 3:17).

These observations come out of the comforting experience of God's love for them. It does not come from analytical study; it comes from heart-based experience. God reveals these aspects of his nature to his children out of his desire to know him as both a father and a nurturing mother.

Towards the end of his prophecy, Isaiah speaks to the broken-hearted people of Israel. He expresses the profound longing in the heart of God to comfort his people.

> *"Comfort, comfort my people, says your God. Speak tenderly to Jerusalem and proclaim to her that her hard service has been completed, that her sin has been paid for, that she has received from the LORD's hand double for all her sins" (Isaiah 40:1 -2).*

The prophet Isaiah has deeper insight revealed to him about God's comforting and nurturing motherly heart. He draws on the imagery of a child relating to its mother. In Isaiah 49, his words come directly from God himself.

> *"Can a mother forget the baby at her breast and have no compassion on the child she has borne? Though she may forget, I will not forget you! See, I have engraved you on the palms of my hands" (Isaiah 49:15 – 16).*

It reaches its fullest expression in Isaiah 66, where he speaks specifically to God's people Israel who are grief stricken over the calamities experienced by the city of Jerusalem.

> *"For you will nurse and be satisfied at her comforting breasts; you will drink deeply and delight in her overflowing abundance." For this is what the LORD says: "I will extend peace to her like a river, and the wealth of nations like a flooding stream; you will nurse and be carried on her arm and dandled on her knees. As a mother comforts her child, so will I comfort you; and you will be comforted over Jerusalem" (Isaiah 66:11 – 13).*

The truth expressed through these verses add great depth to the nature of God who is Father. In his fathering of mankind, he connects with his children as a comforter and nurturer. Many describe this as the "motherheart of God." They are not saying God is a mother or a woman any more than they are saying he is male or a man, but within his revelation of himself as Father he expresses both masculine and feminine qualities which are experienced as fatherly and motherly love.

WHAT DO JEREMIAH AND EZIEKIEL SAY ABOUT OUR HEART?

In God's dealing with his people in the Old Testament, he increasingly draws them to the state of their hearts, never more so than in the Prophecy of Jeremiah. Jeremiah is sometimes referred to as the Weeping Prophet since he is very emotional and wears his heart on his sleeve, so to speak.

He is speaking from Jerusalem in the final years of the southern Kingdom of Judah. He will be there to witness the final siege and the burning of the temple by the Babylonians. He is not taken into exile with the first wave of Jewish exiles but remains until the final catastrophic rebellion and mass deportation of the Jews when he also is taken to Babylon.

Early in his ministry he addresses "faithless Israel" in language coming straight from God's heart. God addresses Israel and says,

> *"I myself said, "How gladly would I treat you like my children and give you a pleasant land, the most beautiful inheritance of any nation.' I thought you would call me 'Father' and not turn away from following me" (Jeremiah 3:19).*

CHAPTER 5

It is the most poignant verse in the Old Testament. It takes us back to the very beginning, the revelation Paul receives in Ephesians 1:4. It reveals God the eternal Father longing for his children to come home and to call him Father. In it he shows he has not changed, and in spite of everything he is still our Father whose arms are wide open to us as his offspring.

Jeremiah, along with Ezekiel, a contemporary of his, both see the root issue separating Israel from their Father God is their blind eyes resulting in hard hearts. All of which are consequences of the Fall. Jeremiah describes the heart as full of deceit.

> *"The heart is deceitful above all things and beyond cure. Who can understand it" (Jeremiah 17:9)?*

Much later in his ministry after the city has fallen, Jeremiah sees a new beginning as people turn back to God with all their hearts.

> *"You will seek me and find me when you seek me with all your heart. I will be found by you," declares the LORD" (Jeremiah 29:13).*

This new relationship Jeremiah sees is going to be a new heart-based covenant between God and man written on our hearts not on tablets of stone.

> *"This is the covenant I will make with the people of Israel after that time," declares the LORD. "I will put my law in their minds and write it on their hearts. I will be their God, and they will be my people. No longer will they teach their neighbour, or say to one another, 'Know the LORD,' because they will all know me, from the least of them to the greatest," declares the LORD" (Jeremiah 31:33 – 34).*

Ezekiel makes it even clearer and sees this will be God's initiative and activity. Man cannot fix their own problem as Adam tries to do. Instead, God our Father will come and do the heart surgery on his people. This is all pointing forward to the coming of his Son as seen by Isaiah.

> *"I will give them an undivided heart and put a new spirit in them; I will remove from them their heart of stone and give them a heart of flesh" (Ezekiel 11:19).*

> *"I will sprinkle clean water on you, and you will be clean; I will cleanse you from all your impurities and from all your idols. I will give you a new heart and put a new spirit in you; I will remove from you your heart of stone and give you a heart of flesh. And I will put my Spirit in you and move you to follow my decrees and be careful to keep my laws" (Ezekiel 36:25 – 26).*

As the Old Testament draws to a close, one last prophet speaks. Malachi who writes about four hundred years before the coming of Jesus sees something.

Almost as a postscript, God makes one last promise. God tells his people another prophet will come like Elijah whose ministry will turn everything upside down like the first Elijah. He will precipitate a returning of the hearts of fathers to their children and vice versa. It will be a time of re-establishing the God given order of hearts relating to hearts. Fathers to children which comes about when we discover God as our real Father.

> *"See, I will send the prophet Elijah to you before that great and dreadful day of the LORD comes. He will turn the hearts of*

the fathers to their children, and the hearts of the children to their fathers" (Malachi 4:5 – 6).

And with that God stops speaking! He has said everything he needs to say to prepare the way for the coming of his son into the world.

CHAPTER 6

THE COMING OF THE SON

Four hundred years of silence. Four hundred years of mankind drifting further from God. Four hundred years of sinking deeper into legalistic interpretations of the Old Testament from a Wrong Tree perspective. Then one day an old man, a Jewish priest, whose family line goes right back to Abijah, who had been high priest in the time of David, stands in line in the temple in Jerusalem. Along with a number of other priests in his division, he is waiting to draw lots on who will have the honour to go into the temple of the Lord and burn incense. As he draws his hand out of the bag, his heart quickens when he sees he has drawn the lot announcing it is his turn. After the usual ritual cleansing, he enters the temple. His name is Zechariah. He and his aged wife Elizabeth are childless.[1]

---

1. Zechariah was not the high priest just one of the priests. In my teaching I have often said the High Priest going into the Holy of Holies had a rope tied around his ankle so he could be dragged out if he made a mistake and was killed as a result by God. I have been looking everywhere for some historical reference for this. To my surprise and embarrassment, I have found absolutely none!

Here is a quote from Jack Wellman one of many scholars who have examined this. He is part of a ministry called "Telling Ministries." He summaries his studies in this paragraph:

"There is not one shred of evidence in the Old and New Testament, in the Apocrypha, or any of the Dead Sea Scrolls, Josephus's writings, the Pseudepigrapha, the Talmud, the Mishna, or any other

CHAPTER 6

Luke, the gospel writer tells us what happens in his first chapter of the Gospel. Zechariah has an angelic encounter that literally leaves him speechless.

An angel name Gabriel informs Zechariah his prayers are answered. His wife will have a baby, a son who will be called John. Specifically, the angel says of the child,

> *"He will be filled with the Holy Spirit even before he is born. He will bring back many of the people of Israel to the Lord their God. And he will go on before the Lord, in the spirit and power of Elijah, to turn the hearts of the fathers to their children and the disobedient to the wisdom of the righteous, to make ready a people prepared for the Lord" (Luke 1:15 – 17).*

This links directly back to the last words of God in the Old Testament. John will be the fulfilment of the prophecy of Malachi. Zechariah's questioning of the angel comes from his rational mind with a distinctly unbelieving undertone. He does not answer from his heart. Not surprisingly, he can't believe it because he and his wife are far too old to have children. In response, the angel tells Zechariah he will not be able to speak until the baby is born.

Dumbstruck, Zechariah goes home on the completion of his priestly duties and lo and behold, Elizabeth becomes pregnant.

Six months later, the angel Gabriel is sent on another mission, this time to Nazareth, a tiny backwater town in Galilee.

---

authoritative source that states the high priest had to have a rope tied around his leg, his feet, or his waist. Just be glad that Jesus is our high priest and has entered into the Holy of Holies once-and-for-all, with His own blood, and did for us all, what no human high priest could ever do. Otherwise, we'd all be at the end of our rope."

Read more: www.whatchristianswanttoknow.com/did-the-high-priest-have-a-rope-tied-around-him-when-entering-the-holy-of-holies

WHAT IS SO SIGNIFICANT ABOUT THE ANGEL'S MESSAGE?

The person Gabriel visits this time is a young unmarried teenage girl called Mary. She is betrothed to be married to a local man called Joseph who is a carpenter. The ceremony has not been conducted or the marriage consummated, so she is still a virgin. We are not told what angels look like and it is extremely unlikely Mary has ever seen one before. So, his appearance and greeting is likely as shocking as it is unexpected. He says to her,

> *"Greetings, you who are highly favoured! The Lord is with you" (Luke 1:28).*

Luke's language is very understated about Mary's reaction.

> *"Mary was greatly troubled at his words and wondered what kind of greeting this might be" (Luke 1:29).*

She becomes extremely agitated and disturbed, which is not surprising for one so young. She is most likely frightened and has no idea what the angel is talking about! To put her at ease the angel helpfully tells her not to be afraid! He repeats how she is on the receiving end of great favour from God. The word for favour is *"charis"* which is used widely in the New Testament and usually describes a special gift of God. In this context, she is honoured highly by God and viewed with great favour by him. Then the angel breaks the news to her,

> *"You will conceive and give birth to a son, and you are to call him Jesus. He will be great and will be called the Son of the Most High. The Lord God will give him the throne of his father*

CHAPTER 6

David, and he will reign over Jacob's descendants forever; his kingdom will never end" (Luke 1:31 – 33).

Each phrase of this astonishing announcement is as pregnant as Mary is about to become. It describes the greatest intervention by Almighty God since the creation of the world. Mary, a virgin will conceive. She has no idea how it will happen. It will be miraculous. She will give birth to a son. No one knew the sex of a baby prior its birth, this will be another miracle. The most incredible revelation comes in the next phrase, the baby will be called the Son of the Most High. No one knew God had a Son! Finally, he will be given a Kingdom like his forefather King David, but this kingdom will never end. The baby will be eternal.

Reeling from this incredible news, almost naively Mary asks how this is going to happen. Maybe her mind has not been able to process past the fact she is going to become pregnant. This in itself is huge given her circumstances, let alone all the other incredible things being said.

"How will this be," Mary asked the angel, "since I have not known a man" (Luke 1:34)?

It is a fair question. The angel's answer is beautiful. It resonates with revelation and truth. It comes straight from the heart of God himself.

"The Holy Spirit will come on you, and the power of the Most High will overshadow you. So the holy one to be born will be called the Son of God" (Luke 1:35).

All three persons of the Godhead are actively participating in the events about to unfold. The Holy Spirit will be the active agent who came upon Mary. The Most High, the Father Almighty will overshadow her. This carries the picture of the mother hen gathering the chicks under her wings, and of being under the shadow of the Almighty as a place of safety and refuge. The result of this will be the eternal Son of God being conceived within her.

This astonishing revelation to Mary, the revealing of something which is eternally true, is quite simply Almighty God has a Son. This is not known by the people of Israel. No one knows this. There are hints of it in the Old Testament. Sometimes the Kings of Israel are referred to as God's sons but not in this way. This is entirely new. The truth of God having a Son by definition means he is also Father. This is the first step of a major uncovering by God of his relational nature as a Father.

The significance of this revelation cannot be over emphasised. It was and is still world changing and life changing. It is the start of a journey of homecoming for the orphan hearted children of God. It is the beginning of a returning of the hearts of the fathers to the children and the children to the fathers. It is the fulfilment of Old Testament prophecy.

WHAT DID MARY DO WITH THIS NEWS?

When something as extraordinary as this happens, there is a natural need in us to find someone to talk to, to help us make sense of it. The final piece of news given by the angel may have really helped Mary. Gabriel tells her about her relative Elizabeth.

> *"Even Elizabeth your relative is going to have a child in her old age, and she who was said to be unable to conceive is in her sixth month. For there is nothing impossible with God's word" (Luke 1:36 – 37).*

To hear this news about Elizabeth is likely great encouragement to Mary. Perhaps Mary's family are already discussing the news of Elizabeth's unusual pregnancy. However, before she does anything, she responds to the angel in such a way as to show why she has been so graciously chosen by God for the task of bearing in her womb his Son. She says,

> *"I am the Lord's servant," Mary answered. "May your word to me be fulfilled." Then the angel left her"* (Luke 1:38).

Her delightful childlike response comes straight from her heart. She willingly offers herself up to God as his handmaid. From this day forward she will think about these events and treasure them in her heart, right up to the day she sits down and tells her story to Luke.

Within just a few days, she sets off to visit Elizabeth. She may not have realised it, but she is already carrying the Son of God in her womb. Whatever she thinks, the news about Elizabeth prompts her to go and see her relative. This family specialises in unusual pregnancies and it is a good idea for the two women to talk.

> *"At that time Mary got ready and hurried to a town in the hill country of Judea, where she entered Zechariah's home and greeted Elizabeth. When Elizabeth heard Mary's greeting, the baby leaped in her womb, and Elizabeth was filled with the Holy Spirit"* (Luke 1:39 – 41).

As soon as Mary arrives at Elizabeth's house, the presence of God manifests through the activity of the Holy Spirit. As Mary greets her, the Holy Spirit falls on Elizabeth and the baby in her womb leaps within her.

> *"In a loud voice she exclaimed: "Blessed are you among women and blessed is the child you will bear! But why am I so favoured, that the mother of my Lord should come to me? As*

soon as the sound of your greeting reached my ears, the baby in my womb leaped for joy. Blessed is she who has believed that the Lord would fulfil his promises to her" (Luke 1:42 – 45)!

This is an amazing encounter. Mary greets Elizabeth, but the Spirit fills her and touches her baby within her and reveals truth to her about Mary's pregnancy. Whether she knows Mary is pregnant or not, Scripture doesn't say. But when she speaks, Elizabeth blesses her and her baby. By Spirit given revelation, she sees it is a boy and he is her Lord.

This must have been a huge encouragement to the young Mary who would have been trying to grapple with her new situation. Here is a relative also supernaturally pregnant who knows Mary's baby is unique and has declared the baby is her Lord. Now there are two people who know God has a Son.

It is astonishing how God the Father gives this revelation to two women, both of whom weren't considered of any status within their communities. Later, Paul will speak of how God works,

"But God chose the foolish things of the world to shame the wise; God chose the weak things of the world to shame the strong. God chose the lowly things of this world" (1 Corinthians 1:27).

In these birth stories recoded by Luke, there are a couple of other things to note. The first is the authenticity of the stories and the strong feeling of eyewitness accounts. In the beginning of his gospel, Luke says he has carefully investigated everything from the beginning. These treasured memories of Mary strongly reflect her personal account of the events.

Secondly, what strikes us in these accounts is the trinitarian nature of the whole process. God the Father is the initiator; the Holy Spirit is the "revelator;" Jesus is the focus. Angels are the servants who communicate the message, and the two women are the receivers.

Luke tells his readers Mary stayed for three months with Elizabeth, presumably until Elizabeth's baby was born. When the baby is born, Zechariah, who has been silent for nine months, speaks. He says the baby will be called John. Like Mary and Elizabeth, he is filled with the Holy Spirit and speaks prophetically over his new-born son.

> *"And you, my child, will be called a prophet of the Most High; for you will go on before the Lord to prepare the way for him, to give his people the knowledge of salvation through the forgiveness of their sins" (Luke 1:76 – 77).*

His prophetic utterance lays out the future ministry of John who will be known as "the baptiser." Thirty years later, he will encounter fulfilling the words spoken by his father at his birth.

When Mary returns to her family and fiancé in Nazareth, she is already three months pregnant. It will be an "interesting" homecoming for her.

HOW DID JOSEPH REACT TO THE NEWS?

Not well is the answer! The gospel writer Matthew takes up this side of the story.

I imagine Mary's return to her family as one of excitement in reporting the news of Elizabeth's safe delivery of her baby. At the same time, it would have been obvious to Mary's mother her daughter is pregnant. This presents a very serious and complicated situation. Mary and her betrothed Joseph are not yet married. In Jewish culture, a pregnant unmarried girl is at risk of being stoned to death for her promiscuous behaviour. The family would feel great social shame. Assumptions would be made most probably by Mary's father. The issue would be, 'who is the father?' There would be a strong desire to fix the situation and exercise damage control. Matthew tells the story.

> *"Because Joseph her betrothed husband was faithful to the law, and yet did not want to expose her to public disgrace, he had in mind to divorce her quietly" (Matthew 1: 19).*

I can imagine Mary's father demanding to know who the father of the baby is. Any talk of an angelic messenger probably does not impress her father. Joseph is likely summoned no doubt to explain himself. He would be shocked, maybe even hurt because he has not made love to Mary. But in his eyes, someone has. We can see from what Matthew says Joseph loves her. He does not want to expose her to public disgrace or worse, stoning. He resolves to officially end the betrothal as quietly as possible.

Joseph likely goes home with a heavy and confused heart. He would go to bed, no doubt turning the day's events over and over in his mind and finally falling asleep. Matthew continues the story.

> *"After he had considered this, an angel of the Lord appeared to him in a dream and said, "Joseph, son of David, do not be afraid to take Mary home as your wife, because what is conceived in her is from the Holy Spirit. She will give birth to a son, and you are to give him the name Jesus, because he will save his people from their sins."*
>
> *All this took place to fulfil what the Lord had said through the prophet: "The virgin will conceive and give birth to a son, and*

they will call him Immanuel" (which means "God with us")"
(Matthew 1:20 -23).

Now there are three people who know the baby was special. It is not clear if Joseph understands Jesus is the Son of God, but the angel has told him the child who was conceived by the Holy Spirit will be a boy, to call him Jesus and he will save the people from their sin. Matthew, as is his custom in his gospel, points to the messianic prophecy given to Isaiah. This virgin birth will be a fulfilment of this prophecy.

Joseph, on waking, goes back to see Mary. I have wondered what sort of reception he receives from her father and mother. He probably wants to speak to her privately so he can tell her about his experience.

They no doubt look into each other's eyes. Perhaps Mary's eyes are red from weeping and no doubt she looks at Joseph with disappointment and hurt after the previous day's developments. Joseph's eyes probably look different this morning as he gazes at the girl he loves. I can imagine he hushes her fears as he says. "I know. The angel came to me too in a dream, I know who he is. Together we can do this."

Joseph rises to the challenge to become the stepfather of Jesus. He marries Mary in spite of the fact she is pregnant. The villagers of Nazareth no doubt have a lot to gossip about. Matthew finishes the story.

> *"When Joseph woke up, he did what the angel of the Lord had commanded him and took Mary home as his wife. But he did not consummate their marriage until she gave birth to a son. And he gave him the name Jesus" (Matthew 1:24 – 25).*

The remaining stories of Jesus's birth are recorded by Matthew and Luke in their respective gospels. Nothing else is known about the childhood of Jesus until he is twelve years old. It is Luke again who tells the story, which reflects Mary's memory of the event.

Growing up in Nazareth in a Jewish community, Jesus becomes familiar with all the Jewish customs and rituals governing their lives. He attends the Synagogue in Nazareth, learns to read and write in Hebrew. He knows all the prophetic longings for the coming of the Messiah, the anointed one. He has heard how the Scriptures are interpreted by the Rabbis. He is intimately familiar with the rhythms of the Jewish festivals and how the agricultural seasons are tied in with these celebrations.

He went to Jerusalem regularly with his parents and had seen the huge temple complex built by King Herod years before. He has stood in the temple precincts with his stepfather Joseph observing the rituals conducted by the priests. He has seen the buying and selling going on in the temple courts and spotted the corruption of the system as poor people struggle to buy ritually acceptable animals for sacrifice.

Luke records one of those visits when Jesus is twelve years old.

> *"Every year Jesus' parents went to Jerusalem for the Festival of the Passover. When he was twelve years old, they went up to the festival, according to the custom"* (Luke 2:41 – 42).

On this particular occasion, the family is returning home to Nazareth at the end of the Passover festival. At dusk as they make camp for the night, his parents have a terrible shock.

> *"After the festival was over, while his parents were returning home, the boy Jesus stayed behind in Jerusalem, but they were unaware of it. Thinking he was in their company, they travelled on for a day. Then they began looking for him among their relatives and friends. When they did not find him, they went back to Jerusalem to look for him"* (Luke 2:43 – 45).

You can feel the panic rising in Joseph and Mary. After travelling for a whole day, to return to Jerusalem will mean they arrive in the middle of the night in the dark city. Where will they begin looking for a twelve-year-old boy?

Their frantic search goes on for three days. Each day must be worse than the day before as each avenue is explored and found to be a dead end. In these situations, the imagination runs wild. Perhaps he is sick or has hurt himself; maybe he has been stolen by slave traders. Worst of all, can he be dead? They know his true identity as the Son of God. They may not have any idea what this means. As far as they are concerned, he is their boy. They have cared for him, watched him take his first steps, taught him to speak. They have told him the stories surrounding his birth. But what does he make of all this?

DID JESUS KNOW WHO HE REALLY WAS?

Perhaps in utter desperation Joseph and Mary go to the temple of Yahweh, Almighty GOD. They know Jesus is the Son of God. Nobody else knows this. They have carried the responsibility of raising Jesus and now they have lost him! They climb the steps up to the Temple mount. Ahead of them is the great gateway and the first of the enormous courts. The outer court known as the Court of the Gentiles is where God fearing Gentiles are permitted to go. A colonnade, known as Solomon's Porch, led around the side. From there they enter into the Court of the Woman. Beyond is the Court of the Men, then the inner court of the Priests and then beyond the innermost sanctuary, the Holy of Holies where they believe Almighty God lives in isolation separated from his people.

Each step is hard, and fear grips them. How will the Most High

God react to the news they carry? They have lost Jesus. Luke tells us what happens.

> *"They found him in the temple courts, sitting among the teachers, listening to them and asking them questions. Everyone who heard him was amazed at his understanding and his answers. When his parents saw him, they were astonished"* (Luke 2:46 – 48a).

They are probably more than astonished. They are relieved and exhausted, elated and maybe angry all mixed in together. Mary may even have burst into tears with the relief of finding him alive. She blurts out her response.

> *"Son, why have you treated us like this? Your father and I have been anxiously searching for you"* (Luke 2:48b).

Here is Jesus, only twelve years old, listening and talking with the sages of the Temple of Yahweh, questioning them. There is a crowd standing around amazed at his understanding and his answers. It would be like listening to a child prodigy.

This is Jesus, the eternal Son of God, the Creator of the universe and he is also the twelve-year-old the son of Mary. He is fully God and fully man. This means he is 100% divine and 100% human, not fifty-fifty. This is one of the great mysteries Paul and other New Testament writers will write about later.

> *"The Son is the image of the invisible God, the firstborn over all creation. For in him all things were created: things in heaven and on earth, visible and invisible, whether thrones or powers or rulers or authorities; all things have been created through him and for him. He is before all things, and in him all things hold together. And he is the head of the body, the church; he is*

the beginning and the firstborn from among the dead, so that in everything he might have the supremacy. For God was pleased to have all his fullness dwell in him, and through him to reconcile to himself all things, whether things on earth or things in heaven, by making peace through his blood, shed on the cross" (Colossians 1:15 – 18).

He is the eternal Son in the human body of an adolescent boy with the physical development of a twelve-year-old, the emotional, psychological and intellectual development of a boy. Jesus's answer to his mother shows graphically the tension of his two-fold nature operating within him. His first response is the twelve-year-old human youngster speaking.

"Why were you searching for me?" he asked (Luke 2:49).

Jesus as a young boy does not grasp the impact of him being missing in Jerusalem has on his parents. He does not seem to comprehend their anxiety or concern for his wellbeing and whereabouts. This is not sin, it is a twelve-year-old talking.

What he says next shows he also knows exactly who he really is.

"Didn't you know I had to be in my Father's house?"

Here he is in the Temple of Almighty God and he is completely at home. "This is my Father's place," his house. The sheer audacity of what he says is probably not missed by the listeners. They do not understand what he means. Nobody ever calls the Temple anything other than God Almighty's habitation, but here is this boy calling it the Father's house. Nobody dares to call God Father; this is blasphemy. Worse still, he calls God his Father. "My Father's house." Maybe they are thinking, "Just who does he think he is?"

By the time Jesus is twelve, he knows exactly who he is. God is his Father, and he is his Son.

Twenty years later, Jesus is back in the Temple and uses the same language when he throws out the money changers. This house, his Father's house has become a den of robbers. However, on this later occasion, the Jewish authorities understands what he means. They accuse him of blasphemy, and it becomes one of the reasons why they plot to kill him.

Joseph and Mary quietly usher the boy out of the temple and take him home to Nazareth where he stays for another eighteen years. Here is Luke's summary,

> *"Then he went down to Nazareth with them and was obedient to them. But his mother treasured all these things in her heart. And Jesus grew in wisdom and stature, and in favour with God and man" (Luke 2:51 – 52).*

Nothing is known of these silent years except those few comments by Luke. What does Jesus do all those years? He spends time growing in every way, in his relationship with his parents and family and fellow men and also in his relationship with God his Father. Presumably, he spends time with his father Joseph learning the craft and skill of a carpenter. Joseph is a father to Jesus in every sense of the word. We don't need to know the detail of those years. By the time the Gospel writers start to talk about Jesus's ministry, Joseph is not mentioned. The assumption is made he has died by then. Luke says Jesus is about thirty years old when he begins his ministry.

CHAPTER 6

WHAT MADE JESUS BEGIN HIS MINISTRY WHEN HE DID?

Luke states John the baptiser prompted by the Spirit begins preaching in the fifteenth year of the reign of Tiberius Caesar, which would be around 26 AD.

> *"The word of God came to John son of Zechariah in the wilderness. He went into all the country around the Jordan, preaching a baptism of repentance for the forgiveness of sins"* (Luke 3:2 – 3).

John is a relative of Jesus. His parents are old when he is born, so he may have grown up on his own. In the Jewish culture the family is important, and it is quite likely Jesus knows John. I have wondered if they have met and talked about their unusual births. Either way, both are on a journey and have a prophetic destiny to fulfil. John will prepare the way for the ministry of Jesus. All the gospel writers speak of John and the things he says. He is even mentioned by the Jewish historian Josephus who writes in the latter part of the first century.

John's significance is in the nature of his message and the revelation he sees. Mark succinctly summarises the ministry of John. He launches straight into it right at the beginning of his version of the Gospel.

> *"The beginning of the good news about Jesus the Messiah, the Son of God, as it is written in Isaiah the prophet:*
>
> *"I will send my messenger ahead of you, who will prepare your way, a voice of one calling in the wilderness, 'Prepare the way for the Lord, make straight paths for him.'"*

And so John the baptiser appeared in the wilderness, preaching a baptism of repentance for the forgiveness of sins. The whole Judean countryside and all the people of Jerusalem went out to him. Confessing their sins, they were baptized by him in the Jordan River. John wore clothing made of camel's hair, with a leather belt around his waist, and he ate locusts and wild honey. And this was his message: "After me comes the one more powerful than I, the straps of whose sandals I am not worthy to stoop down and untie. I baptize you with water, but he will baptize you with the Holy Spirit" (Mark 1:1 – 8).

The content of his preaching was a call to repentance for the forgiveness of sins. The sign of repentance is baptism in the waters of the Jordan River. His appearing and his physical appearance cause huge excitement. John's gospel has a first-hand account of the events. The detail suggests John the apostle is the source. He writes,

"Now this was John's testimony when the Jewish leaders in Jerusalem sent priests and Levites to ask him who he was. He did not fail to confess, but confessed freely, "I am not the Messiah." They asked him, "Then who are you? Are you Elijah?" He said, "I am not." "Are you the Prophet?" He answered, "No." Finally they said, "Who are you? Give us an answer to take back to those who sent us. What do you say about yourself?"

John replied in the words of Isaiah the prophet, "I am the voice of one calling in the wilderness, 'Make straight the way for the Lord.'"

Now the Pharisees who had been sent questioned him, "Why then do you baptize if you are not the Messiah, nor Elijah, nor the Prophet?"

CHAPTER 6

> "I baptize with water," John replied, "but among you stands one you do not know. He is the one who comes after me, the straps of whose sandals I am not worthy to untie."
>
> This all happened at Bethany on the other side of the Jordan, where John was baptizing" (John 1:19 – 28).

John's fiery preaching attracts large crowds from Jerusalem and Judea. Many went out of curiosity but also many are baptised. People come down from Galilee where word has spread about what is happening. This includes Andrew the brother of Simon Peter and also one other, probably John the writer of the Gospel. He is a cousin of Jesus, his mother being Mary's sister making him a relative of John the baptiser also.

Jesus also leaves Nazareth and heads down to Judea. John the gospel writer takes up the story.

> "The next day John saw Jesus coming toward him and said, "Look, the Lamb of God, who takes away the sin of the world" (John 1:29)!

At this moment the Spirit reveals something to John. His preaching and baptising have all been a preparation for the appearing of the "One." On catching sight of Jesus, John suddenly sees it, or more specifically him. To his amazement Jesus walks down the riverbank and into the river and wades purposefully towards him and stands in front of him. I imagine them greeting each other and John looking quizzically at Jesus. Then to his amazement, Jesus asks John to baptise him. Matthew tells us of the exchange.

> "John tried to deter him, saying, "I need to be baptized by you, and do you come to me?"

Jesus replied, "Let it be so now; it is proper for us to do this to fulfil all righteousness" (Matthew 3:13 – 15).

John recognises he is encountering the Lamb of God who is without sin and therefore there is no need for him to be baptised as a sign of repentance. Yet, Jesus insists because he wants to demonstrate something about righteousness. When Jesus speaks about righteousness, he is talking about the nature of God. Paul will later write to the Romans and tell them God's Kingdom is righteousness, peace and joy in the Holy Spirit. Jesus is about to demonstrate this righteousness as he is baptised.

WHY DOES JESUS GET BAPTISED?

When we think like Adam with Wrong Tree thinking, we immediately assume righteousness means behaving in a particular way, doing something good as opposed to doing something evil. Jesus does not think in this way. He is the sinless Son of God. He means something else by fulfilling all righteousness.

All four gospel writers unanimously record the events of Jesus's baptism, the most explicit being the three synoptic gospels, Matthew, Mark and Luke. Each of these writers record the words the Father spoke over his Son. At the moment when Jesus stands in the waters of the River Jordan having been baptised by John, a most amazing sound is heard. The voice of the Lord God Almighty breaks the silence of centuries and speaks. Luke's version has an intimate feel to it.

"And as he was praying, heaven was opened, and the Holy Spirit descended on him in bodily form like a dove. A voice

came from heaven, "You are my Son, whom I love; with you I am well pleased" (Luke 3:21-22).

In this version, the Father addresses Jesus personally rather than speaking generally about him. Luke says Jesus is praying. It is as if we are listening in to a conversation between Jesus and his Father. We don't know what Jesus prays but we hear the Father's answer. These words are likely a great personal encouragement to Jesus. The Father first confirms him as his very own Son. This is his true identity. Then the Father affirms and states his love for him. This is an unconditional statement of fatherly affection and love which many have never heard from their natural fathers. Finally, he asserts his pleasure in him. This is not based on any activity or ministry or accomplishment, it is based on who he is in himself.

The threefold nature at the centre of the Godhead is explicitly and simply revealed at this pivotal moment. The eternal Son is in the water having been baptised. The Holy Spirit alights on him. The Father Almighty speaks lovingly over the Son.

The observers in the crowds on the banks of the River Jordan see another person getting baptised. With their fallen eyes, which are not open to see what is really happening, they may have been surprised by the bird fluttering over the man. They may even point out, in their ignorance, the man with the pigeon on his shoulder. Then there is the strange sound. "Is that thunder?" They miss the significance of what has happened.

One who does not miss the significance is John the baptiser. The eyes of his heart are open. John says the Father himself who sent him to baptise has told him in advance,

> *"The man on whom you see the Spirit come down and remain is the one who will baptise with the Holy Spirit." I have seen and I testify that this is God's Chosen One" (John 1:33 – 34).*

John has seen the Holy Spirit descend on Jesus in the form of a dove and then he hears the Father speak. This confirms to John not only will Jesus baptise with the Holy Spirit, but he is the Lamb of God.

These affirmations come after thirty years of waiting. Jesus has been known as the carpenter's son in Nazareth. In his heart he knows he is God's own Son and God is his true Father. He has stated as much as a young boy in the temple eighteen years before. He is now on the brink of his public ministry. The opening act of the drama of the next three years is about to unfold, the Father himself is announcing who Jesus is, who he has eternally been and will be. The delight and pleasure in the heart of the Father as Jesus begins his great ministry of revealing the Father and bringing redemption to mankind is evident in the Father's words.

> *"You are my Son, whom I love; with you I am well pleased."*

CHAPTER 7

JESUS BEGINS TO REVEAL THE FATHER

We arrive at a major part of the Big Picture. Many have come to see how Jesus reveals the Father. Revelation has been flooding from the heart of God the Father in recent years about the life and ministry of Jesus. We are indebted to so many who have had the eyes of their hearts opened and have come to "see" things previous generations have failed to see. I have written extensively about this in my book *Finding the Father in the Story of the Church* (2016), so I do not intend to repeat myself. However, I would like to acknowledge Jack Winter and James and Denise Jordan who have faithfully revealed the Father through their lives and ministry. I am personally indebted to them for this.

To continue the analogy of the jigsaw puzzle, the revelation of the Father through the life and ministry of Jesus has been a major part of the picture.

For so long the Church has focused on Jesus without fully embracing his revelation of the nature and heart of God as Father. Some religious movements specifically teach it is only Jesus who is important. Others look at the life and work of Jesus through the analytical eyes of their minds and employ Wrong Tree thinking to their deliberations. Jesus is seen as the one who stands between us worm-like sinners and the angry vengeful God who is distant and remote. They pay lip service to his loving nature and interpret it by seeing his love as a reward for human obedience and good behaviour. Historically this thinking flows continually through the rational mind rather than the heart.

There are always some who "see" with the eyes of their hearts, but they are few. When encountered, they are shining lights in the dark centuries that have characterised Christianity and Christendom.

The issue comes back time and time again to Jesus. We have seen how his coming is a specific uncovering of the truth about God the Father who has a Son.

WHAT DID JESUS DO AFTER HIS BAPTISM?

Jesus steps out of the waters of the river Jordan and goes off alone into the wilderness of Judea for forty days as the import of these events sink into his heart. The three synoptic Gospel writers record what happens. Here is Matthew's version.

> *"Then Jesus was led by the Spirit into the wilderness to be tempted by the devil. After fasting forty days and forty nights, he was hungry. The tempter came to him and said, "If you are the Son of God, tell these stones to become bread."*

Jesus answered, "It is written: 'Man shall not live on bread alone, but on every word that comes from the mouth of God.'"

Then the devil took him to the holy city and had him stand on the highest point of the temple. "If you are the Son of God," he said, "throw yourself down. For it is written:

"'He will command his angels concerning you, and they will lift you up in their hands, so that you will not strike your foot against a stone.'"

Jesus answered him, "It is also written: 'Do not put the Lord your God to the test.'"

Again, the devil took him to a very high mountain and showed him all the kingdoms of the world and their splendour. "All this I will give you," he said, "if you will bow down and worship me."

Jesus said to him, "Away from me, Satan! For it is written: 'Worship the Lord your God and serve him only.'"

Then the devil left him, and angels came and attended him" (Matthew 4:1 – 11).

He is not alone for those forty days in the wilderness. Luke says he is led by the Holy Spirit.

The nature of the devil's interaction with Jesus has been the subject of much preaching and study. All I want to add is the way the devil uses the same tactics with Jesus as he did with Eve. He questions the truth about God to try to sow doubt and insecurity into the heart. Twice he says to Jesus, "If you are the Son of God." He is trying to make Jesus doubt what God the Father has said to him. God said, "You *are* my son" (The italics are mine.). The root of these temptations is to try to convince Jesus the devil's way of thinking, Wrong Tree thinking, is what is required. He can get all the worship and respect of the people by doing things in his own strength and through his own plans. In this way he will effectively be worshipping the devil. This is the reason Satan fell according to Isaiah 14. He wants worship.

Jesus is unwilling to listen to any voice other than his Father's. On numerous occasions throughout his ministry he says,

> *"The Son can do nothing by himself; he can do only what he sees his Father doing, because whatever the Father does the Son also does" (John 5:19).*

After this time of spiritual attack, Jesus still full of the Holy Spirit goes back to Galilee and begins speaking to people. Luke tells us news about Jesus spreads through the whole countryside. He teaches in their synagogues, and everyone speaks well of him. Quite early on in his ministry, Jesus goes back to his hometown of Nazareth and on the sabbath day visits his local synagogue as he has done all his life. He stands to read, and the scroll of the prophet Isaiah is handed to him.

> *"Unrolling it, he found the place where it is written:*

> *"The Spirit of the Lord is on me, because he has anointed me to proclaim good news to the poor. He has sent me to proclaim freedom for the prisoners and recovery of sight for the blind, to set the oppressed free, to proclaim the year of the Lord's favour."*

> *Then he rolled up the scroll, gave it back to the attendant and sat down. The eyes of everyone in the synagogue were fastened on him. He began by saying to them, "Today this scripture is fulfilled in your hearing" (Luke 4:17 – 21).*

CHAPTER 7

The passage he chooses to read is no accident. He deliberately chooses to read a messianic passage which would be recognised by everyone present. It prophesies the mission of the promised Messiah whom Israel longs for. In many ways it can be seen as his mission statement. But it is so much more. It touches the deep needs of mankind and how God the Father has stepped in to bring us back into relationship with him.

It is a proclamation of good news to the poor. Those who could never reconnect with the Father because of their poverty-stricken orphan hearted condition. It will be freedom from the slavery and bondage of Wrong Tree thinking and captivity in Satan's kingdom. The eyes of our hearts will be open so we will no longer be spiritually blind. It will be freedom for the oppressed and broken. Only the eternal Son of the Father can set us free from the oppression of being enslaved by satanic thinking and the resulting brokenness of our hearts. This is truly a day of favour, blessing and gift, literally acceptance by the Lord. Jesus has announced how all of this has been lost in the Garden of Eden in the Fall and is about to be restored in and through him.

He says the Spirit is on him for this purpose. Then to crown it all, after he has read the passage, he carefully rolls up the scroll, sits down and says, "Today this scripture is fulfilled in your hearing." Jesus, The Word of God, has just read the word of God, and tells them it is all about him. Astonishing!

Initially, the reaction is very positive. Murmurs of approval and whispers go around the synagogue. Questions are asked, "Isn't this Joseph's son?" They know who he was as he has grown up among them, so perhaps the question is more a case of, "That's a surprise! He's just the carpenter's boy." Jesus sits there in front of them in the full knowledge of who he really is and what his destiny and mission are. Then he speaks again and the whole atmosphere changes. Luke takes up the story.

> *"Jesus said to them, "Surely you will quote this proverb to me: 'Physician, heal yourself!' And you will tell me, 'Do here in your hometown what we have heard that you did in Capernaum.'"*
>
> *"Truly I tell you," he continued, "no prophet is accepted in his hometown. I assure you that there were many widows in Israel in Elijah's time, when the sky was shut for three and a half years and there was a severe famine throughout the land. Yet Elijah was not sent to any of them, but to a widow in Zarephath in the region of Sidon. And there were many in Israel with leprosy in the time of Elisha the prophet, yet not one of them was cleansed—only Naaman the Syrian"* (Luke 4:23 – 27).

He alludes to the Old Testament story of Elijah being sent to Israel's pagan neighbours highlighting Israel's unbelief. The ministry Jesus is about to begin is not to be solely focused on the Jews but will reach beyond to all of broken and fallen humanity. This flies in the face of the exclusive mindset of the Jews who see all non-Jews as unclean and outside of the promises and hope of Messiah. The inference of what he has said is not lost on his hometown crowd.

> *"All the people in the synagogue were furious when they heard this. They got up, drove him out of the town, and took him to the brow of the hill on which the town was built, in order to throw him off the cliff. But he walked right through the crowd and went on his way"* (Luke 4:28 – 30).

Matthew says Jesus leaves Nazareth and moves to Capernaum, a small town on Lake Galilee. In this area he starts to gather a small group of young men around him as disciples. All four gospels recount various stories of the gathering of these men to Jesus.

CHAPTER 7

WHAT WAS THE HEART OF JESUS'S TEACHING ABOUT THE FATHER?

The four Gospels record the events of Jesus's life and teaching. We are not exactly sure when they were written but certainly it is within the living memory of the events they describe. The next generation of followers tell us Mark records the memories of Peter. Matthew and Luke have Mark's Gospel as their template for their gospels but add their own unique material. Luke specifically goes out of his way to investigate and record the stories of eyewitnesses as he has Gentile readers in mind. He begins his gospel story with these words,

> *"Many have undertaken to draw up an account of the things that have been fulfilled among us, just as they were handed down to us by those who from the first were eyewitnesses and servants of the word. With this in mind, since I myself have carefully investigated everything from the beginning, I too decided to write an orderly account" (Luke 1:1 – 3).*

Matthew, who also follows Mark's structure, is writing with a Jewish readership in mind. He shows how all the events are a direct fulfilment of Old Testament prophetic words concerning the coming of the Messiah. He also incorporates a large number of the sayings and teachings of Jesus. Some suggest an early document of Jesus teaching forms the basis of these sayings.

Before looking more closely at what Matthew writes, I want to mention in passing the Gospel of John. Unlike the other three, it is probably written quite a few years later by John the Apostle, one of Jesus's disciples. We are going to look at it in more detail further in the next chapter. But it is noteworthy to say in John chapter 17 when

Jesus is talking to his Father at the end of his ministry, we read some amazing words.

> *"I have brought you glory on earth by finishing the work you gave me to do. And now, Father, glorify me in your presence with the glory I had with you before the world began. I have revealed you to those whom you gave me out of the world"* (John 17:4 – 6).

These words of Jesus show how he views his ministry. He refers back to the time before creation and the glory in the Godhead. His task is to reveal the Father and he has accomplished it by the time he goes to the cross.

We see this in the accounts of all four Gospel writers. Matthew sets the scene by recording a summary of Jesus's early travels and ministry.

> *"Jesus went throughout Galilee, teaching in their synagogues, proclaiming the good news of the kingdom, and healing every disease and sickness among the people. News about him spread all over Syria, and people brought to him all who were ill with various diseases, those suffering severe pain, the demon-possessed, those having seizures, and the paralyzed; and he healed them. Large crowds from Galilee, the Decapolis, Jerusalem, Judea and the region across the Jordan followed him"* (Matthew 4:23 -25).

Without doubt, Matthew gives the earliest record of Jesus's teaching in the Bible. Looking at this material we see how Jesus uses the word Father numerous times when speaking about almighty God. He always locates the Father in Heaven or uses the term heavenly Father seventeen times.

Matthew launches into the teaching of Jesus with a long section referred to as the Sermon on the Mount.

> *"Now when Jesus saw the crowds, he went up on a mountainside and sat down. His disciples came to him, and he began to teach them" (Matthew 5:1 – 2).*

It is difficult to say if the way Matthew presents it is exactly how Jesus taught on the hillside on just one occasion, or if he collects many sayings over a number of different occasions. However, it gives us a clear and detailed record, full of revelation and truth from the heart of God the Father through the words of the one who knows him best, his beloved Son.

The first teachings Matthew records are a group of sayings all beginning with the same opening formula, "*makarioi,*" which means blessed. They are widely referred to as "The Beatitudes." This description doesn't make much sense to most people as it is such an archaic and religious word.

However, the word is full of meaning. It resonates with godly favour and richness. Many translators have tried to find a more modern word to translate it and they come up with 'fortunate' or worse still, 'happy.' Neither carries the richness of this beautiful word. It links back to the first thing the Father said over the newly created Adam. God blesses mankind. His nature has always been to bless, not just for reward but simply out of love. It is the generous God-filled outpouring of his nature on his offspring.

These nine "Blessed" statements designate a human condition usually considered as disadvantaged or in some way weak and not the characteristics of people the world considers successful. The spiritually poor; those in grief and mourning; the meek who are humble and non-aggressive; those hungry and thirsty for a better way of living; the merciful, a characteristic despised as an expression of weakness; those with hearts focused on purity; those who seek peace and seek to make peace; those who suffer persecution and insult and false accusation. They are about to become transformed by the breaking in of God's royal and Fatherly presence. All these people are about to experience the generous God-filled outpouring of his nature into them.

They will receive the tangible real presence of God the Father's realm of love, 'the kingdom of God'. They will be comforted by the nurturing motherly heart of God the Father. They will enter into the inheritance of God's sons on the earth. They will be filled with the righteous relationship at the heart of God's nature. They will receive the compassionate mercy of God. They will see God for who he is as the eyes of their hearts are opened. They will be recognised as the sons of God, not just offspring or children. They will enter into their true identity as sons. The Apostle Paul will receive more revelation about our identity as sons, which we will look at in a later chapter.

These gospel writers record how Jesus uses a phrase throughout his teaching and ministry, 'the kingdom of God', or the phrase 'the kingdom of heaven.' It's a very familiar term used extensively in contemporary Christianity. I define it in this chapter as the tangible and real presence of God the Father in his realm of love. It is God filled; it is real, and it is here and now. Wherever God is at work or his presence is manifested, it is characterised by love in action. It is the realm of the Father's love. As the Apostle John said, 'For God is love" (I John 4:8).

In the following teachings, Jesus continually relates what he says back to God the Father. We are to love our enemies and pray for those who persecute us to show we are living as sons of our Father in heaven (Matthew 5:44 – 45).

Jesus says we are to be like the Father who is perfect in every way

(Matthew 5:48). He says Father will reward us when we seek to live for him in the world without being on show rather serving and giving in secret. Jesus teaches praying to the Father is to be unseen not a public show.

> *"Pray to your Father who is unseen, then your Father who sees what is done in secret will reward you" (Matthew 6:6).*

The synoptic gospel writers all record a version of the prayer Jesus gives his disciples in response to their request for a formula they can use in prayer. Luke records it thus,

> *"He said to them, "When you pray, say: 'Father, hallowed be your name, your kingdom come. Give us each day our daily bread. Forgive us our sins, for we also forgive everyone who sins against us. And lead us not into temptation'" (Luke 11:2 -4).*

It would have been a surprise to the disciples to be told they can personally address God in prayer as Father in the same way Jesus does. Praying in this way to the Father is based on an assurance of Father knowing what we need. We are encouraged to seek first his kingdom and his righteousness, and all the legitimate needs of life will be given to us as well.

The longing of the Father to relate to us as sons is at the heart of Jesus's teaching. He focuses his disciples on this relationship with God as Father.

> *"Which of you, if your son asks for bread, will give him a stone? Or if he asks for a fish, will give him a snake? If you, then, though you are evil, know how to give good gifts to your children, how much more will your Father in heaven give good gifts to those who ask him" (Matthew 7:9 – 11)!*

Jesus focuses on doing what the Father asks him to do. He has come in order to show us what the Father is like. His focus is not missed by the Gospel writers. Matthew and Luke record an incident when Jesus prays.

Luke's version is identical to Matthew's except for the comment made before he prays.

> *"At that time Jesus, full of joy through the Holy Spirit, said...."*
> *(Luke 10:21).*

This reflects Luke's particular interest in the Holy Spirit's involvement in the life and ministry of Jesus. The word translates full of joy is *"agalliao."* This literally means to jump for joy. I love this translation; it captures something of the heart of Jesus when he prays. More serious translators have a reverential and religious mindset in their translations which at times misses this. This is such a case in point. The picture of Jesus full of animation and excitement where he literally leaps in the air for joy is astonishing. I imagine Jesus leaping, punching the air and shouting at the top of his lungs, "Yes!" Maybe this is a bit too twenty-first century for some.

The prayer of Jesus to his Father is to be read in this gloriously joyful way.

> *"At that time Jesus said, "I praise you, Father, Lord of heaven and earth, because you have hidden these things from the wise and learned and revealed them to little children. Yes, Father, for this is what you were pleased to do" (Matthew 11:25 – 26).*

This joy filled prayer reveals something of the way revelation is given. It relates back to the two trees in Genesis. The tree of the knowledge of good and evil demands serious and studious mental contemplation. This is a redundant approach which does not lead to life. The Tree of

Life which symbolises the downward flow of love filled grace and joy from God is received by the childlike heart. This truth is revealed to little children says Jesus.

Another extraordinary comment by Jesus reveals the dialogue happening between Father and Son, "Yes, Father, for this is what you were pleased to do." In the heart of the Godhead there is absolute joy and delight in revealing their nature to their beloved children. It is almost as if they are sharing a great joke.

Jesus turns to his disciples and explains what is happening.

> *"All things have been committed to me by my Father. No one knows the Son except the Father, and no one knows the Father except the Son and those to whom the Son chooses to reveal him" (Matthew 11:27).*

The word translated as 'knows' is *'epiginosko'*- meaning fully knows through experience and relationship. This is a revelation of the Father Jesus chooses to bring to his disciples and all who follow him.

Luke's Gospel includes events and stories unique to his account. He meets and speaks with a number of people who have encountered and interacted with Jesus. One of the most loved and well-known of the stories is often referred to as the Parable of the Prodigal Son.

WHO IS THE REAL PRODIGAL IN THE STORY?

This wonderfully memorable story is set in a context where Jesus is speaking to two distinctly different groups of people. Luke sets the scene.

> *"Now the tax collectors and sinners were all gathering around to hear Jesus. But the Pharisees and the teachers of the law muttered, "This man welcomes sinners and eats with them" (Luke 15:1 -2).*

The first group is described as tax collectors and sinners. These are people who are ostracised by people. Tax collectors have sold their souls to the Roman governing authorities and are employed to collect tax from their own people, people like Matthew and Zacchaeus. They are viewed as parasites sucking the financial life blood out of their neighbours and hated by all. Sinners are a group who are generally considered the low-lifes of the day. Drunkards, prostitutes, gamblers and the like. The other group are the spiritually elite, Pharisees and teachers of the law. The two groups both operate from Wrong Tree thinking. They judge each other and themselves according to harsh rules. One group is never good enough to please God or man and the other is striving for religious perfection and continually failing.

To this eclectic mix, Jesus tells three stories which have a common thread flowing through them. They are known as the parable of the lost sheep, the parable of the lost coin and the parable of the lost son. This description highlights only one aspect of the stories. When these stories are viewed through the fallen eyes of Adam and with minds immersed in a Wrong Tree mindset, we tend to think they are all about the lost being found. Indeed, the sheep, the coin, and the son were "lost" but there is so much more.

The stories have often been approached from the perspective of the need for salvation of the lost, the sinner who needs to repent and get right with God. However, to uncover what else these stories offer, a good question to ask is what is Jesus wanting to say to his audience? Jesus says,

CHAPTER 7

> *"These words you hear are not my own; they belong to the Father who sent me"* (John 14:24).

In these stories Jesus is speaking what the Father gives him to speak and they reveal the nature of God as Father. The overriding message of each story is the joy in the heart of God when the "*lost*" are found. I'm putting the word lost in italics. In what way are they lost?

The sheep has its head down doing what sheep do, eating grass. Its attention is the next tuft of grass and then the next until without realising it, in its busyness, it loses connection with the rest of the flock and the shepherd. It doesn't intentionally get lost; it is just busy eating grass. Also, it is a sheep that belongs in a flock, not a goat. If this is meant to be about the unsaved sinner, Jesus might have had a goat in mind rather than a sheep.

As for the coin, it is one of ten owned by a woman. It has been suggested this valuable coin may have been part of the coins of a dowry chain worn by middle eastern women on special occasions. To have lost one of those coins would have been careless and very obvious to others. Coins don't lose themselves, presumably it becomes detached by accident and is lost. Like the sheep, it belongs to a group but is unexpectedly lost to the group.

Finally, the so-called lost sons. They both are sons yet for different reasons neither have a genuine relationship with the father in the story. The younger is rebellious and selfish. The older is a reluctantly obedient son who exhibits strong passive aggressive attitudes. Jesus puts these words in the boy's mouths. First, the younger of the two.

> *"The younger one said to his father, 'Father, give me my share of the estate.' So he divided his property between them.*

Not long after that, the younger son got together all he had, set off for a distant country and there squandered his wealth in wild living" (Luke 15: 12 – 13).

Then the older son later responds to the invitation to join the homecoming party for his brother by saying to his father,

"The older brother became angry and refused to go in. So his father went out and pleaded with him. But he answered his father, 'Look! All these years I've been slaving for you and never disobeyed your orders. Yet you never gave me even a young goat so I could celebrate with my friends. But when this son of yours who has squandered your property with prostitutes comes home, you kill the fattened calf for him'" (Luke 15:28 – 30)!

The three lost stories describe people who should have been in relationship with their homes, the flock, the chain and the father's house. Yet all are detached in some way. Jesus's use of these images describes the fallen state of mankind. They once belonged but are now alienated. The sheep through self-focused work, heads down getting on with life and ignoring how it has wandered. The coin wrenched out of its honoured place and the sons by their own volition. The audience Jesus addresses represents all of these characteristics.

However, they are not the main focus of the three stories. Jesus wants to reveal the nature of God in these stories. This is his main focus. The first story depicts the shepherd lovingly seeking the sheep and bringing it home, back to the flock where it belongs and having a party to celebrate its return. This image of a shepherd speaks of the Shepherd of Israel, who Jesus describes himself as in John 10. The seeking shepherd is the eternal Son.

The lost coin is found by the woman when she lights a lamp. The

CHAPTER 7

Spirit inspired word is described as a lamp in Psalm 119. The New Testament describes the Holy Spirit illuminating and revealing truth. The lamp in the hand of the woman is the Holy Spirit.

In the final story, it is the father whose welcoming and embracing character Jesus reveals as being the nature of God the Father. The father is the Father Almighty. Three stories, three persons of the Godhead: the Son, the Spirit and the Father all seeking and restoring and bringing home the wayward and the lost.

One other significant part of the three stories is the level of joy in each story. This is deliberate. Jesus is revealing the joyful nature of God. The shepherd joyfully carries the sheep home. He joyfully summons his neighbours to celebrate with him. The woman finding the coin joyfully invites her friends and neighbours to share in her rejoicing. The father stages a celebratory feast on the homecoming of his younger son which includes music and dancing.

Jesus says,

> *"I tell you that in the same way there will be more rejoicing in heaven over one sinner who repents than over ninety-nine righteous persons who do not need to repent" (Luke 15: 7).*

And

> *"In the same way, I tell you, there is rejoicing in the presence of the angels of God over one sinner who repents" (Luke 15:10).*

Jesus's intention in telling these stories to this group of lost and broken people is to show them what God is really like. He is speaking life to them as the Tree of Life. His fullest description is of God the Father in the third parable.

The father in the story responds to both sons in the same way. Facing the demand of the younger boy, he shares their inheritance between them. Later he goes out to the returning younger son and to the older one who refuses to come to the party. Luke describes the return of the son in the story.

> *"But while he was still a long way off, his father saw him and was filled with compassion for him; he ran to his son, threw his arms around him and kissed him.*
>
> *"The son said to him, 'Father, I have sinned against heaven and against you. I am no longer worthy to be called your son.'*
>
> *"But the father said to his servants, 'Quick! Bring the best robe and put it on him. Put a ring on his finger and sandals on his feet. Bring the fattened calf and kill it. Let's have a feast and celebrate. For this son of mine was dead and is alive again; he was lost and is found.' So they began to celebrate" (Luke 15:20 – 24).*

The actions of the father in the story reveal the nature of God the Father. He is ever watching for the wayward son. The father sees him from a distance. This suggests he is watching intently for any movement from the boy. On seeing him in the distance, Jesus says he is filled with compassion for him. This choice of the word compassion by Jesus is not accidental. It is deliberate. In the Old Testament when Moses asks to see God's glory in Exodus 33 and 34, he is instructed by God to hide in the rock as he passes by and declare his name.

> *"And he passed in front of Moses, proclaiming, "The LORD, the LORD, the compassionate and gracious God, slow to anger, abounding in love and faithfulness, maintaining love to thousands, and forgiving wickedness, rebellion and sin (Exodus 34:6 - 7a).*

CHAPTER 7

God reveals himself to Moses as compassionate. Jesus uses this same word to describe his own feelings for the wounded, hurting and broken whom he encounters throughout his ministry. Paul when writing about God in 2 Corinthians says he is,

> *"the Father of compassion and the God of all comfort"*
> *(2 Corinthians 1:3).*

Jesus shows something of the emotions in the heart of the Father in this word when he is dealing with his alienated children. He cares with unfailing love. Then the father in the story runs to the son. This is extraordinary, particularly for the listeners who does not expect a dignified patriarchal figure like this landowning father to hitch up his robe and run to the boy.

This is only a story, but the story would have a very different ending had the older brother met his brother before the father. The judgmental and jealous attitude revealed later by the boy when speaking to his father is typical of the pharisaical Wrong Tree attitude of the listeners.

The father reaches the boy and warmly embraces him. This is not a polite handshake but a passionate hugging of the boy. This is followed by a kiss. This affectionate gesture is of a father fully accepting and welcoming his son home without reservation or recrimination. These beautiful gestures come from the very heart of God the Father. Jesus's inclusion of them in the story is not just a human response but a deliberate description of his Father.

The father does not take any notice of the boy's planned speech. The young man intends to bargain with his father following the realisation his dire straits in the far country can be resolved by going home.

> *"How many of my father's hired servants have food to spare, and here I am starving to death! I will set out and go back to*

my father and say to him: Father, I have sinned against heaven and against you. I am no longer worthy to be called your son; make me like one of your hired servants'" (Luke 15: 17 – 19).

The boy's reasoning is classic Wrong Tree logic of fallen man. He is in trouble and thinks he can fix his problem by his clever plan. He will go home and speak to his father. He will play the religious card, first of all by confessing his sin. It is difficult to say if this repentance is genuine or not. But taking it at face value, it is a realisation his actions have led to the broken relationship with his father. He then adds a very significant conclusion to his thinking. He feels his actions have disqualified him from his position as a son in the family. He feels unworthy to be known as his father's son.

This reaction is the payoff of all Wrong Tree thinking Satan initiates in the Fall in Genesis 3. His objective with Adam and Eve is to alienate them from God as their Father and to feel they consequently are not worthy or good enough to be sons and daughters of God.

The boy then sets out his solution. He will make a deal with his father. In his mind, he is no longer qualified as a son therefore the best he can hope for is to be taken on as a household slave. It is his way of saying if he works harder and does more maybe he can at least survive with food in his belly. Again, this is the tragic mindset of Wrong Tree thinking which says we can work and do things to get back into God's favour. This is the redundant dead end of all religion which strives with human effort to please God.

The father in the story responds quite differently. He interrupts the speech and again acts in a shocking way.

"But the father said to his servants, 'Quick! Bring the best robe and put it on him. Put a ring on his finger and sandals on his

feet. Bring the fattened calf and kill it. Let's have a feast and celebrate. For this son of mine was dead and is alive again; he was lost and is found" (Luke 15:22 - 24).

Every action of the father displays acceptance, love, forgiveness and joy at the return of the son. The best robe is to be found and the boy clothed in it. This probably is the father's robe. He covers the boy so no one will see his bedraggled and unkempt state. A ring is placed on the son's finger. This significant action is perhaps the most telling of all. This ring is reserved by the father for recognition of the boy being his son. Rings are worn by sons who are heirs and carriers of their father's authority. Only sons wear rings like this. He is also given sandals. Slaves and servants wear no shoes. Here again is a strong indication of sonship in the words of Jesus.

Finally, they hold a joyful feast, and the centrepiece is the slaughter of a corn-fed fattened calf. A feast indeed. These luxuries are only used at the most special of family celebrations.

But Jesus is not finished. He adds one more exchange of conversation between the father and his older son who is sulking and, in his anger, has refused to join the party. The young man fires words at his father that are full of pain and venom.

> *"Look! All these years I've been slaving for you and never disobeyed your orders. Yet you never gave me even a young goat so I could celebrate with my friends. But when this son of yours who has squandered your property with prostitutes comes home, you kill the fattened calf for him'" (Luke 15:29 – 30)!*

His Wrong Tree thinking leads him to see his place in the family as a slave who just keeps the rules. The reality is he is a son and heir who works alongside his father, but he cannot see this. There is jealousy in his heart and judgment towards his brother. He cannot even call him brother. He has not spoken with his brother but has judged him as squandering his money on prostitutes. This is a huge judgment. Of course, prostitutes can be found in every town. The son didn't have to go to a foreign country to find them. They even turn up in Pharisees' dining rooms such as the one who appears at the dinner party for Jesus hosted by Simon the Pharisee according to Luke 7: 36 – 50. Maybe Simon is in the crowd and one of the ones moaning about Jesus eating with the likes of this woman.

The father responds to his hurting son in a loving and heart-warming way,

> *"'My son,' the father said, 'you are always with me, and everything I have is yours. But we had to celebrate and be glad, because this brother of yours was dead and is alive again; he was lost and is found'" (Luke 15:31 -32).*

This story is usually called the Parable of the Prodigal son. Prodigal is an old English word not used much these days. How it is interpreted depends on which tree is ruling in our hearts. It has a negative connotation, which includes wasteful, improvident, spendthrift, self-indulgent and extravagant. It also has very positive meanings of generous, lavish, unsparing, and bountiful.

This story of Jesus comes straight from the heart of the Father, who is the real prodigal. God the Father is generous, unsparing, and bountiful in his love for his sons and daughters. The Apostle John many years later expresses it this way,

> *"See what great love the Father has lavished on us, that we should be called the children of God" (I John 3:1)!*

CHAPTER 8

THE FATHER IN JOHN'S GOSPEL

The writer of the fourth Gospel does not name himself and instead uses the description "The disciple Jesus loved." Since the second century, many believe this to be John, the brother of James, the son of Zebedee the fisherman and his wife Salome, the sister of Jesus's mother Mary. This means he is a first cousin of Jesus and has an intimate familial relationship with him unlike any other New Testament writer.

WHY IS JOHN'S GOSPEL SO DIFFERENT?

John is also identified as the author of the three letters bearing his name and the Book of Revelation. They are all similar in language and style. The Gospel is quite different to the first three synoptic Gospels and this reflects John's personal knowledge of the events he writes about. He does not follow the pattern of the other three Gospels. He also appears not to repeat material or stories already written. An example is the account of the events taking place in the upper room. He does not repeat the details of the Passover meal and the way Jesus invests the bread and wine with new meaning. Instead he uses the evening to record a large amount of teaching shared by Jesus.

He seems to have written many years after the events described have taken place. He has a lifetime to reflect on the events and see their significance by the Holy Spirit. As a result, he receives revelation on the importance of the events he witnessed.

My friend Stephen Hill has written a magnificent devotional commentary on John's Gospel which I am very grateful for. I do not need to repeat all he says, but I encourage my readers to obtain it and read it for themselves. I simply want to draw on some themes as they relate to the wider biblical revelation of the Father as part of the Big Picture.

John's Gospel describes the way Jesus's ministry focuses on his disciples and the reaction to him by the Jewish religious hierarchy and the Pharisees. He records many situations where Jesus explains to the disciples personally what is happening. The disciples are on a journey with Jesus over a number of years. John mentions three Passovers which indicates Jesus's ministry is spread over at least three years. His intention seems not to have been to include everything Jesus says or does but rather, in his own words, at the end of chapter 20 he says,

> *"Jesus performed many other signs in the presence of his disciples, which are not recorded in this book. But these are written that you may believe that Jesus is the Messiah, the Son of God, and that by believing you may have life in his name" (John 20:30 -31).*

His final thoughts on the subject are added almost as an afterthought at the end of Chapter 21.

CHAPTER 8

"This is the disciple who testifies to these things and who wrote them down. We know that his testimony is true. Jesus did many other things as well. If every one of them were written down, I suppose that even the whole world would not have room for the books that would be written" (John 21:24 – 25).

The disciples do not know who Jesus is when they join him. John the baptiser has pointed two of them to Jesus as the lamb of God. They seek him out when he is in Judea sometime after he is baptised, following his time in the wilderness. Having spent a day with him, they are drawn to him and accompany him to Galilee where more join. One of their first descriptions of Jesus is as a Rabbi, a teacher.

A group of the disciples join Jesus and his family at a wedding in Cana, where he performs his first miracle turning water into wine. I imagine they are impressed by this first miracle. He then moves to the lakeside town of Capernaum. The three synoptic Gospels record many of the events happening in the area. John says following this, Jesus and his disciples go to Jerusalem for the Passover festival.

While in the city, Jesus visits the temple and drives out the money changers and merchants who are trading in the temple courts. He declares,

"Get these out of here! Stop turning my Father's house into a market" (John 2:16)!

Jesus calls the Temple his Father's house. This is the same expression he uses eighteen or so years earlier when he is there as a boy. On this occasion the reaction from the Jews in the temple is different, they begin to challenge him.

"The Jews then responded to him, "What sign can you show us to prove your authority to do all this?"

> *Jesus answered them, "Destroy this temple, and I will raise it again in three days." They replied, "It has taken forty-six years to build this temple, and you are going to raise it in three days?" But the temple he had spoken of was his body. After he was raised from the dead, his disciples recalled what he had said. Then they believed the scripture and the words that Jesus had spoken" (John 2:18 – 22).*

In this exchange we see how Jesus reaffirms God is his Father and the temple belongs to the Father. Jesus also prefigures his own destiny of death and resurrection after three days. John points out how the disciples don't understand the importance of what he says. It only becomes clearer after the resurrection. The disciples are on a steep learning curve of discovery and revelation.

In Chapter 3, John records the evening meeting Jesus has with Nicodemus, one of the Pharisees, and adds his own commentary on the ministry of Jesus.

John the Apostle gives a beautiful summary of the Big Picture as I call it. Perhaps the most well-known and most frequently quoted verse in the Bible. It encapsulates God the Father's eternal purpose and unchanging love for the world he created. It lays out God the Father's plan to give eternal life to the world. It is in stark contrast to the mindset of seeing God through fallen eyes as one who condemns. John describes him as a loving God who wants to restore his "world" to life.

> *"For God so loved the world that he gave his one and only Son, that whoever believes in him shall not perish but have eternal life. For God did not send his Son into the world to condemn the world, but to save the world through him" (John 3:16 – 17).*

While he does not refer explicitly to the tree of the knowledge of good and evil, the "Wrong Tree" or the Tree of Life, it is implicitly in his words. We can see their power at work. One condemns and the other brings real life.

John the gospel writer also weaves in John the baptiser's assessment of the life and ministry of Jesus. John's legacy continues long after the resurrection of Jesus. Across the Jewish diaspora, in the Roman Empire, there are many groups who follow his teaching for years after his death. Paul encounters some of them on his missionary journey to Ephesus. John the Apostle, writing from a later date in the first century, has these groups in mind when he composes this Gospel. This is John the baptiser's testimony about Jesus,

> *"John replied, "A person can receive only what is given them from heaven. You yourselves can testify that I said, 'I am not the Messiah but am sent ahead of him.' The bride belongs to the bridegroom. The friend who attends the bridegroom waits and listens for him and is full of joy when he hears the bridegroom's voice. That joy is mine, and it is now complete. He must become greater; I must become less" (John 3:27 – 30).*

The beloved disciple then explains the relationship between Jesus and his relative John the baptiser. He has John's followers in mind when he writes showing them how John is the one who prepares the way for the coming of Jesus. He describes Jesus as the 'one who comes from above' and John as the 'one who is from the earth.'

> *"The one who comes from above is above all; the one who is from the earth belongs to the earth and speaks as one from the earth. The one who comes from heaven is above all. He testifies to what he has seen and heard, but no one accepts his testimony. Whoever has accepted it has certified that God is truthful. For the one whom God has sent speaks the words of God, for*

God gives the Spirit without limit. The Father loves the Son and has placed everything in his hands. Whoever believes in the Son has eternal life, but whoever rejects the Son will not see life, for God's wrath remains on them" (John 3:31 – 36).

In Chapter 4, John recounts an unusual conversation Jesus has with a Samaritan woman in which he reveals something about his Father.

WHAT DID JESUS REVEAL TO A NON-JEWISH PROSTITUTE?

The conversation between Jesus and the woman breaks a number of social norms of the day. Respectable Jewish men don't talk to women without their husbands present. They certainly do not engage in a chat with a Samaritan woman who is most likely a prostitute. These cultural norms originate in Wrong Tree thinking based on misogyny, racism and sexual exploitation. Jesus, who is the bringer of life and revelation, ignores these taboos and engages with the woman. There are many facets to the story, but one easily overlooked is their discussion of worship. Jesus says,

"Woman, believe me, a time is coming when you will worship the Father neither on this mountain nor in Jerusalem. You Samaritans worship what you do not know; we worship what we do know, for salvation is from the Jews. Yet a time is coming and has now come when the true worshipers will worship the Father in the Spirit and in truth, for they are the kind of worshipers the Father seeks. God is spirit, and his worshipers must worship in the Spirit and in truth" (John 4:21 - 24).

Three times in this passage Jesus explicitly links the Father to

CHAPTER 8

worship. He foresees a time when worship of the Father will not be focused in a geographical locality, either on Mount Gerizim or in Jerusalem. Jesus makes this statement forty years before the fall of Jerusalem in 70 AD and the burning of the Temple by the Roman general Titus's troops. He disconnects the worship of God the Father from one specific cultural or religious location. Nor will the worship of the Father be the special preserve of the Jews but will be open to all those who will meet him in the Spirit and in truth. He is referring to the new relationship of those who will be filled with the Spirit of the Father. Jesus goes one step further and says the Father is actively seeking worshipers.

For many today, worship is a major part of Christian life and devotion. In many places this is interpreted as a passive activity, where "worshipers" watch and observe a group of professional, musically gifted people lead worship from the front of a church or on a stage. Audience or congregational participation is reduced to little more than the occasional sing-along to some catchy tunes, arm waving or clapping in time with the rhythm of the music, or the adoption of a somewhat mystical, far-away look upwards, locating God somewhere up in the rafters. Invitations are issued to come and worship Jesus, who in many places is the focus and object of the worship.

This style of worship is widespread across the Christian world. In some places there is enthusiastic congregational participation. I have witnessed an African expression of this where worshipers are whipped up into a frenzied, almost hysterical fever pitch. Participants enter into a trance like state. This is engendered by the rhythm, volume and screamed demands of participation by the worship leader.

Many worship songs sung today have a marked absence of biblical content and tend to be self-centred rather than God centred, let alone Father oriented. The lyrics often consist of pleading like desperate orphans for God to come and do something. This is often a cry coming from our brokenness and need to be helped rather than from a heart to worship the Father, or from a place of being in the Spirit as Jesus spoke about.

So much of worship is, at best, Jesus only focused and at worst, man centred, all about our feelings, our needs, including lots of unbelief and poor theology. My friend James Jordan has said on a number of occasions, "We sing heresy before we believe it!"

In speaking these words to the woman at the well, Jesus is specifically saying the focus of worship is to be the Father, his Father and it will be in the power of his Spirit. This seems to be a more full and rounded expression of Trinitarian worship than many are experiencing today. In these sayings, the Son is calling for worship of the Father in the Spirit. This, Jesus says, is true worship.

In John Chapter 5, John introduces a major section of teaching in which Jesus explains his relationship with God his Father.

John sets the scene in Jerusalem at one of the festivals attended by Jesus. While in the city Jesus stops at the pool called Bethesda where he heals a man who had been paralysed for thirty-eight years. Jesus tells him to get up, pick up his mat and walk. The problem is this happens on a Sabbath and the Jewish authorities seize the opportunity to criticise and confront Jesus for having broken the Sabbath law by instructing the man to carry his mat and also to heal him. We read how they are so angry they want to kill Jesus.

CHAPTER 8

WHY DID THE JEWISH LEADERS TRY TO KILL JESUS?

Jesus's response is simple, he is only doing what the Father is doing. John tells us what happens.

> "So, because Jesus was doing these things on the Sabbath, the Jewish leaders began to persecute him. In his defence Jesus said to them, "My Father is always at his work to this very day, and I too am working." For this reason, they tried all the more to kill him; not only was he breaking the Sabbath, but he was even calling God his own Father, making himself equal with God" (John 5:16 – 18).

The issue for the Jewish religious authorities isn't just about breaking the law, they rightly realise Jesus is calling God not just Father but his own Father and this makes him equal with God. Jesus explains the truth to them about his personal relationship with God his Father.

> "I tell you the truth, the Son can do nothing by himself; he can do only what he sees his Father doing, because whatever the Father does the Son also does. For the Father loves the Son and shows him all he does. Yes, and he will show him even greater works than these, so that you will be amazed. For just as the Father raises the dead and gives them life, even so the Son gives life to whom he is pleased to give it" (John 5:19 – 21).

The whole passage lays out the intimate relationship between the Father and the Son. The Son of himself can do nothing but in concert with the Father, together they both work. He describes the love the Father has for his Son by showing him his works. The greatest work is still to come, the Father will raise the dead and because of this, the Son will also bring life. This is completely consistent with receiving from the Tree of Life found in Genesis and through to Revelation. Jesus is symbolically the Tree of Life who brings life to mankind.

> *"For as the Father has life in himself, so he has granted the Son also to have life in himself" (John 5:26).*

Finally, Jesus tells them how their spiritual deafness and blindness comes from their unbelief. They have earnestly sought answers in the Scriptures but because the eyes of their hearts are closed and ears blocked, they can neither see nor hear what the Scriptures actually says. He tells them eternal life does not come through Bible study but through him who is revealed in the Scriptures.

> *"For the works that the Father has given me to finish, the very works that I am doing, testify that the Father has sent me. And the Father who sent me has himself testified concerning me. You have never heard his voice nor seen his form, nor does his word dwell in you, for you do not believe the one he sent. You study the Scriptures diligently because you think that in them you have eternal life. These are the very Scriptures that testify about me, yet you refuse to come to me to have life" (John 5:36 – 40).*

In the following chapters of the Gospel, John records some notable miracles or signs as he calls them. Jesus feeds over five thousand people by miraculously multiplying a few bread rolls and a couple of fish. Then having lingered up a hillside on his own until after dark he re-joins his disciples who are halfway across the lake. He comes walking on the choppy lake water and gets in the boat. Not surprisingly, they are terrified. Jesus's answer is almost funny. "It's only me, don't worry!"

CHAPTER 8

Upon reaching the other side, crowds start to gather, again looking for Jesus. On finding him, there are lots of questions. How did he get there so quickly? How can they do these amazing works like he is doing? What sign will he give them so they can believe?

The crowds know they have experienced something amazing, but they cannot work it out. Their eyes are closed, as Isaiah has once been told,

> "…ever hearing, but never understanding; be ever seeing, but never perceiving" (Isaiah 6:9).

They are looking for free food, for bread rather than real spiritual food. Jesus explains,

> "Very truly I tell you, it is not Moses who has given you the bread from heaven, but it is my Father who gives you the true bread from heaven. For the bread of God is the bread that comes down from heaven and gives life to the world."

> "Sir," they said, "always give us this bread."

> Then Jesus declared, "I am the bread of life. Whoever comes to me will never go hungry, and whoever believes in me will never be thirsty. But as I told you, you have seen me and still you do not believe" (John 6:32 –36).

Sometime later, Jesus goes back to Jerusalem for the feast of Tabernacles. He goes privately without any fanfare and slips into the city incognito. The Jewish leaders are watching out for him to try to have him arrested. In the middle of the feast, Jesus turns up in the temple and begins to teach. His teaching and learning cause great amazement. John records much of the discussion and the reactions of the chief priests and Pharisees in Chapter 7. It begins to come to a head and a trap is set for Jesus involving a hapless woman who has been caught in bed with her adulterous lover. She is dragged from her bed and made to stand before Jesus, who they challenge to pass judgment on her.

This story of male misogyny is a devasting exposé of the judgment coming from the Wrong Tree. The man who is also an adulterer is not there, only the woman. He is probably running home tucking his shirt in his belt. Jesus's loving and sensitive handling of the situation speaks volumes about the nurturing and loving heart of the Father expressed through Jesus's words and actions. The story resonates with grace and mercy and love. For some reason the most ancient copies of John's gospel left it out surprisingly. In the early centuries when the New Testament was copied by hand by scribes, there was an increasing tendency to devalue the place of women in the Church. Maybe this story was too much for some of them. Thankfully, this is not true for all and it is widely accepted by most and has been included in all modern translations with a few caveats about its provenance.

In summary, the Jewish religious authorities plot to kill Jesus because they believed he is blaspheming. They hear him talking about God being his Father and this is too much. They believe their actions are right and what God requires of them. They are victims of Satan's trap of eating from the Tree of the Knowledge of Good and Evil. They believe this is what they must do. Their plot eventually results in the death of Jesus. But he does not die because of their plot. He willingly lays down his life in order to reconcile man to the Father. He continually speaks about his coming death and his resurrection.

In the Garden of Eden, God says to Satan the offspring of the woman,

> "He will crush your head, and you will strike his heel" (Genesis 3: 15).

Jesus knows this and prepares for it. The authorities plot to kill him because of what he says and his relationship with God the Father.

DID JESUS EVER ACTUALLY SAY HE WAS GOD?

In the following three chapters, John gathers together several incidents all pointing to Jesus's knowledge of himself being the Son of God and therefore divine. John chapter 8 tells how the Jews challenge Jesus about the source of his authority and who verifies his claims. In his response, he reveals to them more of his relationship with his Father but first he answers their challenge.

> *"In your own Law it is written that the testimony of two witnesses is true. I am one who testifies for myself; my other witness is the Father, who sent me" (John 8:18).*

They misunderstand him assuming he is talking about his human father and demand to know where this person is. Jesus answers in an enigmatic way which leaves them more mystified than before. Finally he says,

> *"When you have lifted up the Son of Man, then you will know that I am he, and that I do nothing on my own authority, but speak just as the Father taught me. And he who sent me is with me. He has not left me alone, for I always do what is pleasing to him" (John 8:28 – 29).*

Once again Jesus alludes to his crucifixion. He knows crucifixion is the path he will take in bringing reconciliation between fallen man and God. Some of the Jews who are listening claim to believe in what he is saying and announce they are free sons of Abraham. He replies to them with these significant words,

> *"Very truly I tell you, everyone who sins is a slave to sin. Now a slave has no permanent place in the family, but a son belongs to it forever. So if the Son sets you free, you will be free indeed. I know that you are Abraham's descendants. Yet you are looking for a way to kill me, because you have no room for my word. I am telling you what I have seen in the Father's presence, and you are doing what you have heard from your father" (John 8:34 – 38).*

His words describe the condition of fallen humanity, enslaved to sin by the Fall. But he gives them hope by promising freedom and a restoration of their position as sons to those who will be set free by the Son of God.

Their claim to believe in him quickly dissipates and is exposed as hollow. In their hearts they are planning to kill him while still claiming Abraham is their father.

> *"If you were Abraham's children," said Jesus, "then you would do what Abraham did. As it is, you are looking for a way to kill me, a man who has told you the truth that I heard from God. Abraham did not do such things. You are doing the works of your own father" (John 8:39 – 41).*

They indignantly turn on Jesus and accuse him of being illegitimate.

> *"We are not illegitimate children," they protested. "The only Father we have is God himself."*
>
> *Jesus said to them, "If God were your Father, you would love me, for I have come here from God. I have not come on my own;*

God sent me. Why is my language not clear to you? Because you are unable to hear what I say. You belong to your father, the devil, and you want to carry out your father's desires. He was a murderer from the beginning, not holding to the truth, for there is no truth in him. When he lies, he speaks his native language, for he is a liar and the father of lies. Yet because I tell the truth, you do not believe me! Can any of you prove me guilty of sin? If I am telling the truth, why don't you believe me? Whoever belongs to God hears what God says. The reason you do not hear is that you do not belong to God" (John 8:42 – 47).

The tension continues to build in the ensuing debate, getting more heated by the minute. They accuse him of being a Samaritan and demonized. Finally, Jesus says to them,

"Truly, truly, I say to you, before Abraham was born, I am." So they picked up stones to throw at him, but Jesus hid himself slipping away out of the temple" (John 8:58 – 59).

Jesus uses language they instantly recognise. He uses the I AM description used for the name of God and applies it to himself. He is declaring his divinity. The Jews listening are furious and in taking up stones to kill him are acting in accordance with their law which condemns blasphemy with stoning. To them, Jesus has committed an unforgivable sin.

The name of God revealed to Moses in Exodus 3:14 is *"I am who I am."*

It is the name all Jews recognise but fear to say. God says to Moses,

"I AM WHO I AM. This is what you are to say to the Israelites: 'I AM has sent me to you.'"

> *God also said to Moses, "Say to the Israelites, 'The LORD, the God of your fathers, the God of Abraham, the God of Isaac and the God of Jacob, has sent me to you.' "This is my name forever, the name you shall call me from generation to generation" (Exodus 3:14 – 15).*

When Jesus says "before Abraham was born, I am" he is saying he existed before Abraham was born. He knows he is eternal. It is a clear and specific revelation of his name, nature and position in the Godhead.

John records Jesus making seven statements all beginning with *"Ego eimi,"* I AM. All of these "I am" statements point to his divinity and his great reason for coming into the world.

And Jesus says to them,

> *"I am the bread of life. He who comes to Me shall never hunger, and he who believes in Me shall never thirst" (John 6:35).*

> *"I am the light of the world. He who follows Me shall not walk in darkness but have the light of life" (John 8:12).*

> *"I am the door. If anyone enters by Me, he will be saved, and will go in and out and find pasture" (John 10:9).*

> *"I am the good shepherd. The good shepherd gives His life for the sheep" (John 10:11).*

> *"I am the resurrection and the life. He who believes in Me, though he may die, he shall live" (John 11:25).*

> *"I am the way, the truth, and the life. No one comes to the Father except through Me" (John 14:6).*

CHAPTER 8

"I am the true vine, and My Father is the vinedresser" (John 15:1).

John continues to record Jesus's ministry. In Chapter 9, Jesus heals a blind man and following the response of the Pharisees talks about their spiritual blindness. This continues in Chapter 10, where Jesus describes himself as the Good Shepherd. Again, he tells them he will lay down his life for his sheep who are not just Israel but all people. This is a clear statement of the great plan originating in the heart of God to bring all his children home.

> *"I have other sheep that are not of this sheep pen. I must bring them also. They too will listen to my voice, and there shall be one flock and one shepherd. The reason my Father loves me is that I lay down my life only to take it up again. No one takes it from me, but I lay it down of my own accord. I have authority to lay it down and authority to take it up again. This command I received from my Father" (John 10:16 – 18).*

Throughout the Gospel, John builds saying upon saying to prove from Jesus's words he is God. It culminates in this section.

> *"The works I do in my Father's name testify about me, but you do not believe because you are not my sheep. My sheep listen to my voice; I know them, and they follow me. I give them eternal life, and they shall never perish; no one will snatch them out of my hand. My Father, who has given them to me, is greater than all; no one can snatch them out of my Father's hand. I and the Father are one."*
>
> *Again his Jewish opponents picked up stones to stone him, but Jesus said to them, "I have shown you many good works from the Father. For which of these do you stone me?"*

> *"We are not stoning you for any good work," they replied, "but for blasphemy, because you, a mere man, claim to be God"* (John 10:25 – 33).

As the story begins to near its dramatic climax in Jerusalem with Jesus's death and resurrection, John records two important events taking place in Bethany outside the city. The first is the raising from the dead of Jesus's friend Lazarus and the second is Jesus's anointing by Lazarus's sister Mary. Both stories prepare the way for the coming death, burial and resurrection of Jesus which are about to happen in just over a week. The plot to kill Jesus by the Jewish religious leaders is taking shape and his disciples have been infiltrated. Judas Iscariot is already in touch with the High Priest and agrees to deliver Jesus into their hands.

This section ends with yet another unequivocal statement from Jesus about his ministry.

> *"For I did not speak on my own, but the Father who sent me commanded me to say all that I have spoken. I know that his command leads to eternal life. So whatever I say is just what the Father has told me to say"* (John 12:49 – 50).

CHAPTER 9

THE EVENTS IN THE UPPER ROOM

Matthew, Mark and Luke all relate the events taking place in the upper room. Jesus gathers with his disciples to celebrate the feast of Passover in a large upstairs room in Jerusalem. The three Synoptic writers take roughly one chapter to tell their version of the evening's events.

Mark's account is the most detailed of the three, and he takes the story right through to the arrest of Jesus in the Garden of Gethsemane. The flavour of an eyewitness in Mark's version is unmistakeable. It leads me to believe John Mark himself, whose mother Mary owned a large house with an upstairs room in Jerusalem, is an observer of the evening, possibly serving at the meal.

All three of the Synoptic gospel writers focus on the last supper of Jesus and his disciples. In particular, they focus on the Passover meal itself and how Jesus takes the bread and wine of the meal and invests them with new meaning for his followers. According to different Christian traditions, this is referred to as the Lord's Supper, Communion, Breaking Bread, the Eucharist or Mass.

THE EVENTS IN THE UPPER ROOM

WHY IS JOHN'S GOSPEL SO DIFFERENT TO THE OTHERS?

John's Gospel uses the evening's events to highlight a number of other important truths. It is as if he does not feel he needs to repeat what others have written. He follows the leading of the Spirit and writes what the Spirit reminds him. The evening makes a deep personal impression on him as he reclines at the meal alongside Jesus. He is probably a young man, impressionable and vulnerable. He is believed to have lived into the late first century when he writes his Gospel in his old age.

John recounts how Jesus disrobes, wraps a towel around his waist and washes the disciple's feet in an incredible demonstration of humility and servanthood. In light of everything he has told them about his true identity, this act is likely confusing and humbling.

The meal begins and Jesus continues speaking to them about the nature of true servanthood. Suddenly the atmosphere changes. John writes,

> *"Jesus was troubled in spirit and testified, "Very truly I tell you, one of you is going to betray me" (John 13:21).*

John vividly records what happens next.

> *"His disciples stared at one another, at a loss to know which of them he meant. One of them, the disciple whom Jesus loved, was reclining next to him. Simon Peter motioned to this disciple and said, "Ask him which one he means."*
>
> *Leaning back against Jesus, he asked him, "Lord, who is it?"*

> *Jesus answered, "It is the one to whom I will give this piece of bread when I have dipped it in the dish." Then, dipping the piece of bread, he gave it to Judas, the son of Simon Iscariot. As soon as Judas took the bread, Satan entered into him.*
>
> *So Jesus told him, "What you are about to do, do quickly." But no one at the meal understood why Jesus said this to him. Since Judas had charge of the money, some thought Jesus was telling him to buy what was needed for the festival, or to give something to the poor. As soon as Judas had taken the bread, he went out. And it was night" (John 13:22 – 30).*

If this is not bad enough, Jesus continues,

> *"When he was gone, Jesus said, "Now the Son of Man is glorified and God is glorified in him. If God is glorified in him, God will glorify the Son in himself, and will glorify him at once.*
>
> *"My children, I will be with you only a little longer. You will look for me, and just as I told the Jews, so I tell you now: Where I am going, you cannot come. A new command I give you: Love one another. As I have loved you, so you must love one another. By this everyone will know that you are my disciples, if you love one another."*
>
> *Simon Peter asked him, "Lord, where are you going?"*
>
> *Jesus replied, "Where I am going, you cannot follow now, but you will follow later."*
>
> *Peter asked, "Lord, why can't I follow you now? I will lay down my life for you."*

THE EVENTS IN THE UPPER ROOM

Then Jesus answered, "Will you really lay down your life for me? Very truly I tell you, before the cock crows, you will disown me three times" (John 13:31 – 38)!

The evening takes a very dramatic turn from what has been expected by the disciples. Betrayal by one and denial by another. What is quite amazing is in spite of having spent three years with Jesus, the disciples seem not to grasp the importance of what is happening and what Jesus has been saying. They are confused and upset. I can imagine the tension in the room as the evening grows darker and the lamps are lit maybe by John Mark.

What follows next in John's Gospel is the most extraordinary and wonderful summary of all Jesus has personally told his disciples in the preceding three years. John's Upper Room Discourse, as it is known, is the most profound revelation. Its four chapters of truth are unparalleled in the relationship between God and man. If you have a "red letter" version of the New Testament, it is very red.

I cannot do justice to this and will not attempt to write an exposition of it all. My intention is to draw out some of the salient points relating to the Big Picture. For a verse-by-verse uncovering, I refer you again to Stephen Hill's excellent commentary on John.

Chapter 14 begins with an unusual encouragement by Jesus. For weeks, he has been telling them he was going to die in Jerusalem. He has told them he is about to be betrayed by one of their number. He says Simon Peter will deny he knows Jesus. Then Jesus says, "Cheer up boys, trust us, Father and I know what is going on!" or words to that effect.

"Do not let your hearts be troubled. You believe in God; believe also in me. My Father's house has many rooms; if that were not so, would I have told you that I am going there to prepare

a place for you? And if I go and prepare a place for you, I will come back and take you to be with me that you also may be where I am" (John 14:1 – 3).

Jesus is laying out before them the glorious plan originating in the heart of the Father before the creation of the world. He is telling them they belong, and they have a place prepared for them in the Father's house. Many have understood this to mean Jesus is talking about going to "heaven." God is in heaven and his followers will end up there some day. Jesus is more specific, however.

He says the place he is going to prepare for them, where they will be welcomed is where he is at that moment. Not just some future reality. He says definitively, "I will take you to where I am now."

WHERE WAS HE AND WHERE WAS HE GOING?

If we think he is talking about a future state in heaven we can be excused for thinking John muddled up his tenses. Many read this and think Jesus is saying, "I will come back and take you to be with me so you also may be where I will be." But there is no mistake. Jesus is not talking about something far in the future, the place prepared is where Jesus is as he says these words. As he speaks, he is at one with the Father and he is in the bosom of the Father. He is saying this is where we also belong. In him, and like him, in the heart of the Father. This is the destiny prepared for us before creation. At home in the heart of God himself.

Jesus checks to see if they understand him and asks, "You know the way to the place I am going, don't you?"

I imagine there are lots of blank faces and quizzical looks in the room. The silence is broken by Thomas who blurts out they don't know where Jesus is going so consequently don't know the way. Jesus's answer, one of the aforementioned seven 'I Am' sayings, is well known, "I am the way and the truth and the life." I have known this verse since my earliest days as it was painted on the wall of the church I grew up in.

For countless millions, it is the heart of the gospel. Jesus is the way. All that is needed is Jesus. Some have even said there is no need for the Holy Spirit or the Father. The most important thing is following Jesus. However, to leave the quote hanging in the air on the church wall without finishing the rest of the verse is to miss the best bit. Jesus also says, "No one comes to the Father except through me." Jesus is affirming his life's focus is to be the way to the Father, to be the truth and also life of God the Father.

One of the twentieth century's notable Bible teachers was Derek Prince who, after years of preaching about Jesus, had a personal revelation of God being his Father. Prince famously said, "Most of the church has got stuck on the way." He had a definite spiritual experience when God revealed himself to him as his Father. He also said, "I didn't think about it. From then on whenever I addressed God, it just came out of my heart, God my father."

John continues the exchange in Chapter 14 with Philip's request, "Lord show us the Father." It is as if he is saying, "I can see you, but I can't see the Father." The disciples still don't get what Jesus meant. They can see he has direct contact with the Father, but they are trying to rationally work it out in their heads. What does it mean to see the Father in Jesus? They see Jesus relating to God as Father but haven't realised he and the Father are one. Jesus replies,

CHAPTER 9

"Don't you know me, Philip, even after I have been among you such a long time? Anyone who has seen me has seen the Father" (John 14:9).

Jesus has been revealing the Father to them for over three years. What they need is revelation. Jesus says to them if they really knew him, they would know the Father as well. John uses the *"ginosko"* word which is the progressive experience of knowing. Then he changes to the other word translated as 'know", *"oida"* meaning complete knowledge. By knowing Jesus through personal experience and relationship they will also completely know the Father.

Many think in knowing about Jesus and the Father, we automatically know the Father and seeing Jesus is all we need. They suggest emphasising knowing Father is neglecting Jesus. If anyone has been neglected it is the Father.

Throughout the evening Jesus continues teaching them. When John writes these things down, he is reminded by the Holy Spirit what Jesus said at the time. Jesus promises to send his Holy Spirit to be a comforter and encourager who will remind them of all the things he said. The Spirit would only speak what he hears the Father say. Father, Son and Spirit are collectively and individually involved in revealing truth to them.

> *"But the comforter, the Holy Spirit, whom the Father will send in my name, will teach you all things and will remind you of everything I have said to you" (John 14:26).*

The Spirit's role as a comforter is also very important. Jesus says of him,

> *"And I will ask the Father, and he will give you another comforter to help you and be with you forever, the Spirit of*

> truth. The world cannot accept him, because it neither sees him nor knows him. But you know him, for he lives with you and will be in you. I will not leave you as orphans; I will come to you" (John 14:16 – 18).

This passage culminates in an amazing statement by Jesus. He will not leave his disciples as orphans, but he will come to them. In Genesis 3, the Fall of Adam and his wife precipitated by eating the fruit of the Tree of the Knowledge of good and evil results in a loss of intimate connection with the Father as sons. Mankind is effectively orphaned by Satan's plot. The sense of orphan heartedness is exhibited in every interaction between each other and God. We see this tragic outworking in human history. In the glorious 'Big Picture,' we see Jesus declaring this era of orphan heartedness is over. No longer need we live like orphans. The Father himself will come to us in Jesus who is one with the Father. The disciples are not physical orphans but have an orphan heart or attitude and way of behaving. Jesus says those days are over.

They will no longer need to beg and plead like orphans for things from God or to get Jesus to ask on their behalf for things. As free sons in the household, they can go directly to the Father.

As the evening progresses, Jesus uses an image of a vine to help the disciples see more clearly who he is and who they are in relationship with him. He tells them the Father is the gardener who prunes and encourages them to be more fruitful. He exhorts them to remain grafted into him.

In Chapter 15, Jesus shows the disciples how much he loves them.

> "As the Father has loved me, so have I loved you. Now remain in my love. If you keep my commands, you will remain in my love, just as I have kept my Father's commands and remain

in his love. I have told you this so that my joy may be in you and that your joy may be complete. My command is this: Love each other as I have loved you. Greater love has no one than this: to lay down one's life for one's friends" (John 15:9 – 13).

Earlier, Jesus tells them he will send them another comforter, the Holy Spirit (John 14:15). He says the Spirit will be *'another'* comforter. This is because he has already been comforting them. In this passage, he explains how he comforts them. He loves them in the same way as the Father loves him.

HOW DID JESUS LOVE HIS DISCIPLES?

Jesus needs to know and experience his Father loving and comforting him and in this same way he treats his disciples. In effect, he has been a father to them. His relationship with the disciples is not just as a rabbi and a teacher, he fathers them.

When Jesus makes the statement about loving them in the same way the Father loves him, none of them question him about what he means as they did earlier in the evening. They know what he means. They have experienced him loving them. They do not know it intellectually; they know it at heart level. They are young and like all young men have issues in their lives and carry wounds from their childhood. There are petty rivalries between them. They are jealous of each other. Luke records how at the beginning of the meal they are arguing about who is the most important among them (Luke 22:24). They flare up at times. James and John suggest Jesus sending fire from heaven down on an unwelcoming Samaritan village would be a good idea (Luke 9:54). One of them has even been a terrorist, Simon the Zealot! However, Jesus loves them and comforts them on their three-year journey with him, amid their own personal challenges.

When this group of young men becomes disciples of Jesus, they are doing what many young men did in Israel at that time. They attach themselves to a rabbi to learn and study from the teacher. Their relationship with Jesus is fundamentally different. He has chosen them. His ministry to them is to father them as he pours the love of the Father into them. He encourages them to love each other in the same way. This means laying down their lives for each other.

Jesus goes one step further. He continues,

> *"You are my friends if you do what I command. I no longer call you servants, because a servant does not know his master's business. Instead, I have called you friends, for everything that I learned from my Father I have made known to you. You did not choose me, but I chose you" (John 15: 14 – 16).*

He is transitioning them from thinking and behaving like disciples who serve a master or Rabbi to being friends. They are learning how to be friends rather than just obedient servants. This is a change of relationship. Their mindset is like Adam's, serving to find a place, being obedient out of duty and not really knowing the heart of their master. They, however, have been chosen by Jesus who has opened his heart up to them, comforted them, loved them and revealed his Father to them. Because of this he will no longer refer to them as servants or disciples but as his friends.

The intention of God since before creation is to have sons as the focus of the Father's love. These disciples are on a journey out of orphan hearted slavery back home to the Father's house where they have a place of acceptance and belonging as sons. They are not quite there yet. They are moving from slavery into sonship and at this point they are no longer servants but friends.

Jesus shows them how this transition will affect the way they live. Earlier in the evening, he says they are to continue the work the Father has given him to do and there are even greater works prepared for them to do.

AREN'T WE SUPPOSED TO PRAY IN JESUS NAME?

Jesus tells the disciples they can ask anything in his name.

> *"... Very truly I tell you, whoever believes in me will do the works I have been doing, and they will do even greater things than these, because I am going to the Father. And I will do whatever you ask in my name, so that the Father may be glorified in the Son. You may ask me for anything in my name, and I will do it" (John 14:12 – 14).*

He tells them these works will be done in relationship with the Father. He will ask the Father on their behalf, like a go-between taking their requests to the Father as they are unable to do it themselves. But later in the evening, he explains how things will change as the transition from servants to friends and ultimately son takes place.

> *"There is a day coming when you won't ask anything of me, my Father will give you whatever you ask in my name" (John 16:23).*

This is not a contradiction but a transition. Jesus is saying they will no longer need to go to him. Rather, they will be able to go directly to the Father themselves. We now have the same direct access to Father as Jesus has.

The expression "in Jesus's name" has become a formula to be used at the end of a prayer to God. It is almost a mantra and tells everyone we are just about to finish our prayer, so wake up and get ready to say 'Amen.' In our Wrong Tree way of thinking, we believe if we don't say the words right, God will not hear and certainly not answer our prayers!

I was once taken to task by a group of African pastors who were horrified I didn't say "in Jesus's name" at the end of grace before a meal. It was very serious for them and seemed to prevent them hearing very much else I was teaching. A few days later at a question and answer session, it came up again. The same leader addressed the issue to me in a very serious manner. Then he paused and a huge grin spread across his face as he concluded God seemed to answer me anyway.

The expression of asking in Jesus's name is not about correct prayer theology but about where we are asking from. In the new relationship as sons, we are positioned in Christ, in fellowship with him and connected in spirit with him. Relationship with the Father as a son changes everything. When we are in this place, we are in his will and we are able to ask in his name.

It is also about what we are asking for. We tend to make our prayer formulas lists of things we want from God and what we want him to do. I have noted there is a great deal of disappointment among Christians about what appears to be the absence of answers to our prayers. Many suggest the solution is lack of faith, unbelief, unconfessed or secret sin, lack of effort, we didn't shout loud enough and perseverance. When prayer is not answered in the way desired, all manner of reasons are suggested, most of which are rooted in Wrong Tree judgmental thinking.

CHAPTER 9

Prayer has become militaristic with language about warfare, breakthrough, soldiers, and prayer warriors. A group has emerged known as intercessors and these people are given great prominence and credence in contemporary Christianity. There is talk of the gift of intercession and the ministry of intercession. Some churches can become controlled by these people and it can lead to all manner of super spirituality and manipulation. I have known pastors who are unable to exercise their ministries because of these people. If we add a prophetic "Thus says the Lord," it becomes a toxic mix, and we are far removed from what Jesus is saying here in John's Gospel.

The Bible does not talk about the ministry of intercession or a group of intercessors, instead it points to just one intercessor, Jesus. Sons and daughters are in him and we are free to ask the Father directly. We ask the Father to show us the work he is doing and those things he has prepared in advance for us to do with him. It is about our relationship with him. I know many who take great delight and have found deep satisfaction in spending much time in a place of prayer born out of their relationship with Father and Son and Spirit. This is what Jesus is talking about when he tells us to abide in him or remain in his love. Their hearts are focused on receiving life from the Tree of Life himself.

In John 16:26, Jesus says, he is not going to be the one passing on their prayers, the Father himself will be answering them. 'I will not ask the Father on your behalf.' They can ask him themselves.

The key to this approach to prayer and asking is based on the amazing revelation Jesus brings to his friends. It is breath taking when we realise exactly what this means.

"The Father himself loves you" (John 16:27).

They know the Father loves Jesus as his beloved son, but Jesus says the Father himself loves them just as much as he loves Jesus. This is astonishing. Our Wrong Tree thinking since the Fall and the lies Satan continually tells us has convinced us we are unlovable, unworthy, not acceptable and we have to strive and struggle to work in the forlorn hope if we do enough God will be a little less than seriously cross with us.

It appears from what John writes, the disciples are finally beginning to see a little more clearly what Jesus means.

> *"Then Jesus' disciples said, "Now you are speaking clearly and without figures of speech. Now we can see that you know all things and that you do not even need to have anyone ask you questions. This makes us believe that you came from God. "Do you now really believe?" Jesus replied" (John 16:29 – 31).*

Jesus has taken them as far as he can. The events about to happen over the next few days will test them beyond anything they can imagine and whether they really do believe what he has said. He prepares them by saying,

> *"A time is coming and in fact has come when you will be scattered, each to your own home. You will leave me all alone. Yet I am not alone, for my Father is with me. I have told you these things, so that in me you may have peace. In this world you will have trouble. But take heart! I have overcome the world" (John 16:32 – 33).*

As the evening draws to a close, John records Jesus praying. This is sometimes called the High Priestly prayer of Jesus. It is the Son talking to his Father from a place of intimacy and love. It is the conclusion of his ministry before he goes to the cross. The Holy Spirit reminds John of this prayer as he writes the Gospel many years later.

It begins with Jesus speaking directly to his Father then it moves on to Jesus praying for his friends in the room, and finally he prays for all who will believe through their message.

In the first part of the prayer Jesus recognises the moment God has been looking towards since the Fall of man in Eden has come.

> *"Father, the hour has come. Glorify your Son, that your Son may glorify you. For you granted him authority over all people that he might give eternal life to all those you have given him. Now this is eternal life: that they know you, the only true God, and Jesus Christ, whom you have sent. I have brought you glory on earth by finishing the work you gave me to do. And now, Father, glorify me in your presence with the glory I had with you before the world began" (John 17:1 – 6).*

Jesus says eternal life is not some future idyll in heaven, it is knowing the Father, the one true God and Jesus his Son. The word is *"ginosko"* again. Knowing through experience and relationship. For so many, knowing God has been devalued to knowing about God rather than intimacy and personal encounter with the Father which Jesus describes as eternal life.

In addition, Jesus says he has finished the work he has been given by the Father to do.

This statement by Jesus is surprising. Personally, for most of my Christian life, I would have said Jesus came to die on the cross and save us from our sins. One day reading this verse I was stopped in my tracks, and I saw this statement by Jesus saying he had completed or finished the work the Father had given him to do. My response was but what about the cross?

HOW COULD JESUS HAVE FINISHED THE WORK WHEN HE HAD NOT DIED ON THE CROSS YET?

Surely, he is not finished until he dies. His final words are, "It is finished." I rushed back to check out the Greek. Jesus is saying it in the past tense. He has finished the work Father had given him to do. Then Jesus says,

> *"I have revealed you to those whom you gave me out of the world" (John 17:6).*

Jesus's work is to reveal the Father to the disciples and through their testimony to the whole world. Jesus wants them to know what God is really like before he goes to the cross. He wants them to see God is a Father who loves them personally and longs for them to know him. He is about to reconcile the world to himself through his death on the cross, as Paul will later say. If Jesus had gone to the cross without this revelation, they would be confused and think God is distant and angry and will turn his face away as Jesus carries the sin of the world in his body. This is taught and widely believed by many. God is seen as so holy and angry at sin he turns his face away from Jesus when he carries all of the sin of the world on himself because he cannot bear to look at sin. This is a huge assumption arising from an erroneous view of the nature of God which we will look at in more detail in the next chapter. At this point all I want to say is Father has been looking at the sin of the world in man since the Fall in all its horror and degradation.

Before Jesus goes to the cross, he reveals the true heart of God the Father. He completes this work by the end of the evening in the upper room.

CHAPTER 9

His imminent departure and his return to his Father is beginning to unfold and he knows how hard the next few hours will be. At the same time, he wants them to experience the immense joy in his heart about the result.

> *"I am coming to you now, but I say these things while I am still in the world, so that they may have the full measure of my joy within them" (John 17:13).*

The writer to the letter to the Hebrews has seen this also. He writes,

> *"For the joy set before him he (Jesus) endured the cross, scorning its shame, and sat down at the right hand of the throne of God" (Hebrews 12:2).*

At the conclusion of the prayer Jesus prays for all who will come to know the Father through the testimony of his friends, the disciples. Everything he has revealed and given to them is to be given to us too. What the eternal triune God has planned before the creation of the world, the love they share which is their glory, is to be shared with us too.

> *"I have made you known to them and will continue to make you known in order that the love you have for me may be in them and that I myself may be in them" (John 17:26).*

Jesus says he has made the Father known and promises to continue to make the Father known so the Father's love for him will be in us too and he himself will be in us. This is the fulfilment of the plan originating in the heart of God before the world was created. This is the Big Picture. The plan is revealed to Paul who writes it in his letter to the Ephesians.

"For he (the Father) chose us in him before the creation of the world to be holy and blameless in his sight. In love he planned for us to be sons through Jesus Christ, in accordance with his pleasure and will, to the praise of his glorious grace, which he has freely given us in the One he loves" (Ephesians 1:4 – 6).

CHAPTER 10

THE CROSS

At the end of the evening, Jesus and his friends leave the upper room and go out into the night. They leave the city behind them, cross the Kidron ravine and climb up the hill to the Garden of Gethsemane which is on the Mount of Olives overlooking the city.

Mark records the events in the garden.

> *"They went to a place called Gethsemane, and Jesus said to his disciples, "Sit here while I pray." He took Peter, James and John along with him, and he began to be deeply distressed and troubled. "My soul is overwhelmed with sorrow to the point of death," he said to them. "Stay here and keep watch."*
>
> *Going a little farther, he fell to the ground and prayed that if possible, the hour might pass from him. "Abba, Father," he said, "everything is possible for you. Take this cup from me. Yet not what I will, but what you will."*
>
> *Then he returned to his disciples and found them sleeping. "Simon," he said to Peter, "are you asleep? Couldn't you keep watch for one hour? Watch and pray so that you will not fall into temptation. The spirit is willing, but the flesh is weak."*

Once more he went away and prayed the same thing. When he came back, he again found them sleeping, because their eyes were heavy. They did not know what to say to him. Returning the third time, he said to them, "Are you still sleeping and resting? Enough! The hour has come. Look, the Son of Man is delivered into the hands of sinners. Rise! Let us go! Here comes my betrayer!"

Just as he was speaking, Judas, one of the Twelve, appeared. With him was a crowd armed with swords and clubs, sent from the chief priests, the teachers of the law, and the elders. Now the betrayer had arranged a signal with them: "The one I kiss is the man; arrest him and lead him away under guard." Going at once to Jesus, Judas said, "Rabbi!" and kissed him. The men seized Jesus and arrested him. Then one of those standing near drew his sword and struck the servant of the high priest, cutting off his ear.

"Am I leading a rebellion," said Jesus, "that you have come out with swords and clubs to capture me? Every day I was with you, teaching in the temple courts, and you did not arrest me. But the Scriptures must be fulfilled." Then everyone deserted him and fled.

A young man, wearing nothing but a linen garment, was following Jesus. When they seized him, he fled naked, leaving his garment behind" (Mark 14:32 – 52).

CHAPTER 10

WHO IS THIS NAKED BOY?

Jesus is described as going alone to pray some way away from Peter, James and John. We are told after Jesus prays, he returns to find the disciples asleep. It raises the issue of the description of Jesus's prayer Mark records. If all the disciples, including Peter, are asleep, how would they know what he has prayed? Unless someone else is there in the garden listening and watching. It is my conclusion this is John Mark, and he is also the young man who flees naked from the garden

Of the three Gospel writers who record Jesus praying in the garden, only Mark says he addresses God as Abba. This is the most intimate expression a small child uses to speak to his father. It is akin to "papa" or perhaps "daddy." It is the term still used throughout the Middle East by little children when addressing their fathers.

It speaks of home, of love and affection, of closeness and belonging. It speaks of relationship and intimacy. When Jesus prays, he enjoys the closest of connections with his Father. Mark says he is "deeply distressed and troubled." Overwhelmed with sorrow, Jesus falls to the ground. This is the vivid writing of an eyewitness.

In this moment of deep pain and anguish, Jesus cries out to his Abba. The resonance in the word would comfort his aching heart. Mark hears pure revelation and records it for us. It becomes deeply ingrained into the DNA of the early church as they realise they too are sons and daughters to the Father, and they can also address the Father in such terms of intimacy in the same way as Jesus.

Paul, writing to the Galatians, also uses this term *"abba."*

> *"But when the time had fully come, God sent his Son, born of a woman, born under the law, to redeem those under the law, that we might receive the full rights of sons. Because you are sons, God sent the Spirit of his Son into our hearts, the Spirit who calls out, 'Abba, Father'" (Galatians 4:4).*

This letter, written in response to a crisis in the early church is the first piece of Christian writing. It is written before the start of Paul's second missionary journey when Paul revisits Galatia. Therefore, it predates any of the Gospels. We are going to look at this in a later chapter. Paul says we are Abba's sons and daughters in the same way as Jesus is Abba's son. The same level of intimacy and closeness, of belonging and loving affection is ours too.

I have wondered how Paul receives this revelation. Perhaps this is known widely in the early church. Or maybe he hears this from young John Mark who is with him on the first part of the journey. I can imagine they talk about what Mark heard and saw in his brief encounters with the disciples and maybe even his observation of Jesus in the Garden of Gethsemane. Whatever the way this is remembered, it has become part of our glorious inheritance as sons and daughters. We too are Abba's children, and we can relate to him in exactly the same way as Jesus, with the same assurance and intimacy as him.

Then follows the trial of Jesus before the Jewish High Priests and the Sanhedrin, King Herod and finally the Roman Governor Pontius Pilate. After these trials, he is taken out to be crucified after having been whipped and abused. All four gospels record the events; each differs slightly as they reflect their sources of information or personal observations. The Early Church did not fabricate or try to harmonise these accounts. They let them speak for themselves. Different people heard different things including the words Jesus speaks from the cross. There are seven statements made by Jesus as he hangs on the cross.

There is a generally accepted order to each of these words. The first is Jesus asking his Father to forgive those who are crucifying him.

> *"Father, forgive them, for they do not know what they are doing"* (Luke 23:34).

He addresses his Father as nails are hammered into his hands and feet. He asks the Father to forgive the men who are doing this. They represent all humanity, as we are all complicit in the death of Jesus. In this great redemptive moment, he is able to pray for all of us to be forgiven because he knows the purpose the Father has given him is to bring forgiveness and reconciliation. Paul says of this in Colossians:

> *"And you, who were dead in your trespasses and the uncircumcision of your flesh, God the Father made alive together with Jesus, having forgiven us all our trespasses, by cancelling the record of debt that stood against us with its legal demands. This he set aside, nailing it to the cross. He disarmed the rulers and authorities and put them to open shame, by triumphing over them in him"* (Colossians 2:13-15).

Through his death, all mankind will be brought home. The soldiers do not know what they are doing, but the incarnate Son of the Father knows exactly what is happening and he speaks forgiveness.

Then follows Jesus's heartfelt expression of care for his mother, who along with her sister, John's mother, are standing at the foot of the cross with John. John will have had vivid memories of these words.

> *"Dear, woman, here is your son." Then he said to John, "Here is your mother"* (John 19:26).

Jesus lovingly entrusts his mother into the caring hands of his beloved friend and cousin John. Amid his own agony, he is concerned for the well-being of the woman whose womb hosted him and brought him into his humanity. It is touching and full of compassionate comfort. Jesus's Father of compassion and the God of all comfort is ministering his love to his faithful servant, the highly favoured and beloved daughter, Mary of Nazareth.

A desperate thirst soon overwhelms him. It is a terrible feature of crucifixion and Jesus cries out, "I am thirsty" (John 19:28). As his tongue becomes parched, Jesus the Son in his humanity experiences the full agony of crucifixion. This is not some superhuman enduring the pain but an ordinary man who fully embraces our humanity in his life and death. He is thirsty.

As the two criminals on either side address him, one mocking and the other pleading, Jesus compassionately promises one of them. "I tell you the truth today, you will be with me in paradise" (Luke 23:43). One will enter paradise because of Jesus. It is as if for the dying thief on the cross all seven of the 'I Am' sayings of Jesus recorded by John are about to become his personal reality. The Good Shepherd is about to lay down his life for him. Jesus's death on the cross will be the door to the Father's presence for this broken man. It will be the way to the Father bringing truth and life. He will experience Jesus as the light of the world, the bread of life and the living water. All this healing and joy will become his as he steps into the resurrection life with Jesus. Paradise indeed!

As the end draws near, both Mark and Matthew record a great cry in Aramaic comes from the lips of Jesus, *"Eloi, Eloi, lama sabachthani?"* It is the most shocking and challenging of all. Both Gospels translate this as "My God, my God, why have you forsaken me" (Mark 15:34, Matthew 27:46)?

CHAPTER 10

DID GOD ABANDON AND FORSAKE JESUS ON THE CROSS?

Has the Father forsaken Jesus? Does he abandon him to suffer alone? Are these indeed words of dereliction, despair and failure?

Many interpret this to be how Jesus is feeling as the Father turns his back on his Son who has taken on himself all the sins of the world. They are coming from an understanding of God not as a loving Father, but a vengeful angry God whose demands for absolute justice and holiness must have satisfaction for sin. All this sin is loaded onto Jesus on the cross and God must look away and abandon Jesus in his agony. This view of God has been deeply rooted in Western Christianity for centuries.

C. Baxter Kruger addresses this whole issue thoroughly in his writings. He points out nothing can be further from the truth of the Bible. Kruger says,

> *"There are those who want us to believe that on the day Adam fell, God the Father was filled with a bloodthirsty anger that demanded punishment before he would even consider forgiveness. And they want us to believe that when Jesus Christ hung on the cross, the Father's anger and wrath were poured out upon him, instead of us."*

He continues,

> *"Jesus Christ did not go to the cross to change God; he went to the cross to change us. He did not die to appease the Father's anger or to heal the Father's divided heart. Jesus Christ went to the cross to call a halt to the Fall and undo it, to convert fallen*

> *Adamic existence to his Father, to systematically eliminate our estrangement, so that he could accomplish his Father's dream..."*
> *(Jesus and the Undoing of Adam, C. Baxter Kruger, 2003).*

So why is Jesus saying "My God, my God why have you forsaken me?" As a number of commentators have seen, these are the opening lines of Psalm 22. It is as if Jesus is being reminded by the Father of this amazing psalm. The psalm is one of the prophetic psalms of David. In particular, this one describes the feelings of the Son as he hangs on the cross. There are so many verses in the psalm that resonate powerfully with what Jesus is going through.

The Psalm begins with the cry from the cross, "My God, my God, why have you forsaken me? Why are you so far from saving me, so far from my cries of anguish" (Psalm 22:1)? In quoting this, there are those present who know the psalm by heart. Perhaps the Pharisee Nicodemus, if he is there, has heard these words and understands the full import of the incredible revelation contained within them. These words express what Jesus is feeling as he fully embraces our humanity. We have felt so afraid and alienated and far from God. In his death on the cross, Jesus is totally uniting himself with our broken, rotten and fallen humanity. It is the ultimate incarnation of the beloved Son of the Father.

Jesus, unlike us, has not lost hope or lost sight of God his Father. He knows his Father is the enthroned Holy One of Israel (22: 3) who is trustworthy, who delivers Israel and saves them (22:4). At the same time as he hangs on the cross,

> *"scorned by everyone, despised by the people. All who see me mock me; they hurl insults, shaking their heads. "He trusts in the Lord," they say, "let the Lord rescue him. Let him deliver him, since he delights in him" (Psalm 22:7 - 8).*

CHAPTER 10

The mockers at the cross to which Jesus is nailed use almost these same words:

> "In the same way the chief priests, the teachers of the law and the elders mocked him. "He saved others," they said, "but he can't save himself! He's the king of Israel! Let him come down now from the cross, and we will believe in him. He trusts in God. Let God rescue him now if he wants him, for he said, 'I am the Son of God'" (Matthew 27:41- 44).

In quoting this psalm, Jesus is calling on his Father to comfort him.

> "Do not be far from me, for trouble is near and there is no one to help. Many bulls surround me; strong bulls of Bashan encircle me. Roaring lions that tear their prey open their mouths wide against me" (Psalm 22:12 – 13).

Jesus entrusts his mother to John and in the psalm, the psalmist reflects these thoughts:

> "Yet you brought me out of the womb; you made me trust in you, even at my mother's breast. From birth I was cast on you; from my mother's womb you have been my God" (Psalm 22:9 - 10).

The actions of the soldiers and the painful agony of crucifixion and exhaustion are described in the psalm.

> "I am poured out like water, and all my bones are out of joint. My heart has turned to wax; it has melted within me. My mouth is dried up like a potsherd, and my tongue sticks to the roof of my mouth; you lay me in the dust of death. Dogs surround me, a pack of villains encircles me; they pierce my hands and my feet. All my bones are on display; people stare

and gloat over me. They divide my clothes among them and cast lots for my garment" (Psalm 22:12 – 18).

Baxter Kruger says Psalm 22 moves from agony to God's victorious intervention and to a prophecy that the coming generations will look back upon this moment as the salvation of the Lord of Hosts.

"All the ends of the earth will remember and turn to the Lord, and all the families of the nations will bow down before him, for dominion belongs to the Lord and he rules over the nations. All the rich of the earth will feast and worship; all who go down to the dust will kneel before him those who cannot keep themselves alive" (Psalm 22:27 – 29).

Kruger continues,

"In the greatest of ironies, the cry of Jesus, "My God, My God, why have You forsaken me?" actually sets in motion a line of thought that completely reinterprets what is happening on the cross. Far from being a perverse moment when the angry God pours His wrath out upon the Son and utterly rejects him, the cross is the moment when the Father absolutely refuses to forsake His Son, the moment of moments when He does not hide His face or turn His back upon him in disgust. Here, according to the Psalm and its interpretation of the event, there is no forsaking at all. In fact, the Psalm tells us that the coming generations will see this event not as divine rejection, but precisely as divine presence and rescue and salvation." (Kruger, Jesus and the undoing of Adam).

Psalm 22 explicitly and prophetically shows the Father has not abandoned or turned his face away from Jesus.

CHAPTER 10

"For he has not despised or scorned the suffering of the afflicted one; he has not hidden his face from him but has listened to his cry for help" (Psalm 22:24).

The Father has not despised or turned his back on the suffering of the Son nor hidden his face from him, quite the contrary. The triune God, Father, Son and Holy Spirit are all intimately involved in this great consummation of their plan to enter fallen humanity and bring us back home to them.

Psalm 22 continues,

"Future generations will be told about the Lord. They will proclaim his righteousness, declaring to a people yet unborn: He has done it" (Psalm 22:30 – 31)!

In the amazing climax of the psalm, there is the prophetic declaration that the finished work of Christ on the cross will be proclaimed to all future generations since Jesus has died for all. Paul declares this amazing truth,

"For the love of Christ controls us, having concluded this, that one died for all, therefore all died; and He died for all, so that they who live might no longer live for themselves, but for Him who died and rose again on their behalf" (2 Corinthians 5:12 – 14).

Peter also picks up this refrain,

"For Christ also died for sins once for all, the just for the unjust, so that He might bring us to God, having been put to death in the flesh, but made alive in the spirit" (1 Peter 3:18).

Both Luke and John record Jesus's final moments. As Jesus endures the agony of the cross, the words of the psalm resonate within his Spirit. As it reaches its terrible and dramatic climax, Jesus says,

"Father, into your hands I commit my spirit" (Luke 23:46).

The final sentence of the psalm is magnificent. The words are "He has done it" (22:31). The Hebrew verb used here carries a very strong emphasis on completion, accomplishment and finishing. Not abandoned, nor forsaken, but received and welcomed by his Father. Then the great and earth-shattering cry, not of dereliction, failure and despair but of triumph, glorious exaltation and joy, *"tetealestai*!" IT IS ACCOMPLISHED! It is finished.

"And Jesus cried with a loud voice and yielded up his spirit. And at that very moment the veil of the temple was torn in two from the top to the bottom; and the earth quaked and the rocks were split" (Matthew 27:50 – 51).

Earlier, Jesus had said to his disciples,

"The reason my Father loves me is that I lay down my life, only to take it up again. No one takes it from me, but I lay it down of my own accord. I have authority to lay it down and authority to take it up again. This command I received from my Father" (John 10:17 – 18).

CHAPTER 11

RESURRECTION AND ASCENSION

All four gospels recount how after Jesus dies, a rich man called Joseph of Arimathea who is a secret follower of Jesus asks the Roman governor Pilate for permission to remove the body as soon as possible since the Jewish Sabbath is about to begin. Normally crucified victim's bodies are left to rot on their crosses. Permission is granted and Joseph, accompanied by his friend Nicodemus the Pharisee, also a secret follower of Jesus, lovingly takes the dead body of Jesus down from the cross. Nicodemus has brought a large quantity of myrrh and aloe. Taking Jesus's body, the two of them wrap it with the spices in strips of clean linen. This is in accordance with Jewish burial customs.

They place it in Joseph's own new tomb in a garden he has cut out of the rock. He rolls a big stone in front of the entrance to the tomb and goes away, as it is the Jewish day of Preparation for the Sabbath. Mary Magdalene and another Mary are sitting opposite the tomb watching all these things.

Matthew adds on the next day, the one after Preparation Day, the chief priests and the Pharisees go to Pilate with an unusual request.

"Sir," they said, "we remember that while he was still alive that deceiver said, 'After three days I will rise again.' So give the order for the tomb to be made secure until the third day. Otherwise, his disciples may come and steal the body and tell the people that he has been raised from the dead. This last deception will be worse than the first."

"Take a guard," Pilate answered. "Go, make the tomb as secure as you know how." So they went and made the tomb secure by putting a seal on the stone and posting the guard" (Matthew 27:63 – 66).

All four gospels record their versions of what happens when Jesus rises from the dead, as do the Apostles Paul and Peter in their letters. But what happens in between? Where is Jesus the eternal son of God?

WHERE WAS JESUS BETWEEN HIS DEATH AND RESURRECTION?

Christian tradition says after Jesus is crucified and placed in the tomb, his Spirit embarks on a mission of rescue to all those who died before his death. This belief is enshrined in the early creeds of the church and is still recited today in the Creed.

"He was crucified, dead, and buried. He descended into Hell."

This belief is based on several verses in the New Testament difficult to interpret, but primarily comes from 1 Peter 3 where Peter is writing about Jesus's suffering, death and resurrection.

"Christ also suffered once for sins, the righteous for the unrighteous, to bring you to God. He was put to death in the body

but made alive in the Spirit. After being made alive, he went and made proclamation to the imprisoned spirits..." (1 Peter 3:18 – 19).

Peter's comment *"he went and made proclamation to the imprisoned spirits,"* is cited by a number of theologians who believe this refers to Jesus going into Hades or Hell in order to preach the gospel. It first appears in a surviving sermon by Bishop Melito of Sardis before 180 AD. It is not universally believed in the early church era, the first Latin theologian Tertullian disagreed with it. Others such as Origen and Ambrose wrote in support. Augustine of Hippo writing in the beginning of the fifth century says it is allegory rather than true history.

Over time this teaching is given the rather dramatic name of the Harrowing of Hell. It is taken up by the Roman Catholic Church and the Orthodox Churches in the east. It becomes fixed in the literature, art and drama of the Middle Ages. Thousands of medieval paintings, mosaics, and illuminated manuscripts depict Jesus leading Adam by the wrist from the darkest depths of Hades out into the light followed by Eve and a long procession of Old Testament figures. At Jesus's feet lay an array of tools of imprisonment, locks, keys, and chains, and a demon crushed by the gates of Hell, which Jesus has blown open. These are very powerful images. Is this what Peter meant? It's difficult to say.

In the Reformation, Luther included it in his Catechism,

"We believe simply that the entire person, God and human being, descended to Hell after his burial, conquered the devil, destroyed the power of Hell, and took from the devil all his power" (Solid Declaration, Art. IX).

Although the Harrowing of Hell is taught by the Catholic, Orthodox, Lutheran, and Reformed traditions, a number of Christians reject the doctrine of the "harrowing of hell." They claim there is very little biblical evidence for it. Wayne Grudem says the single argument in favour of the "harrowing of hell" clause in the Creed seems to be that it has been around for a very long time. He says an old mistake is still a mistake. Grudem consequently will not say the phrase when reciting the Creed.

C.S. Lewis writes to a friend in 1960 about the Harrowing of Hell and says,

> *"I believe in something like this we understand that Jesus did go to hell to preach to those who came before the cross. We understand that he saved some of them and brought them to heaven with him. The medieval authors, delighted to picture what they called 'the harrowing of hell', Christ descending and knocking on those eternal doors and bringing out those who He chose.... That would explain how what Christ did can save those who lived long before the Incarnation." – Letter to Mrs Sutherland (April 28, 1960)*

Lewis goes on to the point out, "Jesus is the way, truth and life. Heaven is waiting for those who believe in Jesus and his work of redemption. This point reorders all other points; the Truth that makes subservient all other truths; the eighth day of creation." He concludes what happened to human souls prior to Jesus is debatable and it is easier to land in a place of reflection and imagination than in anything sharpened by dogma alone. Lewis says the absence of a heaven made for human beings does explain Jesus's desire to preach to the imprisoned spirits.

Hidden in the debate and the dogma is a simple truth. There is no place where God the Father will not send his Son to find his wayward children in order to lead them home.

CHAPTER 11

Back to the events recorded in the Bible. On the first day of the week everything changes for the whole world.

WHAT HAPPENED AT THE GARDEN TOMB?

Each Gospel writer records their version of events. Like their account of the crucifixion, each reflect their personal memories and the reports of other eyewitnesses. Sometimes there is a bit of confusion about the names of the women who went to the tomb on account of several of the ladies being called Mary.

Matthew begins by reporting there is a violent earthquake, and an angel came to the tomb and rolled back the stone and then sits on it. All the writers agree the angel's appearance is like lightning, and his clothes are white as snow. The guards are terrified by the angel, quaking with fear and become like dead men. Some of the guards flee into the city and report to the chief priests everything that has happened. Matthew tells the story which becomes the official version in Jerusalem. The chief priests meet with the elders and devise a plan. They give the soldiers money and instruct them to say, 'His disciples came during the night and stole him away while we were asleep.' The Jewish authorities hope if this report gets to the governor, it will satisfy him and keep them out of trouble. Matthew says this story is widely circulated among the Jews up to the time he is writing the Gospel.

In John's account it seems Mary Magdalene arrives at the tomb first on her own while it is still dark, sometime after the guards have left and before the other women arrive after sunrise.

She sees the stone has been removed from the entrance. So, she runs back into the city to find Simon Peter and the other disciple, the one Jesus loves, John the Gospel writer. She tells them someone has taken the body of Jesus out of the tomb. She doesn't know where they have put him.

Peter and John immediately leave for the tomb. John outruns Peter and reaches the tomb first. He bends over and looks into the tomb and sees the strips of linen lying there but does not go in. When Simon Peter catches up to him, he goes straight into the tomb. He sees the strips of linen lying there, as well as the cloth that had been wrapped around Jesus's head. The cloth is still lying in its place, separate from the linen. This is not the work of grave robbers who would have stolen the valuable linen. Finally, John who reached the tomb first, also goes inside. John adds they still do not understand that Jesus has to rise from the dead. Then these two go back into the city to where they are staying.

John follows this with a very detailed account of what happens next, which Mary Magdalene no doubt tells him at some point. She is standing outside the tomb crying, and in her distress bends down to look into the tomb and sees two angels in white seated where Jesus's body has been, one at the head and the other at the foot. They ask her why she is crying. This is likely quite a shock. Her response shows she does not realise they are angels. John continues the story,

> *"They have taken my Lord away," she said, "and I don't know where they have put him." At this, she turned around and saw Jesus standing there, but she did not realize that it was Jesus.*
>
> *He asked her, "Woman, why are you crying? Who is it you are looking for?" Thinking he was the gardener, she said, "Sir, if you have carried him away, tell me where you have put him, and I will get him."*

CHAPTER 11

Jesus said to her, "Mary." She turned toward him and cried out in Aramaic, "Rabboni!" (which means "Teacher") (John 20:13 – 16).

This exchange between Jesus and Mary is very human. The distraught, broken hearted and confused woman overwhelmed with grief can barely see through her puffy swollen eyes in the semi darkness before dawn. She is expecting a dead body or worse, grave robbers not angels. In the half-light outside the tomb, she sees a figure who she assumes is the gardener who manages the garden.

Instead, it is the risen Jesus.

He says her name and she turns to him again and says, "Rabboni?" I have added a question mark to this. There is no way of recording a question like this in the Greek, so it is purely an interpretation on my part. Whatever way she says it, she runs to him and throws her arms around him as if to say, "I am never going to let you go again!"

"Jesus said, "Do not hold on to me, for I have not yet ascended to the Father. Go instead to my brothers and tell them, 'I am ascending to my Father and your Father, to my God and your God'" (John 20:17).

This reply by Jesus contains another layer of revelation within the big picture. He gently tells her not to hang on to him as he is still to return to his Father. Instead, he has a very important commission for her. He asks her to give a message to his brothers. In the Upper room four days earlier, he tells his disciples he will no longer refer to them as servants but as friends. He is transitioning them into their new identity. Now he is calling them 'brothers.' The transition has taken place the moment Jesus rose from the dead. He has died and his death has reconciled fallen man to God. They are no longer orphans and alienated from God, they have been brought home and welcomed back into God's household, the Father's family. They are now brothers of Jesus not just friends. They are his family, his brothers.

This is the message Jesus asks Mary to give them. Jesus is going back to not just his Father and his God but their Father and their God. The full transaction is completed. The apostle Paul sees this truth himself and puts it this way,

> *"Once you were alienated from God and were enemies in your minds because of your evil behaviour. But now he has reconciled you by Christ's physical body through death to present you holy in his sight, without blemish and free from accusation"* (Colossians 1:21 – 22).

Father's original plan for mankind is that we are holy and without blemish. This is now accomplished through the death and resurrection of Jesus. The disciples are brothers of Jesus because they have the same Father. They have become sons in the same way Jesus is a son.

Mankind lost this position of sonship in the Garden of Eden. In that ancient garden a woman is trapped and deceived by a fallen angelic being as she stands beneath the tree of the knowledge of good and evil. At his suggestion she reaches out and eats of its noxious fruit. Here in the resurrection garden another woman encounters angelic beings and she turns and meets the risen Christ who is the tree of life. She reaches out and eats of his fruit which is eternal life. Then she is commissioned to be the messenger to Jesus's brothers. As some early church writers have described her, she is the apostle to the apostles.

John says she goes and reports what she has heard to the disciples. In the other gospel narratives, there is some confusion about the other women who went to the tomb after sunrise after these events have happened. Mary Magdalene is included in the list of names. This may have been a simple mistake. As after the event, it is known Mary has been to the tomb and has been the first one to see the risen Jesus.

Matthew says Mary Magdalene and the other Mary go back to the tomb. Mark adds Salome, Mary's sister, accompanies them and brings spices so they can anoint Jesus's body after sunrise. Luke adds more names. He says it is Mary Magdalene, Joanna, Mary the mother of James, and others. It seems it is quite a group of women. While they are on their way to the tomb, they ask each other who will roll the stone away from the entrance of the tomb. When they arrive at the tomb, they see the stone, which is very large, has been rolled away.

Luke tells us what happens next.

> *"They found the stone rolled away from the tomb, but when they entered, they did not find the body of the Lord Jesus. While they were wondering about this, suddenly two men in clothes that gleamed like lightning stood beside them. In their fright the women bowed down with their faces to the ground, but the men said to them, "Why do you look for the living among the dead? He is not here; he has risen! Remember how he told you, while he was still with you in Galilee: 'The Son of Man must be delivered over to the hands of sinners, be crucified and on the third day be raised again.'" Then they remembered his words" (Luke 24:2 – 8).*

Matthew has the next part of the story,

> *"So the women hurried away from the tomb, afraid yet filled with joy, and ran to tell his disciples. Suddenly Jesus met them. "Greetings," he said. They came to him, clasped his feet and worshiped him. Then Jesus said to them, "Do not be afraid.*

Go and tell my brothers to go to Galilee; there they will see me"
(Matthew 28: 8 – 10).

Luke adds the women leave the garden and find the disciples and tell all these things to the Eleven and to all the others. Mary Magdalene gives the disciples the news she has seen the Lord, and she tells them what he said to her. Amazingly, the women's words are not believed because their words seem like nonsense. Luke says Peter goes back to the tomb, sees the strips of linen lying by themselves, and he goes away, wondering to himself what has happened. This may refer to the visit John also mentions or perhaps it is a second visit.

The day is filled with confusion, uncertainty, fear and speculation. In the evening, two of the followers of Jesus, who are returning to Emmaus outside the city, return with astonishing news. They had met Jesus on the road. The same evening, when the disciples are together with the doors locked, for fear of the Jewish leaders, Luke explains what happens,

> *"...while they were still talking about this, Jesus himself stood among them and said to them, "Peace be with you." They were startled and frightened, thinking they saw a ghost. He said to them, "Why are you troubled, and why do doubts rise in your minds? Look at my hands and my feet. It is I myself! Touch me and see; a ghost does not have flesh and bones, as you see I have." After he said this, he showed them his hands and side. And while they still did not believe it because of joy and amazement, he asked them, "Do you have anything here to eat?" They gave him a piece of broiled fish, and he took it and ate it in their presence (Luke 24: 36 – 39).*

John's gospel gives more detail of the evening's events.

CHAPTER 11

"Again Jesus said, "Peace be with you! As the Father has sent me, I am sending you." And with that he breathed on them and said, "Receive the Holy Spirit. If you forgive anyone's sins, their sins are forgiven; if you do not forgive them, they are not forgiven."

Now Thomas (also known as Didymus), one of the Twelve, was not with the disciples when Jesus came. So the other disciples told him, "We have seen the Lord!" But he said to them, "Unless I see the nail marks in his hands and put my finger where the nails were, and put my hand into his side, I will not believe."

A week later his disciples were in the house again, and Thomas was with them. Though the doors were locked, Jesus came and stood among them and said, "Peace be with you!" Then he said to Thomas, "Put your finger here; see my hands. Reach out your hand and put it into my side. Stop doubting and believe."

Thomas said to him, "My Lord and my God!" Then Jesus told him, "Because you have seen me, you have believed; blessed are those who have not seen and yet have believed" (John 20: 21 – 29).

HOW MANY TIMES DID JESUS APPEAR AFTER THE RESURRECTION?

These gospel accounts, whilst they may appear confused, capture the drama of the first few days following the resurrection of Jesus. The number of appearances of the risen Jesus and the specific details vary because witnesses reported different perspectives. We are not told of all of the appearances. There are others. Paul, writing to the Corinthians, tells of a number of appearances. He writes this letter some years before the Gospels are written and they provide the earliest written record of the resurrection.

> *"For what I received I passed on to you as of first importance: that Christ died for our sins according to the Scriptures, that he was buried, that he was raised on the third day according to the Scriptures, and that he appeared to Cephas, and then to the Twelve. After that, he appeared to more than five hundred of the brothers and sisters at the same time, most of whom are still living, though some have fallen asleep. Then he appeared to James, then to all the apostles, and last of all he appeared to me also, as to one abnormally born"* (1 Corinthians 15: 3 – 8).

Paul follows this with his explanation of the significance of the resurrection. He is living in a flow of revelation, which we will look at in the next few chapters.

> *"If Christ has not been raised, your faith is futile; you are still in your sins. Then those also who have fallen asleep in Christ are lost. If only for this life we have hope in Christ, we are of all people most to be pitied.*
>
> *"But Christ has indeed been raised from the dead, the first fruits of those who have fallen asleep. For since death came through a man, the resurrection of the dead comes also through a man. For as in Adam all die, so in Christ all will be made alive. But each in turn: Christ, the first fruits; then, when he comes, those who belong to him. Then the end will come, when he hands over the kingdom to God the Father after he has destroyed all dominion, authority and power. For he must reign until he has put all his enemies under his feet. The last enemy to be destroyed is death. For he "has put everything under his*

> *feet." Now when it says that "everything" has been put under him, it is clear that this does not include God himself, who put everything under Christ. When he has done this, then the Son himself will be made subject to him who put everything under him, so that God may be all in all" (1 Corinthians 15:14 – 28).*

Jesus continues to appear to the disciples over the next forty days. In the beginning of the Acts of the Apostles, Luke tells us about these encounters.

> *"After his suffering, he presented himself to them and gave many convincing proofs that he was alive. He appeared to them over a period of forty days and spoke about the kingdom of God. On one occasion, while he was eating with them, he gave them this command: "Do not leave Jerusalem, but wait for the gift my Father promised, which you have heard me speak about. For John baptized with water, but in a few days, you will be baptized with the Holy Spirit."*

> *Then they gathered around him and asked him, "Lord, are you at this time going to restore the kingdom to Israel?" He said to them: "It is not for you to know the times or dates the Father has set by his own authority. But you will receive power when the Holy Spirit comes on you; and you will be my witnesses in Jerusalem, and in all Judea and Samaria, and to the ends of the earth" (Acts 1: 3 – 8).*

Forty days after his resurrection Jesus returns to his Father. Only Luke gives any details of this event in his Gospel and then also in the Acts of the Apostles. He says this event takes place outside Jerusalem near Bethany. Jesus has told his followers he would return to his Father and following this they should wait for the Holy Spirit to come upon them to empower them for the proclamation of the good news. Putting

Luke's two accounts together Jesus leads them out to the vicinity of Bethany. He lifts up his hands and blesses them. While he is doing this, he is taken up before their eyes, and a cloud hides him from their sight as he is taken into heaven. As they are looking intently into the sky, two men dressed in white stand beside them. "Men of Galilee," they say, "why do you stand here looking into the sky? This same Jesus, who has been taken from you into heaven, will come back in the same way you have seen him go into heaven" (Luke 24:50 – 51; Acts 1:9 – 11).

Jesus's disciples then return to the city and await the coming of the Holy Spirit. Significantly, Luke records the reaction of the disciples after the ascension.

> *"Then they worshiped him and returned to Jerusalem with great joy. And they stayed continually at the temple, praising God" (Luke 24:52 – 53).*

These people, who after the resurrection were confused and in need of convincing, have been transformed. They respond with worship and joy.

BUT WHAT IS SO IMPORTANT ABOUT THE ASCENSION?

For many, the ascension is just a day in the Church calendar to commemorate Jesus's return to heaven. It is a gap filler between Easter and Pentecost. It is the part of the story that almost feels like a mere footnote; the part some of the gospel writers don't mention at all; and the part doesn't even have a holiday attached to it. Many wonder why it is important.

One thing Jesus does can be easily overlooked. His final act on earth is not another teaching, it is very moving action. It is a blessing. When Jesus ascends, the disciples understand it. They worship him. Jesus isn't the teacher anymore; he is not the prophet. They know he is God. They are worshiping the way you worship God alone. Jesus stays for forty days. He gives his final teachings in those days, and those teachings transform the fearful and confused disciples into men who are prepared to go into the world.

Augustine, one of the theological fathers of the Church in the early fifth century, considers the ascension as important as Good Friday, Easter and Pentecost. The Apostle Paul sees the ascension as the moment when Jesus does not just ascend but also when he is inaugurated, when he takes office, when he takes his seat at the right hand of God.

As I write this, I have just seen a US president inaugurated and seen how authority is invested as a result of the inauguration. This is very much in Paul's thinking about Jesus. He writes in Ephesians 1:20 – 21, God the Father has seated Jesus at his right hand in the heavenly realms, far above all rule and authority, power and dominion, and every title that can be given, not only in the present age but also in the one to come.

In Philippians 2:9 – 11, Paul says God exalts Jesus to the highest place and gives him the name above every name, to which every knee would bow, in heaven and on earth and under the earth, and every tongue acknowledge that Jesus Christ is Lord, to the glory of God the Father.

The whole letter to the Hebrews is based on the idea of the ascension or exaltation of Jesus. In his opening statement the writer says,

RESURRECTION AND ASCENSION

"After he had provided purification for sins, he sat down at the right hand of the Majesty in heaven" (Hebrews 1:3).

Sitting down is important. It is the point here; Jesus has finished his work of dealing with sin and now reigns in heaven interceding for us. This is another task Jesus is doing for us.

Hebrews memorably portrays Jesus as our great high priest who is perfectly qualified not only to deal once and for all with our sin, but to intercede for us with God. The writer says,

> *"Therefore he is able to save completely those who come to God through him, because he always lives to intercede for them" (Hebrews 7:25).*

Paul sees something of this and writes in his letter to the Romans,

> *"Christ Jesus, who died, more than that, who was raised to life, is at the right hand of God and is also interceding for us" (Romans 8:34).*

Just as Jesus prays for his disciples during his earthly ministry, he prays and intercedes for us now.

There is also one last important part of the ascension. The writer to the Hebrews receives revelation from God about something else happening in that moment. In Hebrews 2, the writer is considering the place of God's sons and daughters who have been redeemed by the death of Jesus and brought to life by his resurrection. He is looking to the future world and quotes Psalm 8 using it to describe the authority all of redeemed humanity has.

> *"What is mankind that you are mindful of them, a son of man that you care for him? You made them a little lower than the*

angels; you crowned them with glory and honour and put everything under their feet" (Psalm 8:4-6).

He continues by saying God has put everything under the authority of the redeemed sons of God. He has left nothing that is not subject to them. Even though at this time we do not see everything subject to us, he says, we do see Jesus. He is made lower than the angels for a little while but has now been crowned with glory and honour because he suffered death, so that by the grace of God he might taste death for everyone. This takes us right to the moment of his ascension.

The revelation the writer has been given is simply this: as Jesus ascended, he brought with him many sons and daughters to glory. Jesus blesses the disciples by raising his arms over them. It is as if he stretched out his arms to all of redeemed humanity who will be placed back in their true identity as sons and daughters of God and gathers them in his arms and takes us all home to glory. He is truly,

"…bringing many sons and daughters to glory" (Hebrews 2:10).

The writer sees the full implication of this glorious transaction. We are brought home and once again included in God's family. We are the brothers and sisters of Jesus.

> *"It was fitting that God, for whom and through whom everything exists, should make the pioneer of their salvation perfect through what he suffered. Both the one who makes people holy and those who are made holy are of the same family. So Jesus is not ashamed to call them brothers and sisters. He says, "I will declare your name to my brothers and sisters; in the assembly I will sing your praises." And again, "I will put my trust in him." And again he says, "Here am I, and the children God has given me" (Hebrews 2:10 – 13).*

The ascension of Jesus is the glorious and magnificent last act of the great drama that began with the visit of the angel Gabriel to Mary in Nazareth announcing the coming of the Son of God into our world. In the concluding act of this great drama, he brings us home. The Big Picture is almost complete.

CHAPTER 12

PENTECOST AND BEYOND

Before Jesus returns to his Father, he tells his followers to go back to Jerusalem and await the coming of the Holy Spirit. In the Upper Room, he tells them he will not leave them as orphans but will come to them. He promises the Holy Spirit will come and be alongside them as a comforter and encourager who will continue to explain truth and teach them.

> *"The Holy Spirit, whom the Father will send in my name, will teach you all things and will remind you of everything I have said to you" (John 14:26).*

WHAT IS THE ROLE OF THE HOLY SPIRIT?

A huge amount of the focus of modern Christianity has been on the work and ministry of the Holy Spirit in the Church and the lives of believers and the world. This has been a helpful reminder of his role which in many ways has been overlooked in previous centuries.

The emphasis has often been on his power and gifts. This has been a very necessary refocusing. However, the pendulum swung far in this direction and the Spirit and his gifts have dominated many churches almost to the neglect of Jesus and most certainly the Father. Many chase after power encounters, spiritual gifts, anointing and supernatural ministries at the expense of a more balanced trinitarian and biblical approach. Some of the reasons for this can be found in the early chapters of the Acts of the Apostles. Before looking at Acts we need to be reminded what Jesus says about the Spirit and how he will reveal more truth to them.

> *"I have much more to say to you, more than you can now bear. But when he, the Spirit of truth, comes, he will guide you into all the truth. He will not speak on his own; he will speak only what he hears, and he will tell you what is yet to come. He will glorify me because it is from me that he will receive what he will make known to you. All that belongs to the Father is mine. That is why I said the Spirit will receive from me what he will make known to you" (John 16:12 – 15).*

The gospel writer Luke is also the author of the Acts of the Apostles. He is a Gentile and writes for non-Jewish readers who are not familiar with the beginnings of the Church. The pagan Greco Roman world is deeply fascinated and afraid of the supernatural realm. One of Luke's particular interests and a major emphasis is the work of the Holy Spirit, and he describes many of the supernatural interventions of the Spirit in individuals and the Church. It is an exciting and dramatic story.

The story begins with the outpouring of the Holy Spirit on the day of Pentecost ten days after Jesus has ascended. It is dramatic and full of the supernatural power of the Spirit. Jesus has told the apostles and the wider group of followers they will receive power when the Holy Spirit came. On the day of Pentecost, they certainly do.

CHAPTER 12

> *"When the day of Pentecost came, they were all together in one place. Suddenly a sound like the blowing of a violent wind came from heaven and filled the whole house where they were sitting. They saw what seemed to be tongues of fire that separated and came to rest on each of them. All of them were filled with the Holy Spirit and began to speak in other tongues as the Spirit enabled them" (Acts 2:1 – 4).*

This account has captivated the imaginations of believers ever since. It has given birth to great movements seeking to emulate and continually repeat this experience. The terms Pentecostal and Charismatic stem from this iconic event. Throughout history many powerful moments when God has moved are interpreted as a second Pentecost. I am not sure how many of these there have been, but we are certainly far beyond the second one!

It is no surprise these movements have been longed for and sought because they are rooted in an experience of God. People are hungry for encounter and renewal, especially when the prevailing mood of church becomes dry, cerebral and faithless. But the Holy Spirit has an even more important role to play in the unfolding of the Big Picture. He is going to bring more revelation from the Father through a very unusual and most unlikely person, Paul. More about him later.

When Paul is writing to the Corinthians and the Romans he also speaks about the work and gifts of the Holy Spirit. In Romans 5, he makes a very clear statement of what the Holy Spirit is doing in us continually, beginning with the Day of Pentecost. He says,

> *"God's love has been poured out into our hearts through the Holy Spirit, who has been given to us" (Romans 5:5).*

The greatest gift of the Spirit is the dynamic, life changing love of the Father being poured into our wounded and broken hearts.

WHAT DID THE EARLY CHURCH DO NEXT?

Acts describes the beginnings of the church in Jerusalem which is essentially a Jewish church. In Acts chapters 1 through 7, the activity takes place in and around Jerusalem. Then the church begins to touch the Gentile world in Acts chapters 8 through 12, as the apostles encounter Gentiles such as Cornelius the Roman centurion and the Ethiopian eunuch. The church also begins to face persecution and later, James the son of Zebedee, Jesus's cousin, is the first of the apostles to be martyred.

The Followers of the Way is the name they use to describe themselves. They are mostly Jewish converts and followers of Jesus. In the upper room, on the last night he is with his disciples, Jesus describes himself, amongst other things, as 'the Way.' These Jewish followers are people from the immediate vicinity of Jerusalem and surrounding areas, including Galilee. Luke reports many Jews from faraway cities and provinces of the Roman empire who have been in Jerusalem for the Feast of Pentecost join the band of followers of Jesus. The list Luke provides shows the extraordinary spread of the Jewish Diaspora at that time.

Luke writes about thousands responding to the preaching of the leaders of the church. Three thousand alone are baptised on the Day of Pentecost following Simon Peter's sermon in Acts 2:41. After the remarkable healing of a lame man at the Temple gate by Peter and John and their subsequent arrest, many more respond and become followers.

CHAPTER 12

We get some idea of the community life of these early Followers of the Way in this passage from Acts 4. They are united and share everything with each other.

> *"With great power the apostles continued to testify to the resurrection of the Lord Jesus. And God's grace was so powerfully at work in them all that there were no needy persons among them" (Acts 4:33).*

Luke continues,

> *"The apostles performed many signs and wonders among the people. And all the believers used to meet together in Solomon's Colonnade. No one else dared join them, even though they were highly regarded by the people. Nevertheless, more and more men and women believed in the Lord and were added to their number. As a result, people brought the sick into the streets and laid them on beds and mats so that at least Peter's shadow might fall on some of them as he passed by. Crowds gathered also from the towns around Jerusalem, bringing their sick and those tormented by impure spirits, and all of them were healed" (Acts 5:12 – 16).*

The numbers of new converts continue to grow. Soon there are over five thousand of them. There are miracles and healings, and because it is lots of people growing together there are issues among them. Repenting and being baptised in the Spirit is one thing, learning to live in the day to day as followers of Jesus is another thing altogether. Many in modern times have tried to live like the early church in Acts and long for this. Count me out! It is not easy or ideal or even a blueprint for future church life. They are still thinking and behaving from the Wrong Tree. It is extremely challenging and, in the end, their version of community living ends up disastrously. It will take persecution of the Jerusalem church to scatter them and send them off to their home cities and provinces where they are meant to be living out their new life in Jesus. Twenty-five years later, the churches in Asia, Macedonia and Greece are sending money to support the Jerusalem church because of the ongoing issue of poverty among them.

For the Followers of the Way, the primary issue identifying them is they believe Jesus is the promised Messiah, the anointed Son of God who has been unjustly arrested, tried and crucified. However, after he is declared dead and buried, he is miraculously raised from the dead on the day following the Jewish sabbath. He then appears alive to a large number of people over many days who confirms his resurrection before he is taken up in a cloud, returning to his Father in heaven.

Some of their earliest statements describe what they believe. On the day of Pentecost soon after the Holy Spirit has fallen on the one hundred and twenty who are gathered together, Peter stands to explain what has happened and announces,

> *"Jesus of Nazareth was a man accredited by God to you by miracles, wonders and signs, which God did among you through him, as you yourselves know. This man was handed over to you by God's deliberate plan and foreknowledge; and you, with the help of wicked men, put him to death by nailing him to the cross. But God raised him from the dead, freeing him from the agony of death, because it was impossible for death to keep its hold on him" (Acts 2:20 – 24).*

A few days later, following the healing of a lame man, this explanation is given,

"It is by the name of Jesus Christ of Nazareth, whom you crucified but whom God raised from the dead, that this man stands before you healed" (Acts 4:10).

The early chapters of Acts show the Followers of the Way believe and teach about Jesus and who he is. Their teaching is accompanied by powerful demonstrations of Holy Spirit power. Astonishingly, there is no reference to God as Father.

WHY IS THERE NO MENTION OF GOD THE FATHER IN ACTS?

When Jesus is still with his followers before he ascends back to his Father, he tells them to remain in Jerusalem.

"Do not leave Jerusalem, but wait for the gift my Father promised, which you have heard me speak about. For John baptized with water, but in a few days, you will be baptized with the Holy Spirit

Then they gathered around him and asked him, "Lord, are you at this time going to restore the kingdom to Israel?"

He said to them: "It is not for you to know the times or dates the Father has set by his own authority. But you will receive power when the Holy Spirit comes on you; and you will be my witnesses in Jerusalem, and in all Judea and Samaria, and to the ends of the earth" (Acts 1:4 – 8).

He speaks in the same ways as he does in the gospels. He continually references everything back to his Father. The Holy Spirit will be the gift of the Father to them. The answer Jesus gives in response to the disciple's odd question about the restoration of the physical kingdom of Israel takes it back to the Father. Future events such as this were not the issue. He has told them before, he will come back. The date and timing of this second coming is completely in the gift of the Father and they do not need to worry about it.

His response is to go back and wait. The Holy Spirit will empower them to be witnesses over all the earth.

On the day of Pentecost, when Peter addresses the crowds who gather to find out what all the noise and commotion is about, he makes the one and only direct reference in Acts to God the Father. All other references are more general of God rather than describing him as Father.

> *"God has raised this Jesus to life, and we are all witnesses of it. Exalted to the right hand of God, he has received from the Father the promised Holy Spirit and has poured out what you now see and hear" (Acts 2:32 – 33).*

This a wonderfully brief statement of what transpires. It is pure revelation.

Beyond these references, Luke does not mention the Father at all throughout the rest of Acts. This is surprising given the huge emphasis Jesus places on his relationship with his Father in his teaching and ministry. Some use this as an argument to say it is unnecessary to emphasise the Father and focus on Jesus only. To see what is happening we need to look at the disciples. Seven or so weeks earlier, they are sitting in the Upper Room listening to Jesus explain what he has been teaching them over the previous three years.

When they begin following him, they have no idea who he is except an amazing teacher who also does some extraordinary things. The first miracle they witness is turning water into wine. What a showstopper that would have been. Over the three years, slowly they begin to "see" things more clearly, but even in the Upper Room their questions are very revealing. Then it all fell apart; Jesus is arrested, tried and crucified. They go into hiding in Jerusalem for fear they might also be arrested as his followers.

Then come the resurrection. The gospels are brutally honest about showing them as confused and fearful and, in the case of Thomas, downright sceptical and unbelieving. It must have been a massive challenge to them, and we can see the rollercoaster it must have been to them. All through this, they are beginning to see who Jesus really is. They have heard him say God is his Father, and then he tells them God is their Father too. They are now his brothers. It is a huge amount to take in.

Our fallen Adamic way of thinking makes us try to process and rationalise spiritual realities and truth. We try to work things out in our heads, but these things are received by revelation in our hearts given by the Spirit. Paul will later explain this to the Corinthians.

> *"No one knows the thoughts of God except the Spirit of God. What we have received is not the spirit of the world, but the Spirit who is from God, so that we may understand what God has freely given us. This is what we speak, not in words taught us by human wisdom but in words taught by the Spirit, explaining spiritual realities with Spirit-taught words. The person without the Spirit does not accept the things that come from the Spirit of God but considers them foolishness and cannot understand them because they are discerned only through the Spirit"* (1 Corinthians 2:11 – 14).

For the disciples, the day of Pentecost and the outpouring of the

Holy Spirit on them is a significant part of their journey. They suddenly find themselves thrust into the open in Jerusalem trying to explain what is happening.

As a result, they speak of what they have experienced and try to find language to explain it. Peter starts off,

> *"Fellow Jews and all of you who live in Jerusalem, let me explain this to you; listen carefully to what I say" (Acts 2:14).*

He is speaking to a Jewish crowd from all over the Roman world. They are passionate Jewish people, monotheists in a pagan world full of gods and superstition. They know their Hebrew scriptures, and Peter sensibly references what is happening to prophetic words in the Old Testament. He appeals to their hearts through their own scriptures. The key issue is Jesus. He has been crucified because the Jewish religious authorities accused him of blasphemy. They heard him describe God as his Father. He called himself "I am." All these things are heresy as far as the Jews are concerned. To talk about God as Father at this point would prevent people from opening their hearts as their minds would be closed. Peter goes to the root issue. Who is Jesus?

> *"Fellow Israelites, listen to this: Jesus of Nazareth was a man accredited by God to you by miracles, wonders and signs, which God did among you through him, as you yourselves know. This man was handed over to you by God's deliberate plan and foreknowledge; and you, with the help of wicked men, put him to death by nailing him to the cross. But God raised him from the dead, freeing him from the agony of death, because it was impossible for death to keep its hold on him" (Acts 2:22 – 24).*

He quotes the prophets and the Psalms and continually points them to Jesus and the importance of Jesus being both the Messiah and the son of God. He concludes,

> *"Therefore, let all Israel be assured of this: God has made this Jesus, whom you crucified, both Lord and Messiah" (Acts 2:36).*

The listeners are convicted in their hearts by Peter's words and the response is amazing. He carries on speaking and reasoning and soon hundreds respond to his anointed preaching. They receive Jesus by faith having accepted his forgiveness and then are baptised. Luke makes it sound exciting and easy. The administrator in me wants to work out how long baptising three thousand people would take. Each apostle would have had to baptise about 250 each. That's quite a challenge!

All these new believers are on a journey as the apostles have been. First and foremost, they have to see who Jesus is. When they know Jesus, they will come to know his Father also. The apostles are speaking from what they have experienced; their own journey of revelation will continue. They do not fully see it all at this point. Jesus has said there is more, and the Holy Spirit will instruct them himself. They are all in a process of revelation.

Meanwhile the pressing concern is what to do with all the new believers? Luke offers a vivid picture in the first twelve chapters of the Acts of how the story unfolds. The way it reads, we think it all happens in a very short span of time. The reality is these events take place over a number of years.

Amid the excitement of growth Luke reports some members of the priestly class in Jerusalem become Followers of the Way. In Acts 15:5, he says some of the believers also belong to the party of the Pharisees. None are named, but there are references in the Gospels specifically referring to a number of Pharisees by name who are sympathetic to the teaching of Jesus and the early church.

Nicodemus is a Pharisee and Joseph of Arimathea is a member of the Sanhedrin and is most likely a Pharisee. Luke also reports Jesus has dinner with a Galilean Pharisee who is mentioned by name as Simon. The detail in Luke's story include the inner thoughts of this Pharisee which suggests he personally relates the story to Luke and as a result allows his name to be mentioned. Whether any of these three Pharisees are also Followers of the Way is impossible to conclude from the biblical record. However, the traditions of the church from very early days accorded them the status of sainthood and named saint days after them.

Persecution very quickly becomes the order of the day for the Followers of the Way. A significant persecution breaks out following the stoning death of Stephen, one of the Hellenistic Greek-speaking Jews who is one of the leaders of the community. Trumped up charges are levelled against him based on his alleged blasphemous words against Moses and against God. Acts 7 records in detail his defence before the Sanhedrin. Like Peter, Stephen draws heavily from the Old Testament scriptures to prove his points. Finally, he says something totally offensive to his judges.

> *"You stiff-necked people! Your hearts and ears are still uncircumcised. You are just like your ancestors: You always resist the Holy Spirit! Was there ever a prophet your ancestors did not persecute? They even killed those who predicted the coming of the Righteous One. And now you have betrayed and murdered him, you who have received the law that was given through angels but have not obeyed it" (Acts 7:51 – 53).*

These words seal Stephen's fate. He is dragged out of the city and stoned to death for blasphemy. Almost as a footnote, but more importantly, Luke introduces the next main character in the story, Saul of Tarsus later to be known as the Apostle Paul.

CHAPTER 12

> *"Meanwhile, the witnesses laid their coats at the feet of a young man named Saul. While they were stoning him, Stephen prayed, "Lord Jesus, receive my spirit." Then he fell on his knees and cried out, "Lord, do not hold this sin against them." When he had said this, he fell asleep. And Saul approved of their killing him" (Acts 7:58 – 8:1).*

Luke recounts how a persecution breaks out against the church in Jerusalem, and all except the apostles are scattered throughout Judea and Samaria. The persecution is led by Saul. In an attempt to destroy the church he goes from house to house, dragging off both men and women and putting them in prison.

This very unlikely candidate will be the one who receives major revelation completing the Big Picture.

CHAPTER 13

PAUL THE APOSTLE

Paul is known as Saul in his early years but for ease of reading, I'm going to refer to him throughout as Paul. He makes his debut in Acts as mentioned at the stoning of Stephen. From his own account of his early life, he grew up in Tarsus in Syria and moves to Jerusalem to study under Gamaliel, a renown Rabbi and Pharisee. Paul's own words record his early life in his defence before King Agrippa when he is on trial many years later.

> *"The Jewish people all know the way I have lived ever since I was a child, from the beginning of my life in my own country, and also in Jerusalem. They have known me for a long time and can testify, if they are willing, that I conformed to the strictest sect of our religion, living as a Pharisee" (Acts 26:4 – 5).*

WHO WERE THE PHARISEES?

The Pharisees are a group within Judaism who are both a religious sect and a political movement. They are mentioned many times in the

New Testament and also in the writings of the first century Jewish historian Josephus. They emerge in the intertestamental period in the centuries before the Christian Era. The root meaning of the word "Pharisee" is probably related to the Hebrew root meaning "separate" or "detach."

Pharisees are like scribes who interpret the Jewish writings and seek to leave nothing to doubt. Their interpretation of the law of Moses governs every part of life, and part of the out working of this is the way they separate themselves from almost every part of society for fear of ritual contamination. This is not a physical separation, more a religious and ideological separation. They especially separate from the priestly classes represented by the Saducees who interpret the Law differently than them.

They avoid the common people of the land whom they consider law breakers and are very judgmental towards them. They particularly avoid Gentiles or Jews who embrace the Hellenistic culture. The Pharisees are determined to separate themselves from any type of impurity proscribed by the Levitical law or, more specifically, their strict interpretation of it. This brings them into conflict with Jesus and then the Followers of the Way in Israel.

The Pharisees' behaviour is criticised in the New Testament. They are cold and legalistic. At the same time, the Pharisees are mostly holy men who try to keep the law. They pursue purity with a passion and want nothing more than to live lives pleasing God. They are sincere, albeit sincerely misguided.

There were never any more than six thousand Pharisees in the country. They are known as the "chaburah," or "the brotherhood." They enter into this brotherhood by taking a pledge in front of three witnesses to spend all their lives observing every detail of the scribal law.

The scribes created the Mishnah, the writings that codify scribal law. Then there is the Talmud, which is the commentary on the Mishnah. This thinking deeply influences every area of their lives. It is classic Wrong Tree thinking. Every part of life is affected, and they judge severely any who do not subscribe to their views.

An example is seen in the simple Sabbath law. The Law of Moses, the Torah clearly tell the Jews, "Do not work, do not bear burdens, but rest and keep it a holy day."

Their response is to define work. Carrying burdens has to be defined. For example, they can carry milk from a cow enough for one swallow and carry a spoon weighing no more than one fig. They argue over whether or not a woman can wear a brooch, a mother can pick up her child, or a man can wear his wooden leg on the Sabbath. These are burdens.

Not surprisingly, they see Jesus as a law breaker and his followers are considered extremely dangerous. This motivates Paul, as a Pharisee, to persecute the church. However, as pointed out earlier, Luke records a number of them become believers and Followers of the Way. Not least Paul or Saul of Tarsus as he was known.

I have written extensively about Paul's life prior to his conversion in my book *The Story of Paul, the Early Years*, so a summary is all I will attempt here.

The best summary is found in Paul's own words. Luke recounts his conversion in Acts chapter 9 and then Paul tells his own story when on trial before the Jewish Council, the Sanhedrin, in Jerusalem in Acts 22.

> *"Then Paul said: "I am a Jew, born in Tarsus of Cilicia, but brought up in this city. I studied under Gamaliel and was thoroughly trained in the law of our ancestors. I was just*

as zealous for God as any of you are today. I persecuted the followers of this Way to their death, arresting both men and women and throwing them into prison, as the high priest and all the Council can themselves testify. I even obtained letters from them to their associates in Damascus and went there to bring these people as prisoners to Jerusalem to be punished.

"About noon as I came near Damascus, suddenly a bright light from heaven flashed around me. I fell to the ground and heard a voice say to me, 'Saul! Saul! Why do you persecute me?'

"'Who are you, Lord?' I asked.

"'I am Jesus of Nazareth, whom you are persecuting,' he replied. My companions saw the light, but they did not understand the voice of him who was speaking to me.

"'What shall I do, Lord?' I asked.

"'Get up,' the Lord said, 'and go into Damascus. There you will be told all that you have been assigned to do.' My companions led me by the hand into Damascus, because the brilliance of the light had blinded me.

"A man named Ananias came to see me. He was a devout observer of the law and highly respected by all the Jews living there. He stood beside me and said, 'Brother Saul, receive your sight!' And at that very moment I was able to see him.

"Then he said: 'The God of our ancestors has chosen you to know his will and to see the Righteous One and to hear words from his mouth. You will be his witness to all people of what you have seen and heard. And now what are you waiting for?

Get up, be baptized and wash your sins away, calling on his name'" (Acts 22:2 – 18).

When he is on trial before King Agrippa in Acts 26, Paul adds some significant details about the words Jesus says to him on the road to Damascus. He adds Jesus saying,

"Now get up and stand on your feet. I have appeared to you to appoint you as a servant and as a witness of what you have seen and will see of me. I will rescue you from your own people and from the Gentiles. I am sending you to them to open their eyes and turn them from darkness to light, and from the power of Satan to God, so that they may receive forgiveness of sins and a place among those who are sanctified by faith in me'" (Acts 26: 16 – 18).

The words Jesus speaks to Paul will define his ministry. Jesus appoints Paul to be a servant and a witness of what he has seen and will see of Jesus. This points to the past and to future things. The rest of Paul's life will be defined by this moment. Whenever he looks back on his life, this moment and the call he experienced on the Damascus road was the defining moment of transformation, recounting how Jesus appears to him personally in order to convince him he is alive and appoint him for a special task in a specific role. When Jesus says he will bear witness to things he has seen, it suggests Paul may have seen Jesus before this encounter on the road to Damascus.

HAD PAUL SEEN JESUS BEFORE HIS CONVERSION?

In Paul's letters and his sermons recorded by Luke in Acts, there are very few suggestions he has heard Jesus speak. However, there is evidence he has knowledge of a number of the events surrounding Jesus's life and more particularly the ministry of John the baptiser.

Paul mentions the ministry of John the Baptist when addressing Jewish hearers in his early missionary travels. In Pisidian, Antioch, whilst preaching in the synagogue, Paul says,

> *"Before the coming of Jesus, John preached repentance and baptism to all the people of Israel. As John was completing his work, he said: 'Who do you suppose I am? I am not the one you are looking for. But there is one coming after me whose sandals I am not worthy to untie'" (Acts 13: 24 – 25).*

This reference is similar to the sayings of John recorded in the gospels. Significantly, Matthew writes people went out to hear John speak from Jerusalem and all Judea. This includes many of the Pharisees and Sadducees. It is not inconceivable that the young Pharisee, Saul of Tarsus, may have been one of those who went out to hear John preach in the Jordan Valley and hears these words for himself.

The question whether Paul had ever heard or seen Jesus is more difficult. There are no quotations or very few allusions to any of the teachings or words of Jesus in Paul's preaching or letters. The one time he does quote a saying of Jesus it is one not found in any of the gospels. When saying goodbye to the leaders of the church in Ephesus, he says,

> *"In everything I showed you that by working hard in this manner you must help the weak and remember the words of the Lord Jesus, that he himself said, 'It is more blessed to give than to receive'" (Acts 20:35).*

The only other time Paul quotes the words of Jesus relates to the institution of the Lord's supper which is an occasion where Paul could not have heard them spoken in their original context. They do, however, indicate the widespread use of these words by Christians from the earliest times when celebrating the Lord's Supper.

One thing Paul is absolutely convinced about is Jesus's death. In Paul's first major recorded sermon in Acts 13, some years before the gospels are written, Luke quotes Paul's account of the final days of Jesus's life,

> *"The people of Jerusalem and their rulers did not recognise Jesus, yet in condemning him they fulfilled the words of the prophets that are read every Sabbath. Though they found no proper ground for a death sentence, they asked Pilate to have him executed. When they had carried out all that was written about him, they took him down from the cross and laid him in a tomb. But God raised him from the dead, and for many days he was seen by those who had travelled with him from Galilee to Jerusalem. They are now his witnesses to our people"* (Acts 13:27 – 31).

Paul's obsessive persecution of the Followers of the Way is because they are just as convinced Jesus is alive as he is that Jesus is dead. Paul's insistence of Jesus not being alive may have been because he personally witnesses the crucifixion. Although there is no hard evidence of this in anything he specifically says or writes, an explanation of what happens on the cross and its significance is very prominent in Paul's preaching and writing.

The 'preaching of the cross' is the distinctive message of the apostle Paul. The gospel he preaches is Christ died for our sins and rose from the dead for our salvation. No other New Testament writer has such clear and detailed understanding of the significance of the death of Jesus on the cross as Paul, coupled with an emphasis on the blood of Christ.

Jesus tells Paul he wants him to testify about what he has seen. Jesus also says he will show him things. Jesus will reveal truth to Paul, things others may not yet see or understand. Later, he writes to the church in Galatia,

> *"I want you to know, brothers and sisters, that the gospel I preached is not of human origin. I did not receive it from any man, nor was I taught it; rather, I received it by revelation from Jesus Christ" (Galatians 1:11 – 12).*

Throughout his life and ministry, Paul is on the receiving end of direct revelation from Jesus about the nature of all God is doing in Christ. To use my words in the title of this book, Paul is shown the Big Picture.

Before we look at the nature of this revelation in more detail, we need to see what else Jesus says to Paul and what unfolds when he goes to Damascus. Jesus, having appointed and commissioned Paul to be his servant and a witness to the things he has seen and will be shown, goes on to reassure Paul he will be with him, and specifically Paul will testify before the Gentiles. Jesus promises to rescue Paul from all those who will oppose him, both among his own people, the Jews, and also the non-Jewish Gentiles.

> *"I will rescue you from your own people and from the Gentiles. I am sending you to them to open their eyes and turn them from darkness to light, and from the power of Satan to God so that they may receive forgiveness of sins and a place among those who are sanctified by faith in me" (Acts 26:17 – 18).*

Jesus tells Paul what his ministry will fundamentally be about. He is sending him to the Gentiles to open their eyes. Once their eyes are opened, the effect will turn them from darkness to light, from living under Satan's power to living under God's power. This will result in forgiveness of sins and a place where they will belong and live the holy and blameless life of faith. The term 'open their eyes' links back to the events of the Fall in Genesis where the eyes of reason and the satanic way of thinking begin. From then on mankind cannot see with the eyes of their hearts. The coming of the eternal Son will be the beginning of the opening of these eyes. Here, Paul is commissioned to take this revelation to the Gentiles as well as the Jews.

Luke's account in Acts 9 records what follows.

> *"Saul spent several days with the disciples in Damascus. At once he began to preach in the synagogues that Jesus is the Son of God. All those who heard him were astonished and asked, "Isn't he the man who raised havoc in Jerusalem among those who call on this name? And hasn't he come here to take them as prisoners to the chief priests?" Yet Saul grew more and more powerful and baffled the Jews living in Damascus by proving that Jesus is the Christ" (Acts 9:19 – 22).*

Once Paul meets Jesus, he needs no further convincing. Jesus is indeed the Messiah the Jews are anticipating. The Greek speaking Jews use the word Christos, the Christ, to describe Jesus, which means the anointed one. Paul is now convinced Jesus is the son of God. This is a huge change in Paul's thinking. For a Pharisee or any other Jew to say Jesus is the 'Son' of God, and by inference to say God has a son, is blasphemous. For God to have a son means God is a Father.

For the grand persecutor to stand in the synagogue in Damascus and declare he and they have been wrong about Jesus is astonishing, if not downright confusing. Every time he speaks there are lots of questions and discussion. Paul is not holding back. He has only just recovered from his three days of blindness and he is preaching. This says a lot about his character, personality, energy and enthusiasm. Every day, he becomes stronger and stauncher in his preaching and explanations. Paul is used to arguing and debating. He is used to being right and pointing out who is wrong. This has been Paul's modus operandi as a Pharisee for years. It is as if without hardly pausing for breath, he transitions from being the persecutor of the Followers of the Way to being, at the very least, the baffler of those who do not believe Jesus is the Way.

During his trial before Agrippa in Acts 26, he reports what he actually said.

> *"I preached that they should repent and turn to God and demonstrate their repentance by their deeds" (Acts 26:20).*

The language is very similar to John the Baptist's words. It indicates Paul's initial preaching reflects John's preaching rather than what he will receive through revelation some years later. In his preaching, there is a recognition of the need to repent for sin and turn to God, but he adds a thought at this point which is unusual and not typical of his later teaching. He says he looks for clear evidence of repentance being genuine and has really taken place. The evidence he looks for is deeds and actions of perhaps contrition and change of behaviour.

Typically, when genuine repentance has happened, the resulting change in behaviour and life is self-evident. To place this in the proclamation of the gospel at this point indicates a more legalistic approach than is intended and suggests this is the converted Pharisee speaking who is used to defining right and wrong and judging others by his own wisdom of who has and who has not demonstrated proper repentance. This feels like the Wrong Tree.

Whatever the intention, the result causes a huge reaction among the Jewish community in Damascus. Luke tells us in Acts a conspiracy to kill Paul is hatched. The local Jews are trying to catch him and set men watching at the city gates night and day in order to kill him. Somehow, the plot comes to Paul's ears. Luke says the local believers hide Paul in order to save him and find a way to help him escape the city by lowering him in a basket through an opening in the city walls at night.

Paul's reputation and the news of what happened to him in Damascus somehow filters back to the authorities in Jerusalem and is likely a contributing factor in Paul's decision to not go up to Jerusalem to see those who are apostles before he is. In his letter to the Galatians, he says he instead went into Arabia.

WHAT DID PAUL DO IN ARABIA?

We cannot know for sure, except Paul says later he is there for three years. When he arrives in Arabia, he is newly converted, and no doubt reflects on his new situation and the nature of forgiveness. He has not received much instruction in his new-found faith. He has not met any of the apostles or leaders. He has only met a few of the Followers of the Way in Damascus and picked up rudimentary elements of his new faith. He has not heard Jesus teach, as far as we know, though he does have an extensive knowledge of the Old Testament.

One of the major revelations Paul receives quite early in his journey is about the true nature of what happened when Jesus died on the cross. His meeting with Jesus on the way to Damascus has convinced him of the truth of his resurrection. It is more than a vision; it is a real encounter. This has a profound effect on Paul. If he has indeed witnessed the crucifixion, it will be vivid in his mind.

As the years unfold, Paul preaches specifically about the cross. It is a distinct message of his, becoming the essence of the gospel he preaches. He says,

> "*Christ died for our sins and rose from the dead for our salvation*" *(1 Corinthians. 15:1 – 4).*

Paul's gospel is faith in the work of Jesus on the cross and nothing else. None of the other writers of the New Testament or the apostles whose preaching we read about in the early chapters of Acts preach this gospel of the cross until they learn about it from Paul.

The word in the New Testament translates into English as 'cross' is '*stauros.*' In the gospels, this word is used seventeen times collectively by the four writers in their accounts of Christ's crucifixion to describe the instrument of execution. In context, the '*stauros*' is the instrument of torture and death the Romans have invented and use to execute criminals. In Paul's writings, he uses the same word ten times. No other writer uses the word outside of the Gospels, except Paul. "The apostolic preaching of the cross" is a phrase Paul receives by revelation from Jesus and is unique to him.

More important than the translation of the word is to recognise the apparent lack of understanding of its significance by writers other than Paul. Other writers appear to have no understanding that Jesus's death on the cross is the means by which God has solved the problem of sin. This significance of the cross is revealed through the apostle Paul alone.

Paul's revelation and understanding of Jesus's crucifixion is in stark contrast to that of Peter. For Peter, the crucifixion is all about accusation and condemnation which requires Jewish repentance before God can establish his earthly kingdom. We see this in his preaching in Acts 2:36 and 4:10. For Paul, Jesus's crucifixion is the message of salvation not an event to be repented of but an event to boast about continually

(1 Cor. 1:23; 2:2; 2 Cor. 13:4; Gal. 2:20, 3:1; 6:14). For Paul, Jesus's crucifixion and resurrection are his victory over sin and death.

The early sermons Peter preaches recorded in Acts focus on the amazing fact of God raising Jesus from the dead. The references to the death of Jesus made by Peter and the others focus on accusation of the complicity by both the Jewish authorities and the Romans rather than what God does in the death of his son. By contrast, they highlight the work of God in raising Jesus to life as proof he is the Son of God. The response they call for is repentance and turning to God and the evidence of their repentance is baptism.

Paul does not take this approach. In 1 Corinthians, Paul says,

> *"For Christ did not send me to baptise, but to preach the gospel, not with wisdom and eloquence, lest the cross of Christ be emptied of its power. For the message of the cross is foolishness to those who are perishing, but to us who are being saved it is the power of God" (1 Corinthians 1:17).*

On Paul's first missionary journey, his first sermon is to Jews in the synagogue in Pisidian, Antioch. Paul begins in a similar way as Peter in his early sermons in Acts. However, the conclusion he draws is different. Jesus's death and resurrection not only prove him to be the promised Messiah, the Son of God but through his death there is also forgiveness of sins.

> *"Therefore, my friends, I want you to know that through Jesus the forgiveness of sins is proclaimed to you. Through him everyone who believes is set free from every sin, a justification you were not able to obtain under the law of Moses" (Acts 13:38-39).*

In the last paragraph, Paul states his revelation of what happens in the death of Jesus on the cross. Forgiveness of sins is given to those who believe. Stating this is not possible under the law of Moses, Paul shows his message is different from the message of John the Baptist.

To Paul, the 'word' of the cross, the doctrine of the cross, is foolishness to unbelievers but for those who are being saved, it is the very power of God at work (1 Cor. 1:18). The doctrine of the cross is Jesus died for our sins and solves the sin problem once and for all. This proves to be a stumbling block to those who preach the necessity of circumcision and keeping the law of Moses for salvation.

Paul boasts it is the work of the cross, not man's self-effort, which brings salvation. He sees both Jews and Gentiles being united and reconciled to each other and to God by the work of Jesus on the cross.

Paul also receives revelation and fully understands the suffering Jesus experiences on the cross. He sees how Jesus embraces his suffering on behalf of mankind. Paul sees how Jesus humbles himself in dying on the cross as he writes in Philippians 2:8. It is so important to Paul nothing be added to or taken away from this revelation of Jesus's work. Those who oppose this teaching, he declares makes themselves enemies of the cross.

Paul sees God the Father reconciling man to himself and making peace with mankind through the shedding of Jesus's blood on the cross. Quite literally, the cross is the crux of all history. The event towards which all history is moving since the Fall of man is the death of Jesus on the cross. The debt against man which has separated mankind from God is cancelled by the cross. In Colossians 2:14, he says it is as if the debt is nailed to the cross. The vivid language Paul uses suggests strongly he has personal knowledge of the events of the crucifixion.

Closely associated with the cross of Christ is the "blood of Christ," and again, it is with Paul we find the greatest emphasis. Jesus explains the significance of his blood to the disciples at the last supper as mentioned in Matthew 26:28, Mark 14:24 and Luke 22:20. Yet they do not seem to understand it, for they do not preach it. We do not discover the significance of the "blood of Christ" until Paul writes about it after his conversion. Only after Paul taught it do the other apostles mention it.

Paul learns the significance of Christ's work on the cross by direct revelation from the risen and glorified Christ. Paul tells the Romans,

> *"The message I proclaim about Jesus Christ, is in keeping with the revelation of the mystery hidden for long ages past, but now revealed and made known through the prophetic writings by the command of the eternal God, so that all the Gentiles might come to the obedience that comes from faith (Romans. 16:25 - 26).*

Only later, through Paul's teaching, does Peter understand and write of the significance of Christ's death on the cross (1 Peter 1:18 – 19). Peter recognises the special wisdom given to Paul in this regard.

> *"Bear in mind that our Lord's patience means salvation, just as our dear brother Paul also wrote you with the wisdom that God gave him. He writes the same way in all his letters, speaking in them of these matters. His letters contain some things that are hard to understand, which ignorant and unstable people distort, as they do the other Scriptures, to their own destruction" (2 Peter 3:15-16).*

In this season of revelation in Arabia, Paul sees God the Father initiates the work of the Son of God, Jesus on the cross. It is the kindness and love of God reaching out to man which brings about this reconciliation. It is initiated by the mercy and compassion of God for his estranged creation. He finds God the Father of our Lord Jesus Christ to be the Father of compassion and the God of all comfort. He describes God in this way in 2 Corinthians 1.

The two terms are rich in meaning. Paul has a revelation of the nature of the heart of God the Father as being one who has compassion. This word speaks of emotion in the heart of God the Father. Paul knows the story in Exodus 34 where the Lord God reveals his glory to Moses.

> *"Then the Lord came down in the cloud and stood there with him and proclaimed his name, the Lord. And he passed in front of Moses, proclaiming, "The Lord, the Lord, the compassionate and gracious God, slow to anger, abounding in love and faithfulness, maintaining love to thousands, and forgiving wickedness, rebellion and sin" (Exodus 34:5 – 7).*

In many ways, Paul has a similar experience. He has seen the glory of the risen Christ. In this passage, the Lord God describes himself to Moses as first and foremost, "the compassionate and gracious God." Paul's experience on the Damascus road, in the city and in Arabia is similar. Paul experiences God's amazing compassion, his kindness and grace, his slowness to be angry, his abundance of love, his committed faithfulness, his love that embraces thousands, his forgiveness for Paul's own personal wickedness, rebellion and sin. He sees this through the eyes of his heart which has opened. Having done absolutely nothing to merit it, Paul experiences the comfort of God's love and the unconditional nature of his grace. None of his works justify him receiving it, it is the Father's unconditional gift to him. This comforting, embracing Father of compassion deeply heals the wounds in Paul's heart.

The eye-opening revelation of the nature of God is in stark contrast to Paul's pharisaical mindset. The time in Arabia is a time of change in every way where Paul begins to see things differently. He begins to eat from the Tree of Life, receiving the gift of life from God the Father. This is an outpouring of love, grace, mercy, comfort and joy. In fact, all the treasures of heaven God plans to give us, Paul is receiving by what Jesus has done for him. He begins to see what Jesus has done is incredible. He tries to put it in simple words, and the only ones that come are we are "in him." We are in Christ.

The realisation dawning on Paul is God the Father had always planned to pour the treasures of heaven into his creation. He wants to freely give us all the spiritual blessings of heaven and share them with us. This is made possible because we are included in Jesus. Paul sees how before the creation of the world the Father chooses us to be united with his son Jesus. God has planned to have sons and daughters who will be special and set apart for him, blameless and guilt free. Paul sees this plan has been set in motion before anything existed. It has always existed in the heart of God. He sees God's purpose is to always have offspring, sons whom he can lavish his love upon. He sees the Father wants to view mankind as his sons, fully recognised as sons in every way. This love is the overriding motive in the heart of God. When he writes about this in Ephesians 1, his words flow like a river of revelation.

He sees how the Father's heart is full of pleasure. In his son Jesus, the eternal son of God, all this will come about. Paul sees how in Jesus we have redemption through his blood, the forgiveness of sins, in accordance with the riches of God's grace he lavishes on us. It is with God's wisdom and understanding, he makes known the mystery of his will. This is God's good pleasure purposed in Christ. All this will be fulfilled in Christ, and all things in heaven and on earth will be united in Christ.

Whatever the process and whenever it happens, by the time Paul begins to preach "his gospel," it is rich with revelations no one else

CHAPTER 13

has seen and it will change the way we relate to God and know him. After Jesus stands Paul, who is a colossus in terms of revelation. Paul's gospel will be a major part of the returning to God the Father of his sons and daughters and the unfolding of the Big Picture.

CHAPTER 14

THE GOSPEL

Following Paul's time in Arabia, he says he went to Jerusalem. In Galatians, he writes,

> *"I did not go up to Jerusalem to see those who were apostles before I was, but I went into Arabia. Later I returned to Damascus.*
>
> *Then after three years, I went up to Jerusalem to get acquainted with Cephas and stayed with him fifteen days. I saw none of the other apostles, only James, the Lord's brother. I assure you before God that what I am writing you is no lie.*
>
> *Then I went to Syria and Cilicia. I was personally unknown to the churches of Judea that are in Christ. They only heard the report: "The man who formerly persecuted us is now preaching the faith he once tried to destroy." And they praised God because of me. Then after fourteen years, I went up again to Jerusalem, this time with Barnabas"* (Galatians 1:17 – 2:1).

There are many years between Paul's conversion and when he begins his active ministry. Barnabas has gone to look for him in Tarsus where he has been for about fourteen years and asks him to join him in Antioch. Together they encourage and teach the church there. From

CHAPTER 14

Antioch, they are sent out to take the message of the Gospel to other places. First, they visit Cyprus then they cross over to the mainland and start churches in Pamphylia and Galatia before returning to Antioch.

Once back, Luke picks up the story.

> *"From Attalia they sailed back to Antioch, where they had been committed to the grace of God for the work they had now completed. On arriving there, they gathered the church together and reported all that God had done through them and how he had opened a door of faith to the Gentiles. And they stayed there a long time with the disciples.*
>
> *Certain people came down from Judea to Antioch and were teaching the believers: "Unless you are circumcised, according to the custom taught by Moses, you cannot be saved." This brought Paul and Barnabas into sharp dispute and debate with them. So Paul and Barnabas were appointed, along with some other believers, to go up to Jerusalem to see the apostles and elders about this question" (Acts 14:26 – 15:2).*

We can only imagine how Paul and Barnabas react and what is said in the sharp dispute and debate. The Bible is not afraid to hide things where there are disagreements and differences. What we are seeing at this point in the story is of uttermost importance. Paul rightly sees this as a fundamental issue about the very nature of the Gospel he preaches and the nature of the Gospel itself. In Paul's eyes this issue goes to the very heart of the gospel. To use the terminology of the two trees in Genesis, this is Wrong Tree versus the Tree of Life. Man-made attempts to please God versus the free gift of life in Christ Jesus. The Pharisees are saying what God has done in Christ is not enough.

WAS WHAT GOD HAD DONE IN CHRIST SUFFICIENT FOR SALVATION?

Paul and Barnabas, along with some other believers, are appointed to go up to Jerusalem to see the apostles and elders about this question.

In his letter to the Galatians which is written sometime later, Paul says he went up again to Jerusalem, this time with Barnabas and he also took Titus. He says he went in response to a revelation. He does not say what the revelation is. However, in the context of the first part of his letter to the Galatians, Paul writes about receiving revelation about the gospel directly from Jesus. It can be assumed he is receiving confirmation from Jesus about the truth.

When they get to Jerusalem the church and the apostles and elders, to whom they report everything God has done, welcomes them. Rather than rush headlong into a heated public debate and confrontation, Paul says he and Barnabas have a private meeting with the leaders. In this meeting, he presents to them the gospel he preaches among the Gentiles.

Paul's account in Galatians 2 displays a humility towards the leaders and respect for the leadership in Jerusalem. He says he wants to be sure he has not been running his race in vain. They have a full discussion about the issue of circumcision of the Gentile converts which has been the major challenge presented to the Antioch church by the visitors from Jerusalem. Paul relates Titus is not compelled to be circumcised, even though he is a Greek.

In Galatians, he uses strong language to explain how the matter arose. In Paul's mind, these people are false believers who have infiltrated their ranks to spy on the freedom the Christians have in Christ Jesus and to make them slaves to the law. In the letter, he makes it very clear they do not give in to them for a moment, in order for truth of the gospel to be preserved.

As the church in Jerusalem gathers to discuss the issue, Luke says some of the believers who belong to the party of the Pharisees stand and say, "The Gentiles must be circumcised and required to keep the law of Moses." Here is the heart of the problem. These believers are Jewish converts who still belong to the party of the Pharisees. Their words are the same words used in Antioch that has caused much alarm and disagreement. These people have accepted the truth about Jesus, but it has not really changed them. They still owe their allegiance to the Pharisees and pharisaical thinking. Essentially, they are still living and eating from the Wrong Tree.

The backstory to this issue is the apparent complication for Jewish believers which arose when increasingly large numbers of Gentiles became Christians. For Jewish followers of Jesus, it is hard to literally break a lifelong habit of viewing Gentiles as ritually unclean. To meet with them, eat with them and relate to them as brothers is a very big change. It is only possible when their hearts and eyes are open by revelation to truth. As long as they try to rationalise and impose their position on the newcomers, there will be conflict. It is trying to find answers by eating from the fruit of the Wrong Tree again. This pitfall has plagued the church ever since.

Luke writes in Acts 15,

> *"The apostles and elders met to consider this question. After much discussion, Peter got up and addressed them: "Brothers, you know that some time ago God made a choice among you that the Gentiles might hear from my lips the message of the*

gospel and believe. God, who knows the heart, showed that he accepted them by giving the Holy Spirit to them, just as he did to us. He did not discriminate between us and them, for he purified their hearts by faith" (Acts 15:6 - 9).

Peter leads the discussion, speaking from his own experience when he was in Joppa on the coast of Judea. As a Jewish follower of Jesus, he also had to face the challenges of relating to Gentiles. Luke records this incident in great detail in Acts 10 and 11, perhaps because this issue is a pivotal one for the early church. The fact it is Peter who is the focus of the story is important and shows the high regard in which he is held by the Jewish Christians.

The story shows the internal struggle Simon Peter goes through and how it takes an angelic visitation, a supernatural dream and direct instruction by the Holy Spirit to get him to move.

The outcome of the visit Peter makes to Cornelius is Peter preached the gospel to Gentiles. This story is important to Jewish believers. They need to see what the Spirit is doing as it will pave the way for what is about to happen. The gospel is about to be preached and spread all over the non-Jewish Gentile world. Everything is about to change.

After the conversion of a group of these Romans, the news has spread rapidly the Gentiles have received the word of God. But when Peter returns to Jerusalem, the circumcised believers criticise him, accusing him of going into the house of uncircumcised men and eating with them.

Peter tells them the whole story and concludes by telling them how the Holy Spirit came upon them.

"As I began to speak, the Holy Spirit came on them as he had come on us at the beginning. Then I remembered what the Lord

> had said: 'John baptised with water, but you will be baptised with the Holy Spirit.' So if God gave them the same gift he gave us who believed in the Lord Jesus Christ, who was I to think that I could stand in God's way?"
>
> When they heard this, they had no further objections and praised God, saying, "So then, even to Gentiles God has granted repentance that leads to life" (Acts 11:15 – 18).

As the council being held in Jerusalem listens to Peter's statements, they likely remember these events happening some years before. They remember the door of the gospel has been opened by God to the Gentiles through Peter.

Peter's concluding remarks to the gathered leaders of the church and the other apostles are a magnificent statement. He succinctly sums up the whole problem for them of the Old Testament Law, how it is in reality a yoke the Jewish people cannot carry, let alone put on the Gentile believers.

> 'Now then, why do you try to test God by putting on the necks of Gentiles a yoke that neither we nor our ancestors have been able to bear. No! We believe it is through the grace of our Lord Jesus that we are saved, just as they are" (Acts 15:10 – 11).

This should have been the end of the matter. It is a foundational and concise apostolic statement which succinctly defines and states the nature of salvation. It remains today a clear defining statement of Christian faith and doctrine. In saying this, Peter, full of the Holy Spirit at that moment, is speaking with profound anointing.

After he finishes speaking, the gathered assembly listens in silence as Barnabas and Paul tell them about the amazing miracles God has done among the Gentiles on their recent missionary travels in Cyprus and on the mainland as far north as southern Galatia.

When they finish speaking, James the brother of Jesus speaks. James seeks to affirm Peter's description of how God has intervened to include the Gentiles as part of the chosen people by quoting from the prophecy of Amos.

James then makes a unilateral pronouncement.

> *"It is my judgment, therefore, that we should not make it difficult for the Gentiles who are turning to God. Instead, we should write to them, telling them to abstain from food polluted by idols, from sexual immorality, from the meat of strangled animals and from blood. For the law of Moses has been preached in every city from the earliest times and is read in the synagogues on every Sabbath" (Acts 15:19 – 21).*

This statement seems unrelated to the previous discussions. Peter has been speaking with the authority of an apostle, this pronouncement by James is different. In many ways, it is a pastoral response to a pastoral situation rather than an apostolic decree. The conflict is experienced at the level of most people in the church, in their relationships with each other, between Jewish believers and Gentile believers. It is as practical as can they eat together without compromise or at worst ritual contamination?

James's judgment may have been driven by a pastoral imperative and might have been an attempt to apply the principle, but it lacks the clarity of Peter's declaration.

It certainly says they should not make it difficult for Gentiles to turn to God, but it needs to be more specific. It needs to say circumcision is not a requirement for becoming a Christian nor obedience to Mosaic laws, but it stops short of that. James's response lacks the revelation

Peter expresses in his statement. Whilst James is not a Pharisee, his response is characteristic of the Pharisees. It is a response driven by the Tree of the Knowledge of Good and Evil. It defines everything as either good and acceptable behaviour and wrong or evil behaviour. When James's decision is put into a letter, it still does not get to the main point because the judgment of James lacks revelation. It will take someone else to bring this revelation in an apostolic way and get to the heart of the issue.

If it had been clearer, the problems which develop after this in Antioch may not have happened, and Paul may not have written his letter to the Galatians. The apostles and elders, with the whole church, agree to send a letter to the church in Antioch. They decide to send some of their own men to Antioch with Paul and Barnabas. They choose Judas who also called Barsabbas and Silas, men who are leaders among the believers. With them, they send the following letter:

The apostles and elders, your brothers. To the Gentile believers in Antioch, Syria and Cilicia:

Greetings.

We have heard that some went out from us without our authorisation and disturbed you, troubling your minds by what they said. So we all agreed to choose some men and send them to you with our dear friends Barnabas and Paul— men who have risked their lives for the name of our Lord Jesus Christ. Therefore, we are sending Judas and Silas to confirm by word of mouth what we are writing. It seemed good to the Holy Spirit and to us not to burden you with anything beyond the following requirements: You are to abstain from food sacrificed to idols, from blood, from the meat of strangled animals and from sexual immorality. You will do well to avoid these things.

Farewell (Acts 15:23 – 29).

The letter is distinctly pastoral in tone. There is a clear recognition those who advocated circumcision for the Gentile believers did so on their own initiative and not with the support or authorisation of the Jerusalem leaders.

However, the letter is somewhat understated about the impact of these people and it implies the response of the Gentile believers in Antioch is the main problem not the wrong teaching of the believers who are Pharisees. The Antioch church is "disturbed," their minds are troubled. It would have helped if the letter had come straight out with it and said the teaching not only came without Jerusalem's authorisation, it is actually wrong. This needed to be done with conciliatory grace, otherwise it would also have been Wrong Tree.

Armed with the letter from the Council of Jerusalem, the men set off for Antioch. When they arrive, they gather the church together and read the letter. Everything settles down for a while.

The issue of circumcision goes away, and everyone breathes a sigh of relief, especially the male Gentile believers. The church continues to grow. There is a sense of togetherness and belonging among them all. Peter comes to visit after some months and moves freely among the people. At times, it is hard to recognise he has been born a Jew. The level of freedom they enjoy in this life of God in Jesus is wonderful. News came from time to time from the new churches around the coast and up into southern Galatia. All seems to be well, then visitors arrive from Jerusalem. Peter, who used to eat with the Gentiles, begins to draw back and separate himself from the Gentiles because he is afraid of these "certain men" who belong to the circumcision group. Paul says even Barnabas is led astray and joins in this hypocrisy.

CHAPTER 14

WHO WERE THESE 'CERTAIN MEN' AND WHAT DID THEY TEACH?

The traditional view has been Paul's opponents are Jewish Christians, possibly former Pharisees who seek to "Judaise" the Gentile Christians of Antioch and further afield. The specific motivation of these Jewish Christian opponents is they view their cause as righteous and biblical. They seem to use the Abraham and Sarah-Hagar stories to point to such a perspective, as numerous commentators have noted. When Paul writes to the Galatians, he picks up this theme. The Judaisers consider it imperative for Gentiles to be saved in continuity with Israel and in accord with the Law and customs of Moses by becoming Jewish converts.

Everything about Paul's ministry and preaching seems to contradict what they believe. The confrontation he describes in Antioch is a skirmish in the ensuing conflict between Paul and these men, and it will ultimately lead to his arrest in Jerusalem and trial before the Roman authorities years later.

These Judaisers claim to come to Antioch with the support of James, the leader in Jerusalem. It is difficult to say how much of their behaviour is encouraged by James, nonetheless, Paul takes a very strong stand against it.

In Antioch, Paul has to confront Peter specifically for his compromising behaviour which must have been disappointing and discouraging. Peter is after all a key figure in the church, and many would have been influenced by his actions. We are not told what happens after Paul's confrontation with Peter and the others. It is quite conceivable the Judaisers move on and travel to Cilicia and beyond into Galatia spreading their version of the gospel. It is widely accepted these Judaisers from Jerusalem visit the churches established by Paul on his first missionary journey in order to correct them and explain the 'true' nature of the gospel to them.

Paul realises the church faces a very significant challenge. It is a pivotal moment for the church and the future of Christianity. Paul has been a lone voice for some time. At some point after this, Paul writes his letter to the Galatians in which he addresses the issues raised by all these events and the attacks on him personally by the Judaisers. He addresses the issue head on. What is the gospel? Does it include circumcision and obedience to Jewish customs? Is the work of Jesus on the cross sufficient? What is the status of those who believe and are now "in Christ?"

WHAT IS THE GOSPEL?

Paul's response to the Judaisers's challenge is to write a letter to the churches he has planted in Galatia to define what the Gospel is. It is the first New Testament document written by anyone. The themes Paul highlights in Galatians are taken up and developed in a number of his other letters, particularly Romans and Ephesians. The thrust of the letter to Galatia describes fully the reality of being 'in Christ.' He explains how being redeemed by Jesus results in us being placed in the position of sons and daughters to God the Father. Drawing together truth he has received over a number of years by revelation from Jesus, Paul introduces his readers to the glorious truth of sonship which is our true identity and position in Christ. The importance of this letter cannot be overemphasised.

In Paul's opening statement, he launches straight into the issue of his own position and credentials as an apostle appointed by Jesus and the Father. The memory of his encounter with Jesus on the road to Damascus is included in this opening statement. If there is any doubt about what Paul believes about Jesus, it is clarified in the first sentence. Paul states categorically the Father raised Jesus from the dead,

> *"Paul, an apostle, sent not from men nor by a man, but by Jesus Christ and God the Father, who raised him from the dead, and all the brothers and sisters with me" (Galatians 1:1).*

Paul launches into the issue of the true nature of the gospel.

> *"I am astonished that you are so quickly deserting the one who called you to live in the grace of Christ and are turning to a different gospel, which is really no gospel at all. Evidently some people are throwing you into confusion and are trying to pervert the gospel of Christ" (Galatians 1:6 – 7).*

Blunt and to the point, Paul believes this teaching by the Judaisers is another gospel and not the one received from Jesus. He says any other gospel other than the one he preaches is not the gospel at all, even if an angel preaches it. He accuses those who preach 'another gospel' of creating confusion and perverting the truth. In defending his gospel, Paul writes,

> *"For I want you know, brothers, that the gospel I preached is not something man made up. I did not receive it from any man, nor was I taught it, rather I received it by revelation of Jesus Christ" (Galatians 1:11 – 12).*

It is important for Paul, from the outset, to make clear the gospel came to him by revelation directly from Jesus. As an apostle appointed by Jesus, he speaks only what he hears from Jesus not from man. What he preaches is directly from God and to challenge it or try to change it will bring them under the judgment of God.

Paul lays out before his readers the truth of the gospel he preaches.

> *"We who are Jews by birth and not sinful Gentiles know that a person is not justified by the works of the law, but by the faith of Jesus Christ. So we, too, have put our faith in Christ Jesus that we may be justified by the faithfulness of Christ and not by the works of the law, because by the works of the law no one will be justified. But if, in seeking to be justified by Christ, we Jews find ourselves also among the sinners, doesn't that mean that Christ promotes sin? Absolutely not! If I rebuild what I destroyed, then I really would be a lawbreaker.*
>
> *For through the law I died to the law so that I might live for God. I have been crucified with Christ and I no longer live, but Christ lives in me. The life I now live in the body, I live by the faith of the Son of God, who loved me and gave himself for me. I do not set aside the grace of God, for if righteousness could be gained through the law, Christ died for nothing"* (Galatians 2:15 – 21).

This crucial passage explains how Paul sees and understands the gospel. When Paul writes this letter, he writes in Greek, the language most people spoke and understood at that time. We, however, do not speak Greek and need to have it translated into our own languages. Throughout all my books, I consistently use the New International Version (NIV) translation. It is important to remember this translation, whilst it tries to be as close a translation of the original Greek as it can be, it is nonetheless, to some level, an interpretation by the translators and may reflect the translators' theological bias and understanding. This is never more true than in this passage.

CHAPTER 14

Several words in the passage need careful translation to reflect the original intent and message Paul is communicating to the Galatians. The overriding message is we can do nothing ourselves to bring about our own salvation. It has all been done and accomplished by the work of Jesus on the cross. When Paul writes, "[we] know that a person is not justified by the works of the law, but by the faith of Jesus Christ," in Galatians 2:16, he is saying we are not justified or made righteous by works of the law. Rather, we are justified by the faith of Jesus Christ. Jesus's faith brings about our justification.

However, the translators of the NIV translated this sentence, "a person is not justified by the works of the law, but by faith **in** Jesus Christ." The sense is completely opposite when translated as 'faith **in** Jesus' rather than the 'faith **of** Jesus.' It is saying we have to have faith **in** Jesus to receive justification.

This has led some to believe we are not justified if our faith in Jesus is not strong enough or is inadequate. We are equally in danger of self-righteousness if we think our faith is sufficient. It is subtle, but it is like the words of the Pharisees or Judaisers who were inserting circumcision as a requirement for salvation. Even faith, if it is our faith that leads to salvation takes away the work of the cross. Paul makes it clear it is what Jesus has done. This is fundamental for Paul. He would be appalled at the inference this simple translation error has led to.

Paul says in Galatians 2:16, "So we, too, have put our faith in Christ Jesus that we may be justified by the faith of Christ and not by the works of the law." He says we put our faith in Christ Jesus, that is, we believe what he says and has done is true and we are justified and made right with God because of the faithfulness of Jesus.

The same applies to one of the first verses I was encouraged to memorise after becoming a Christian, the oft quoted Galatians 2:20.

I always felt condemned by it because I felt my faith was never strong enough to live the Christian life.

> "I have been crucified with Christ and I no longer live, but Christ lives in me. The life I now live in the body, I live by faith **in** the Son of God, who loved me and gave himself for me."

When I saw it was the faithfulness of Jesus at work in me that enables me to live the Christian life rather than my efforts to have sufficient faith in Jesus, it changed everything. There is joy and freedom in this, not striving and condemnation.

> "I have been crucified with Christ and I no longer live, but Christ lives in me. The life I now live in the body, I live by faith **of** the Son of God, who loved me and gave himself for me."

Paul's gospel is a gospel of freedom and receiving the grace the Lord Jesus freely gives to us. His faithfulness brings about our salvation.

IS BEING OBEDIENT TO GOD'S LAW WRONG TREE?

Not at all, is Paul's answer, but Satan has set a trap in it. In Galatians Chapter 3, Paul continues and further elaborates his thinking. He is speaking directly to people in Galatia, many of whom he knows personally, and his frustration boils over. He restates the importance of the cross in his teaching.

> "You foolish Galatians! Who has bewitched you? Before your very eyes Jesus Christ was clearly portrayed as crucified. I would like to learn just one thing from you: Did you receive the Spirit by the works of the law, or by believing what you

CHAPTER 14

heard? Are you so foolish? After beginning by means of the Spirit, are you now trying to finish by means of the flesh? Have you experienced so much in vain, if it really was in vain? So again I ask, does God give you his Spirit and work miracles among you by the works of the law, or by your believing what you heard" (Galatians. 3:1 – 5).

Paul is not being offensive when he calls them foolish, he is exercising tough love. He loves them, but he cannot abide what happened to them. He concludes they have been "bewitched." This is a strong word to use. In English, the clue is easily recognised in the word. The word speaks of witchcraft, entrapment and the malign activity of Satan. This is absolutely the right word to use because the origin of this teaching forces them to try to get right with God through their own effort, their own self-righteousness, through their own futile attempts. This, as we have seen now many times, finds its origins in the Garden of Eden and the fruit of the Tree of the Knowledge of Good and Evil and Satan's corrupt wisdom. Keeping the rules and obeying the law in order to find peace with God is satanic in origin. What the Galatians are being told to do is to essentially eat from the fruit of the Wrong Tree rather than the Tree of Life.

Paul asks a simple and obvious question. Did they receive the Spirit by the works of the law or by believing what they heard? Their introduction to the good news Paul brought is accompanied by miracles and the anointing of the Holy Spirit on them.

Paul continues the argument calling Abraham into the discussion. In Galatians 3:6, he cites Abraham's faith and how it is credited to him as righteousness. He then goes on to show those who have this gift of faith are the true children and spiritual descendants of Abraham and this includes believing Gentiles. "All nations will be blessed through you." So those who rely on faith are blessed along with Abraham, the man of faith. In contrast, Paul writes those who rely on the works of the law are under a curse, as it is written: "Cursed is everyone who does not continue to do everything written in the Book of the Law," quoting Deuteronomy 27:26. Paul draws on his own deep, extensive knowledge of Old Testament scripture. He is, in some ways, beating the Judaisers at their own game. Paul continues,

> *"Clearly no one who relies on the law is justified before God, because "the righteous will live by faith." The law is not based on faith; on the contrary, it says, "The person who does these things will live by them." Christ redeemed us from the curse of the law by becoming a curse for us, for it is written: "Cursed is everyone who is hung on a tree" (Galatians 3:11 – 13).*

Paul then explains what Jesus has done for us. He receives this by revelation from Jesus himself.

> *"He redeemed us in order that the blessing given to Abraham might come to the Gentiles through Christ Jesus, so that by faith we might receive the promise of the Spirit" (Galatians 3:14).*

WHAT DOES PAUL MEAN BY REDEMPTION?

The use of the word redeemed is important as Paul's explanation unfolds in the next part of Galatians. What Jesus has done in redeeming us has a significant impact on how we understand what Paul writes. The teaching on redemption has its roots in the Old Testament, but in the New Testament it is almost exclusively used by Paul. Redemption is the act of buying something back or paying a price or ransom to return something to your possession.

CHAPTER 14

Redemption is the English translation of the Greek word *'agorazo,'* meaning "to purchase in the marketplace." In ancient times, it often refers to the act of buying a slave. It carries the meaning of freeing someone from chains, prison, or slavery. Paul uses the word four times, twice in Galatians 3:13 and 4:5, then in Ephesians 5:16 and Colossians 4:5. Redemption always involves going from something to something else. In this case, it is Christ freeing us from the bondage of the law to freedom of a new life in him.

The other Greek word connected with redemption is *'lutroo,'* meaning "to obtain release by the payment of a price. The price, or ransom is Christ's precious blood obtaining our release from sin and death. It is used ten times in the New Testament, seven of which are by Paul. In Romans 3:24, Paul expands what he first writes in Galatians.

> *"There is no difference between Jew and Gentile, for all have sinned and fall short of the glory of God, and all are justified freely by his grace through the redemption that came by Christ Jesus" (Romans 3:22 – 24).*

The most important issue in redemption and Paul's use of the word is how it describes the process of salvation. It brings together the two strains of 'redemption' and 'being redeemed.' Something once owned or possessed but has been lost is bought back. A price has been paid in order to get it back into its original owner's possession. The process is the initiative of God the Father in redeeming his wayward and lost children. God does this by sending his son Jesus to redeem us, to buy back what belongs to him in the first place. In Paul's teaching, he recognises by revelation we are God the Father's creation and offspring in the first instance.

Much of what Paul writes about in Galatians, he amplifies and expounds upon in other letters. We have seen this in Ephesians chapter 1. I am going to repeat it here again simply because it is just so magnificent.

> *"Praise be to the God and Father of our Lord Jesus Christ, who has blessed us in the heavenly realms with every spiritual blessing in Christ. For he chose us in him before the creation of the world to be holy and blameless in his sight. In love he predestined us to be placed as sons through Jesus Christ, in accordance with his pleasure and will, to the praise of his glorious grace, which he has freely given us in the One he loves. In him we have redemption through his blood, the forgiveness of sin, in accordance with the riches of God's grace that he lavished on us with all wisdom and understanding"* (Ephesians 1:3 – 8).

Redemption is in the background of the rest of Chapter 4 of Galatians. Before getting there, Paul takes another look at the Law. This has been a focus of the Judaisers, so Paul looks at what the point of the law is in the first place. Again, he later expands on this in Romans Chapter 7.

In Galatians, he continues by writing the covenants based on law cannot be changed. Promises spoken to Abraham and his Seed, Jesus, still stand. The law of Moses given 430 years later did not set aside the covenant or promise given to Abraham. Paul asks a series of obvious questions. Why, then, is the law given at all? Is the law opposed to the promises of God? His answer is the law is given because of man's sin and is in place until the 'Seed,' that is Jesus, to whom the promise refers has come. For if the Law of Moses could impart life, then righteousness would certainly have come by the law.

CHAPTER 14

"But Scripture has locked up everything under the control of sin, so that what was promised, being given through faith of Jesus Christ, might be given to those who believe" (Galatians 3:22).

Note again the difference 'in' and 'of' makes in relation to this last phrase.

Paul also writes about the coming of faith in Galatians 3:23, describing how we are held in custody under the law, locked up until the faith to come is revealed. The faith he writes of is the faith of Jesus and his faithfulness and commitment to being obedient to his Father. His willingness to suffer and die on the cross and by the shedding of his blood to bring redemption and reconciliation. Paul's revelation about the faith of Jesus not our faith in Jesus is a very important part of the Big Picture. Miss this truth and the jigsaw will have missing pieces and it won't get finished.

CHAPTER 15

SONSHIP

In explaining the nature of the gospel and how as a result we are 'in Christ,' Paul comes to another game changing revelation. He sees how the work of Jesus for us and on our behalf restores to us our lost position as children of God. He begins to explain how our status changes or rather is restored to what it is intended to be before creation when God the Father first thought of us and conceived of us in his heart. He receives the glorious revelation and truth of "sonship" which makes us God's sons.

HOW DOES THE FAITH OF JESUS MAKE US SONS?

He writes in Galatians,

> "So the law was our guardian until Christ came that we might be justified by faith. Now that this faith has come, we are no longer under a guardian. Instead you are all sons of God through the faith of Christ Jesus, for all of you who were baptized into Christ have clothed yourselves with Christ. There is neither Jew nor Gentile, neither slave nor free, there

CHAPTER 15

is neither male and nor female, for you are all one in Christ Jesus. If you belong to Christ, then you are Abraham's seed, and heirs according to the promise" (Galatians 3:24 – 29).

As he is writing, more revelation comes to him. Paul sees how Jesus's faithfulness of going to the cross removes us from the constraints of the old Mosaic Law. The law has been like a guardian or schoolmaster controlling us and giving structure to our lives until Jesus came. When he came, we moved out of the schoolroom or nursery and are brought into a new place. We are brought into a place of sonship.

God the Father of the Lord Jesus is central to Paul's thinking and he proclaims how as Christians, we are brought into a relationship with God as Father through the faith of Christ. He specifically uses the term *"huios"* which means *"sons"* in this passage. Some translations, in a nod to equality of the sexes translate this as *"children"* but if Paul had meant children, he would have used the word *"teknon."* But he doesn't, he deliberately uses the word *"sons"* because he is making a very important point. He explains in this chapter how being a son is not about gender but about position and status.

The revelation Paul receives is what this book is about. It is the truth that God the Father has always planned to have sons and how Jesus restores this lost sonship to us. He says it is the faith of Jesus that brings this about, not our faith in him. This verse, "you are all sons of God through the faith of Christ Jesus" (Galatians 3:26), is another crucial example of mistranslation of the little Greek word *"ev."* As we have seen previously, this word can change the whole interpretation of scripture. If it is translated as "in" then the sense becomes man focused. We become sons when we put our faith in Jesus. However, this is contrary to the whole flow of the arguments used by Paul to oppose the Judaisers.

When we think about our faith, many feel it is not strong enough or subject to change if doubt and struggles come into our lives. Trying to maintain enough faith is a Wrong Tree way of thinking. It becomes man centred and prone to failure.

Instead, if the word is translated "*of*" instead of "*in*" the whole emphasis changes. This is a perfectly legitimate translation of the word. It changes everything. We become sons because of the faith of Jesus. It is his faithfulness and kindness, his willingness to go to the cross for us and redeem us that brings us back into our intended position as sons. This is completely in line with everything Paul says and has taught. Jesus brings us into our true identity as sons.

Paul adds, the proof of Jesus's work of bringing us into sonship is evidenced by baptism and being clothed in Christ. When Paul talks about being baptised into Christ, he no doubt thought about his own baptism in Damascus many years before. There is a sense of washing and cleansing of his sinful life. Jesus has dealt with it by the shedding of his blood on the cross. Baptism for Paul is rich with symbolism. It is like a burial of his old life and being raised to a new life in Christ as he later writes in Colossians.

Jesus's own baptism is also an important thought here. Paul says we are baptised into Christ. At Jesus's baptism in the river Jordan by John the baptiser something very significant happens to Jesus. The Holy Spirit falls on him and God the Father declares he is his son, he loves him, and he is proud of him. The Father's affirmation of Jesus's sonship is significant for Jesus. Here, Paul sees how being in Christ brings us into the same place through our baptism. Our baptism affirms we, too, are sons who are loved and of whom the Father is proud.

My background and theological training are within the Baptist tradition. I have taught baptism and baptised hundreds of people. I thought

I knew everything about baptism, but when I "saw" this I was stunned. I realised part of the act of baptising is the thrilling affirmation to the person being baptised. They are God's beloved son also, and Father is proud of them, just as he is of Jesus. Being in Christ brings us into the same position as him, loved, affirmed with a Father who is proud of us. I have had the joy and privilege of baptising many others since I saw this. To be able to say to them as they rise up from the waters of baptism, "The Father says to you, 'You are my son. I love you, and I am proud of you,'" is wonderful.

Paul adds we have clothed ourselves with Christ. Our willingness to step into the waters of baptism shows our willingness to embrace all Jesus has done for us and given us. It is like being clothed in his love. The picture of the Father in Luke's story of the lost sons in Luke 15 comes to mind. The younger son, when he comes home, is embraced and kissed by his father. Then he is clothed with the best robe. It is a symbol of the father covering his son's brokenness and dirt and covering him with a powerful public expression of his love for the boy. This is exactly how the Father treats us.

As Paul continues writing his letter to the Galatians, he is seeing new things he has only glimpsed before. Revelation after revelation fills his heart. Things Jesus has been saying to him over many years are coming together as he writes.

BUT WHY SONS AND NOT DAUGHTERS TOO?

After saying we have clothed ourselves in Christ, he adds,

> *"There is neither Jew nor Gentile, neither slave nor free, nor is there male and female, for you are all one in Christ Jesus" (Galatians 3:28).*

Some have accused Paul of being sexist in his use of the word sons and have carried this thinking through into their translations of the scriptures. The updated versions of many Bibles, including the NIV have opted to use the word children. Here is their rendering of Galatians 3:26. "So in Christ Jesus you are all children of God through faith." In the light of everything I've been saying, this translation totally misrepresents Paul and the truth. But why sons and not children?

For Paul, sonship or being sons is about our position and status in Christ. He categorically says sonship is not about race or ethnicity or previous religious association. It is neither Jew nor Gentile. This was what the Judaisers have been promoting, separation and division. Neither is sonship about being a slave or free person. The Roman world was divided into these two categories where slaves had no rights whatsoever. Then Paul adds there is neither male and nor female. Women in the Roman world had no rights at all. They were considered goods and chattel. Here, he is elevating their status in an unprecedented way. They are in Christ and fully equal with men as "sons." Sonship is not about gender and to argue for gender equality by changing the word to a gender neutral one in this passage is a mistake. Misogyny and the hatred of women which originates in the Fall are completely the antithesis of the Gospel and the heart of God revealed through Jesus. Sonship is not promoting this. Rather the opposite, for as Paul concludes, "For you are all one in Christ Jesus."

Paul says sons are baptised into Christ and have clothed themselves with Christ, then he adds sonship means we are the seed or descendants of Abraham and therefore heirs.

CHAPTER 15

HOW DOES BEING HEIRS SHOW WE ARE SONS?

In the cultures of the twenty-first century, being an heir implies one day the heir will get an inheritance when a father or relatives dies. Being an heir doesn't mean anything until a death occurs. So, the question needs to be asked. What does Paul mean by linking being an heir to being a son?

The language of the nursery and the place of the pedagogues or guardians and trustees who look after the children fills his heart. He sees the child in a wealthy family in the nursery. Even though one day the child will be the heir, as a child he has no more rights than a slave. The Law of Moses has been like these guardians, like a schoolmaster. But when Jesus came, all of this changed. We are recognised by God the Father as his sons and daughters because of the faithfulness of Jesus. Paul continues,

> *"What I am saying is that as long as an heir is a child, he is no different from a slave, although he owns the whole estate. The heir is subject to guardians and trustees until the time set by his father. So also, when we were children, we were in slavery under the elemental spiritual forces of the world. But when the set time had fully come, God sent his Son, born of a woman, born under the law, to redeem those under the law, that we might receive the full rights of sons. Because you are his sons, God sent the Spirit of his Son into our hearts, the Spirit who calls out, "Abba, Father." So you are no longer a slave, but a son and since you are his son, God has made you also an heir"* (Galatians 4:1 – 7).

Paul sees the process of bringing us into sonship is redemption through the death of Jesus for us on the cross. The result of redemption is we are re-placed in our true status as sons, and this means we are heirs. Sonship is all about receiving the gift the Father has given us as an inheritance.

Paul introduces this in verses 1 and 2 by referring to a ceremony known as 'Son Placing." He must have witnessed this on many occasions as would have the Galatians. He is referring to a common practice in the Roman world.

This ceremony of 'son placing,' of recognising a son and heir by a father is referred to in Greek as '*huiothesia*,' which Paul introduces us to in Galatians 4:5. I like the translation of it in this passage as a phrase, "*receive the full rights of sons.*" He uses this word five times in his letters in Galatians 4:5; Romans 8:15,23; Romans 9:4; and Ephesians 1:5. However, it has proven difficult to translate. It is a compound word made up of two Greek words, '*huios*' which means '*son*' and '*thesia*' which means '*placing*' from the verb 'to place.'

"*Huiothesia*" describes a ceremony occurring within Roman culture in which a male child of a citizen achieves the status of manhood and is officially recognised as the son and heir by his father, the paterfamilias. Prior to the ceremony, a son is considered to have the status of a slave in his father's house, even though he has the potential to inherit his father's wealth.[2] The 'son placing ceremony' occurs sometime in a boy's teenage years when his father determines it was time for him to pass from being a child under the absolute power of his father into adulthood and his true status as son and heir.

In this public ceremony, the young man removes the toga he has

---

2. *The Story of Civilization, Vol. 3: Caesar and Christ*, 1972, p. 57.

worn as a boy and puts on the *'toga virallis,'* the toga of manhood. This ceremony marks his entry into full citizenship in the empire and the right to vote in the assembly. Not only this, but also after the 'son placing ceremony,' the son becomes fully legally invested with all of the rights, powers, and privileges of being a son and heir to his father's possessions, wealth, and status. No longer is he viewed as a child, he is a fully participating member of his society and family.[3]

When the father publicly introduces his designated son and heir, he announces this by declaring this boy is his son whom he loved and of whom he was proud. This would have resonated with Paul as these are the words spoken by God the Father over Jesus at his baptism by John in the River Jordan. The Roman father then places the toga on his heir along with a ring of authority on his finger. In the story told by Jesus in Luke 15 there is the same imagery. The returning son is clothed in the best robe and a ring is placed on his finger denoting his status again as a son.

The one who is 'placed as a son' is the biological child of the father. It is not an adoption into the father's household.

However, within Roman and Greek culture, many times there were no male sons to appoint as heir. Infant mortality was high, and many children did not reach adulthood. To overcome this difficulty, the Romans introduced the idea of adoption. They called it *'adoptio filio,' adoption of a son.* This allowed a Roman father to adopt a boy and go through the son placing ceremony with the adopted boy. These adoptions were not necessarily of orphans. Many times, they were spare sons. That is, sons of a man who had more than one. He could effectively sell a son to a friend or colleague who was childless. This practice was seen many times in the imperial family where murder and assassination

---

3. Harrill, 2002; Fraschetti, 1997; *"Roman Children,"* Classics Unveiled.com

were tragically very common. The reigning emperor would adopt and appoint new heirs after the last one died.

By the fourth century AD, the church in the west is predominantly Latin speaking and has as much trouble reading the Greek New Testament as we do. There are a number of poor Latin versions of the bible circulating including one used by Augustine of Hippo in all his writings. Then around 400 AD, Jerome, a Roman scholar and monk, who is a contemporary of Augustine, undertakes the task of producing a translation of the whole Bible from Greek and Hebrew. This is referred to as the Vulgate and is the accepted translation used by the Roman Catholic Church right into the twentieth century. When Jerome encounters this Greek word *'huiothesia,'* he chooses to translate this word in Latin as *'adoptio.'* Like a number of Jerome's translations in the Vulgate, it leaves a lot to be desired. Consequently, this is taken up by other translators and adoption becomes a common translation of this word.

In 1382, when John Wycliffe produces his first translation of the Bible into English, he translates it from Jerome's Latin Vulgate. Thus, when he comes to this word, he translates it into English as 'adoption.' The idea of adoption is still understood and practiced, but the 'son placing ceremony' of the ancient world has long gone from conscious memory.

In the Reformation of the sixteenth century when the Bible is being translated into many European languages, the translators encounter this word and have to decide how to translate it. In the English-speaking world, the first serious translation of the New Testament from Greek is undertaken in 1530 by William Tyndale who has a very clear understanding of the Fatherhood of God and how he recognises us as sons. In his translation, he tries to avoid the word adoption. In Galatians 4, Tyndale translates, *"we through election might receive the inheritance that belongeth unto the natural sons.*" However, his translation is not accepted, and he is burnt as a heretic in Brussels in 1536. When the 1611 authorised King James Version of the Bible is published, the translators use 75% of Tyndale's words but they consider Tyndale's "*huiothesia*" rather cumbersome and in all five references, Wycliffe's word adoption is used instead.

Only in recent years has the English-speaking world revisited this translation. For example, N.T. Wright in his commentaries translates 'huiothesia' as 'sonship.' Northern European languages follow Luther's translation which does not carry the idea of adoption at all. In the Latin-based languages such as Spanish and especially French, which follows Calvin's teaching, they have gone for adoption.

WHAT DID PAUL MEAN BY THIS WORD *HUIOTHESIA?*

Paul's original imagery of 'huiothesia,' literally "placing as a son" as opposed to being adopted within God's kingdom profoundly affects our relationship with God. Adoption, applied to our relationship with God, is problematic as it changes our fundamental status as God's offspring. When a child is adopted into a family, he remains physically the same person. No change of name or falsification of birth records will ever eliminate the biological reality. The child is still the offspring of the natural parents. The child's DNA will always remain different, separate, and unrelated to his adoptive parents.

However, Paul teaches we are God's offspring, created in his image, especially as we consider he is the Father of Adam and Eve. Paul uses this argument in Acts 17:28 - 29 when talking to Greeks in Athens on his second missionary journey. He says, "We are his offspring."

In the genealogy of Jesus in Luke 3:38, Luke traces the family line of Jesus through his mother back to Adam who is described as a son of God. As their descendants, our own DNA carries the fingerprints of divine origins. God even tells us he is intimately involved with the physical creation of each one of us. He 'knits' us together in our mother's womb, according to Psalm 139:13 - 16. This is because God is our real Father.

When we are born, we essentially become slaves of the fallen world of men we have been born into. However, this does not change our original status as God's offspring. We are still his children. We are just separated from intimate relationship with him because of our sin. The gospel Paul preaches is about a loving Father who provides a way for us to be reconciled to him, to have those chains of slavery broken. Paul says this is through the blood Jesus, God's son, shed for us on the cross. The act of becoming a follower of Jesus allows us to receive his redemption, and *'Huiothesia'* is the end result of this process. We become a full and participatory member of the Father's family, with the full rights belonging to his children. God the Father does not adopt us. He restores things to their proper order and reinstates us into his family where we belonged in the first place.

The way Paul uses this word in Galatians 4:5, shows it is obvious the English translation of the word as *'adoption'* does not fit the context, whereas *'sonship'* or *'receiving the full rights of a son,'* or something like it is precisely what Paul speaks of. Paul is using this picture of son placing to illustrate our position in Christ.

Like all illustrations, it has its limitations. In this case the Roman practice only related to one son and not to daughters at all. Paul is not saying only a male child can be a son. He addresses this by saying we are all sons of God through the faith of Christ, and this applies to all, Jews and Greeks, slaves and free, men and women.

CHAPTER 15

"As proof that you are sons, God sent the spirit of his Son into our hearts, crying out 'Abba, Father!' So you are no longer a slave, but God's son; and since you are his son, God has made you also an heir" (Galatians 4:6 – 7).

The translation of *'huiothesia'* as *"adoption"* does not convey the meaning Paul intended. Yet many eminent and famous theologians and Christian leaders have written whole books about adoption. Their premise is God adopts us into his family. The English word adoption refers to a legal process by which a person who wants to have a child can legally recognise and adopt a child who is not biologically their own. Thus, the child will be officially recognised as their own, and consequently have the same legal status as any other children they may have. They see this as a legal transaction on God's part.

It has been suggested Jesus's words in John 14:18, "I will no longer leave you as orphans I will come to you," is a reference to our adoption. But he is not using this in any way as physical orphans, rather it is the attitude of the heart which is orphan like. The way we behave can be very orphan hearted, but we are not orphans who have no father. We have a Father, God. Our "orphaness" is in our inability to "see" who he really is. Satan's Wrong Tree thinking wants us to believe we have been abandoned and disowned by God and he is not our Father.

At first glance, this seems to fit with what God has done, but the premise is fundamentally wrong. There are a number of reasons why adoption is not the proper English word to convey Paul's meaning in the passages where he uses *'huiothesia.'*

In English, adoption means the child who is adopted is not a person's child in any sense before the adoption takes place. This conflicts with the way Paul uses *'huiothesia'* in Galatians 4:5. According to Paul, we have always been God's offspring.

Second, adoption in English refers to the legal contract of making a person one's child. The thinking emerged of adoption being the means of salvation. People speak of the legal transaction undertaken by God on our behalf to adopt us. Whereas, in Paul's use, "*huiothesia*" is the end result of the process of redemption. Redemption is the process by which God the Father reconciles us to himself, saves us and brings us into a position of sons in relationship with the Father. This removes much of the theological confusion.

Equally significant, there is a serious emotional and psychological problem with using the word adoption. Many children who have been adopted are troubled about the fact of their adoption. They may be very comfortable with the idea of their adoptive parents who wanted them and were happy to adopt them. However, they often wonder who their birth parents are. Why did they not want to keep them? Many then try to seek out and locate their biological mother or father. In some cases, these kinds of thoughts can result in children suspecting there must have been something wrong with them, or their birth parents did not want them and then gave them up. It is obvious thoughts of this kind are completely out of place in the contexts where Paul uses '*huiothesia*.'

In the situation Paul refers to, there are no other parents who have given up the children first in order for God to adopt them. God has always been our Father and we have always been his offspring, but we have lost the relationship because of the Fall and our sinful rebellion. He sent Jesus into the world to reveal who he is and always was, our true Father. Through the faithfulness of Christ and his redeeming work on the cross, we are brought home to receive back our status as sons.

As Paul uses the term '*huiothesia*,' the meaning refers to our status of being a son. In particular, two great truths result from this status. First, we recognise ourselves to be God's child, and therefore we feel it is right to address God as "Father." Paul connects this very strongly with the receiving of the Spirit of God in Galatians 4:6.

> *"As proof that you are sons, God sent the spirit of his Son into our hearts, crying out 'Abba, Father!"*

He also picks this up in Romans 8:15 – 16,

> *"The Spirit you received brought about your repositioning to sonship. And by him we cry, "Abba, Father."*

Then again in Ephesians 1:13.

> *"When you believed, you were marked in him with a seal, the promised Holy Spirit."*

Secondly, the promises God has made to his people are made to us as his sons. As God's sons, we can expect to receive everything God has promised his people. Paul introduces the idea we are God's 'heirs' in Galatians 4:7,

> *"So you are no longer a slave, but God's son; and since you are his son, God has made you also an heir."*

And also in Romans 8:17,

> *"Now if we are children, then we are heirs, heirs of God and co-heirs with Christ"*

And in Ephesians 1:14,

> *"(The Holy Spirit), who is a deposit guaranteeing our inheritance."*

Through his faithfulness, we are then placed in a position of sons or as Paul said, we receive from the Holy Spirit, the Father's gift of sonship. It cannot be overstated this first letter written by Paul is of immense significance in setting out the doctrine of the revelation of God as a Father who redeems us and puts us in place as his sons. The doctrine of sonship is central to understanding the rest of the New Testament and God's dealings with mankind.

CHAPTER 16

THE LAST WORD

The last word goes to the writer whose work completes the New Testament. This is believed to be the Apostle John who refers to himself in his Gospel as 'the disciple Jesus loved." His gospel is believed to have been the last written of the four Gospels. Some suggest it is written late in the first century. The three letters of John are attributed to the same writer. Revelation has historically been considered John's writing also. The language used in the Gospel and the three letters are similar.

More significant is the way the writer talks about God as Father. In the gospel from time to time he adds his own words. The most important place this occurs is in John 3 which records Jesus's evening conversation with Nicodemus. Here John writes,

> *"For God so loved the world that he gave his one and only Son, that whoever believes in him shall not perish but have eternal life. For God did not send his Son into the world to condemn the world, but to save the world through him. Whoever believes in him is not condemned, but whoever does not believe stands condemned already because they have not believed in the name of God's one and only Son" (John 3:16 – 18).*

This may be one of the most loved passages in the Bible. John's beautiful description of the Gospel is a summary of the Big Picture. It describes God's unchanging eternal love for the world he has created. Traditionally, we focus on the latter part of the verse which emphasises believing in Jesus in order to receive eternal life. This is very important when it is assumed eternal life means living forever. However, this is man centred and requires something man has to do. Ultimately this tends to lead back into Wrong Tree thinking where we have to do something to be right with God. However, on the last evening Jesus spent with his disciples before going to the cross, he says in his prayer to the Father,

> *"For you granted him (Jesus the Son) authority over all people that he might give eternal life to all those you have given him. Now this is eternal life: that they know you, the only true God, and Jesus Christ, whom you have sent" (John 17: 2 – 3).*

In this prayer Jesus defines eternal life. It is to know God the Father and Jesus his son. He uses *"ginosko"* for knowing, the experiential relational knowing which describes real knowledge of God the Father. Putting these two verses together we see how God the Father's eternal love for the world is a longing for mankind to come back home to be fully known by him as our Father for eternity.

We have already looked in detail at the revealing of God the Father in John's Gospel. Here, I want to look at how John explains this in his first letter and how everything changes for him.

HOW DID EVERYTHING CHANGE FOR JOHN?

This letter is John's personal expression of all he has seen and heard about Jesus. In his Gospel, he is writing with an expressed intention of helping the readers discover life.

> *"But these are written that you may believe that Jesus is the Messiah, the Son of God, and that by believing you may have life in his name" (John 20:31).*

In his first letter, it is John the apostle, beloved by Jesus, writing to those he has led to faith, the churches he has served and ultimately all who will read his words. It is deeply personal and comes after a lifetime of reflection and intimate relationship with the Father and Jesus his Son. He begins his letter expressing this personal connection.

> *"That which was from the beginning, which we have heard, which we have seen with our eyes, which we have looked at and our hands have touched, this we proclaim concerning the Word of life" (I John 1:1).*

John has known Jesus all his life since his childhood growing up in Galilee. His mother and Jesus's mother are sisters. He has a connection unlike any of the other apostles. His brother James has been martyred many years before and only he is left. He has been entrusted by Jesus from the cross with the care of his mother Mary. Early church tradition says the two of them end up living in Ephesus until Mary departs this life. In his old age, John looks back on a lifetime of heart connection with Jesus.

John describes how more than just through family ties he really knew Jesus. He heard what Jesus said. His heart has been opened, and he heard truth in the words of Jesus. He has seen him do extraordinary things with his own eyes. The eyes of his heart are opened to see things beyond the natural seeing of day-to-day life. He says he has touched Jesus. All his human senses have experienced Jesus and he knew him.

He knew him beyond human family relationship and beyond human friendship. John saw with the eyes of his heart. He says Jesus is the Word of life. He receives revelation of the true nature of Jesus. His description of Jesus as the Word of Life links back to his revelatory words at the beginning of his Gospel where he describes Jesus as the "*logos*," the Word.

> *"In the beginning was the Word, and the Word was with God, and the Word was God. He was with God in the beginning. Through him all things were made; without him nothing was made that has been made. In him was life, and that life was the light of all mankind. The light shines in the darkness, and the darkness has not overcome it" (John 1:1 – 5).*

John has been given this amazing revelation by the Father of who Jesus is, the eternal Son, the agent of God's creative power. In him is life. The tree of life in the Garden of Eden is an expression of the life of Jesus. Those who receive of his life, eat of this fruit, live eternally in relationship with the Father, Son, and Spirit. This is John's astonishing summary of the Big Picture.

John describes how this life is manifested in the world in the beginning of his letter.

> *"The life appeared; we have seen it and testify to it, and we proclaim to you the eternal life, which was with the Father and has appeared to us. We proclaim to you what we have seen and heard, so that you also may have fellowship with us. And our fellowship is with the Father and with his Son, Jesus Christ. We write this to make our joy complete." (1 John 1: 2 – 4).*

When John discovers the truth about Jesus and the eternal life given by the Father it changes everything for him. He gives of himself for the rest of his life proclaiming what he has seen and heard in order to bring others into this knowledge also. He longs to share the fellowship he enjoys with the Father and the Son with us too. When I read these words of John, my heart resonates deeply with them. All of my life and ministry is now secondary to this. Once I began to see and hear and be touched by this life, everything else pales into insignificance for me. This is also what gives me joy.

John writes his letter in many ways from a pastoral perspective. He addresses real issues about living the life of sons in relationship with the Father. He writes about the ongoing battle with sin and its impact on our lives and how Jesus is an advocate for us with the Father.

He uses language similar to Paul in this letter as he sees our position as God's children as being 'in Christ.' John writes,

> *"This is how we know we are in him: Whoever claims to live in him must walk as Jesus did" (1 John 2: 5 – 6).*

He says because we are "in him," we walk as Jesus walked.

HOW DID JESUS WALK?

We live our lives in him and through him. We live to do the things Jesus did. This does not mean we have to wear a plastic wristband with WWJD (What Would Jesus Do?) on it, which turns it from relationship to a tortuous struggle to assess every situation as how Jesus would do this. The implication being, if we do not do it, we somehow do not make the grade or pass the test. This downgrades the walking as Jesus walked to yet more pharisaical wrong tree behaviour.

John remembers it well. He mentions it so many times in his Gospel.

Jesus walks in a daily relationship with the Father, hearing his voice, watching his actions and doing what he sees the Father doing, and saying what he hears the Father saying. Jesus claimed no credit for himself. All the glory went to the Father because he only did the Father's works and spoke the Father's words. He said on occasion his words are not his own. His teaching is not his own. Everything has been given to him by his Father.

This, says John, is how Jesus walked, in relationship with the Father.

All of this flows out of the love the Father has for the Son and the love the Son has for the Father. This love then flows from them into us, Jesus's brothers and sisters. John remembers Jesus's words in the Upper Room,

> *"As the Father has loved me, so have I loved you. Now remain in my love. If you keep my commands, you will remain in my love, just as I have kept my Father's commands and remain in his love. I have told you this so that my joy may be in you and that your joy may be complete" (John 15: 9 – 11).*

In the same vein, John continues in his letter to say the practical out-working of being in him and walking as Jesus walked is to love one another. He says,

> *"Dear friends, I am not writing you a new command but an old one, which you have had since the beginning. This old command is the message you have heard. Yet I am writing you a new command; its truth is seen in him and in you, because the darkness is passing and the true light is already shining" (1 John 2:7 – 8).*

Then towards the end of Chapter 2, after having explored some practical out workings of how to live in love with one another,

CHAPTER 16

John continues,

> *"I am writing these things to you about those who are trying to lead you astray. As for you, the anointing you received from him remains in you, and you do not need anyone to teach you. But as his anointing teaches you about all things and as that anointing is real, not counterfeit, just as it has taught you, remain in him"* (1 John 2:26 – 27).

Walking as Jesus walked is to remain in him in relationship with the Father with the anointing of the Spirit. All these words echo the words of Jesus in the Upper Room.

Finally, words explode onto the page of his letter. John's heart is so full it is as if he cannot hold back any longer.

> *"See what great love the Father has lavished on us, that we should be called children of God! And that is what we are"* (1 John 3:1)!

I want to give the last words to John without comment or further explanation. I have said enough. The Word speaks for itself.

> *"Dear friends, let us love one another, for love comes from God. Everyone who loves has been born of God and knows God. Whoever does not love does not know God, because God is love. This is how God showed his love among us: He sent his one and only Son into the world that we might live through him. This is love: not that we loved God, but that he loved us and sent his Son as an atoning sacrifice for our sins. Dear friends, since God so loved us, we also ought to love one another. No one has ever seen God; but if we love one another, God lives in us and his love is made complete in us.*

"This is how we know that we live in him and he in us: He has given us of his Spirit. And we have seen and testify that the Father has sent his Son to be the Saviour of the world. If anyone acknowledges that Jesus is the Son of God, God lives in them and they in God. And so we know and rely on the love God has for us.

God is love. Whoever lives in love lives in God, and God in them. This is how love is made complete among us so that we will have confidence on the day of judgment: In this world we are like Jesus. There is no fear in love. But perfect love drives out fear, because fear has to do with punishment. The one who fears is not made perfect in love.

We love because he first loved us. Whoever claims to love God yet hates a brother or sister is a liar. For whoever does not love their brother and sister, whom they have seen, cannot love God, whom they have not seen. And he has given us this command: Anyone who loves God must also love their brother and sister (1 John 4:7 – 21).

"*God has given us eternal life, and this life is in his Son. Whoever has the Son has life; whoever does not have the Son of God does not have life*" *(1 John 5: 11 – 12).*

WHAT IS THE LAST PIECE OF THE BIG PICTURE?

In the very end of the Bible, the Apostle John writes down the extraordinary visions he has when a prisoner on the Island of Patmos. He writes them to encourage the believers of his day who are suffering persecution and attack. To show them the Father will one day wrap up everything and there will be a new heaven and new earth.

In the final chapter of Revelation, he sees in this new heaven and earth a restored picture of what looks like the Garden of Eden, the place where the story began for the human race. In it is the Tree of Life. This is what John sees.

> *"Then the angel showed me the river of the water of life, as clear as crystal, flowing from the throne of God and of the Lamb down the middle of the great street of the city. On each side of the river stood the tree of life, bearing twelve crops of fruit, yielding its fruit every month. And the leaves of the tree are for the healing of the nations. No longer will there be any curse. The throne of God and of the Lamb will be in the city, and his servants will serve him. They will see his face, and his name will be on their foreheads. There will be no more night. They will not need the light of a lamp or the light of the sun, for the Lord God will give them light. And they will reign forever and ever" (Revelation 22:1 – 5).*

The Tree of Life is bringing healing to the nations. The power of the curse is broken.

The big picture is now complete. We have come full circle; all the edge pieces are connected. There are no gaps. No one is holding a piece to leave the picture unfinished.

As sons and daughters, chosen and loved by our Father, redeemed by his Son our dear brother Jesus, united in him, anointed and filled with his life-giving Spirit, we will reign forever and ever.

OTHER BOOKS BY TREVOR GALPIN

FALLING FROM GRACE
and being caught by the Father (2021)

Newly republished re titled and up dated with additional insights and stories, this is Trevor's own story of his journey of homecoming to the Father. It tracks through the many stages of his spiritual journey including a ministry fall and the journey of recovery orchestrated by God the Father. James Jordon in his Foreword to the book says "Trevor has been extremely transparent in his pathway in the life we call Christianity. He has faced himself, He lost everything including reputation, the most freeing thing to lose. He lost all security and many of his friends. He lost himself and his calling and destiny in ministry. It as a source of satisfaction and joy to me to have been able to play a part in the redemption and restoration God has done in Trevor's life. I highly recommend this book to you and know many will find great encouragement in it."

OTHER BOOKS BY TREVOR GALPIN

JESUS AND HIS FATHER
by his family and friends (2014)

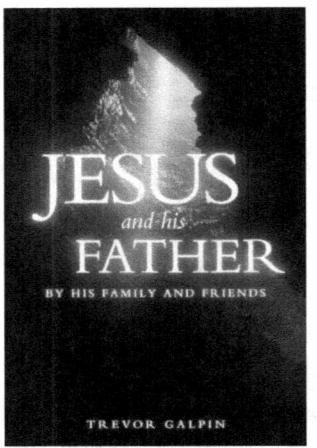

The revealing of God as Father was the primary ministry of Jesus. He revealed this through conversations with his family and friends. This book is the story of fourteen people who heard Jesus say things about God as a Father as recorded in the Gospels.

This book is also available in Dutch and Mandarin Chinese.

FINDING THE FATHER
in the Story of the Church *(2016)*

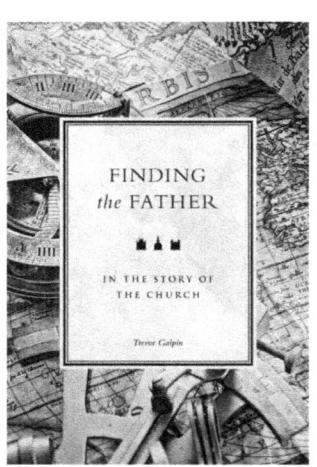

When Jesus returned to his Father he commissioned his followers to continue his work. This is the story of how the church has tried to do this through 2000 years. It looks specifically at the place the truth about the Father heart of God has had in the story. Sometimes it was almost forgotten but gloriously has not been lost.

OTHER BOOKS BY TREVOR GALPIN

THE STORY OF PAUL
The Early Years *(2018)*

This book is about Paul, the apostle who had an amazing revelation of the love of God the Father expressed through Jesus Christ his beloved Son. The revelation of the God who was in Christ. How did Paul receive such an incredible revelation? How was this legalistic Jewish Pharisee who persecuted the early church transformed into the man who has this profound revelation? Who was the man behind the words? What was the back story? Paul's story unfolds in the pages of the New Testament. His story is pieced together from the account written by Luke in the Acts of the Apostles along with some pieces of biographical information scattered through the thirteen letters written by Paul himself. It explores Paul's revelation and teaching because they are relevant for the Church today. Paul saw things with the eyes of his heart that very few have seen, and he still has much to teach us. James Jordan says of this book, "In this very easy to read, informative and entertaining book by my friend, brother and fellow servant of the Body of Christ, Trevor Galpin, you will be introduced to Paul in a deeper and more full way than I have ever known to be in print."

This book is also available in Finnish.

OTHER BOOKS BY TREVOR GALPIN

THE STORY OF PAUL PART 2
The Middle Years (*2020)*

Where was Paul when he wrote the letter to the Romans? Did the church in Corinth manage to sort out its problems? Did Paul get reconciled to John Mark and Barnabas? These are some of the questions addressed in this historical narrative set during Paul's the second and third missionary journeys. Written in story form it draws the reader in to the world of the Early Church and the heart and mind of Paul.

You can contact Trevor Galpin via his website:
www.trevorlindafhm.com

All the above books are available at Book Depository and Amazon.com in paperback and on Kindle. The Story of Paul - Part 1 is also available in audio book format, read by Trevor himself.

RECOMMENDED READING LIST

- **Sonship, A Journey into Father's Heart**
  M. James Jordan (2012)
  Available from www.fatherheart.net

- **The Ancient Road Rediscovered**
  M. James Jordan (2014)
  Available from www.fatherheart.net

- **The Forgotten Feminine**
  Denise Jordan (2013)
  Available from www.fatherheart.net

- **Finding Confidence Beyond Religion**
  Stephen Hill (2016)
  Available from www.ancientfuture.co.nz

- **John: A Prophetic Revelation**
  Stephen Hill (2017)
  Available from www.ancientfuture.co.nz

- **Made in His Image**
  John MacDonald (2020)
  Available from www.amazon.com

- **Jesus and the Undoing of Adam**
  C. Baxter Kruger (2007)
  Available from www.amazon.com

RESOURCES

- **Trevor and Linda Galpin's website:**
  www.trevorlindafhm.com
  This website includes Trevor's blog, resources, itinerary and ways of supporting them in their ministry.

- **Father Heart UK:**
  www.fatherheart.uk
  News and events from the Father Heart team in the UK.

- **A Father to You:**
  www.afathertoyou.com
  Mark Gyde's website with lots of audio and video teachings, teaching materials and inspirational videos.

- **Fatherheart Ministries:**
  www.fatherheart.net

- **James and Denise Jordan:**
  www.jordaninternational.net

- **Stephen Hill:**
  www.ancientfuture.co.nz

www.ingramcontent.com/pod-product-compliance
Lightning Source LLC
Chambersburg PA
CBHW071601080526
44588CB00010B/979